Talent Disruption

Talent Disruption

People Are The Brands

Alexander Mirza

BUSINESS EXPERT PRESS

Leader in applied, concise business books

First published in 2023 by
Business Expert Press, LLC
222 East 46th Street, New York, NY 10017
www.businessexpertpress.com

ISBN-13: 978-1-63742-835-1 (paperback)
ISBN-13: 978-1-63742-837-5 (hardcover)
ISBN-13: 978-1-63742-836-8 (e-book)

Business Expert Press Tourism and Hospitality Management Collection

First edition: 2023

10 9 8 7 6 5 4 3 2 1

EU SAFETY REPRESENTATIVE
Mare Nostrum Group B.V.
Mauritskade 21D
1091 GC Amsterdam
The Netherlands
gpsr@mare-nostrum.co.uk

For my grandfather, a classic Gandhian, a Commonwealth multiculturalist, and an advocate of teaching for those who can do. And for my wife, an old-stock Canadian, whose talent is only equaled by her work ethic and whose unconditional backing of this endeavor made it imaginable.

Description

This book proposes a solution to the human capital challenges faced by service industries amidst unprecedented labor shortages and technological and geopolitical shifts. It offers a framework for diagnosing the root causes of talent disruption.

Talent Disruption provides a detailed roadmap and tools for building a talent engine powered by AI, big data, and analytics. The results are a growing talent pipeline, greater productivity, and **higher profit margins**.

Keywords

talent disruption; labor shortage; employee ownership; hotel labor crisis; workforce management; internal talent marketplace; hospitality management

About the Cover

The cover page illustrates a disruption in the talent market, where individual talents have become the most valuable brands or hubs in a global marketplace. These elite talents are ranked dynamically by an algorithm that assigns them a value or worth based on their performance. Talents are connected to each other, and their peer reviews and reputations can expand their professional networks.

In this marketplace, talents have more control over their careers and can either choose to work for a single employer or build their own brand as freelancers for multiple employers. Their value is determined by their performance, reputation, and connections in the talent marketplace.

The Artificial intelligence (AI) arms race impacts the talent markets. Talents are connected to each other through either solid lines, indicating open digital platforms between their civilizations, or dotted lines, indicating a digital wall separating their civilizations. In the coming years, the digital war between civilizations may eliminate lines altogether, bifurcating talents even within an organization.

Contents

"Workers are the Treasure of a Factory.
They are important to me."

—Sakichi Toyoda, founder of Toyota Industries

Testimonials

"Alex Mirza's research provides compelling insights for what hospitality stake-holders must do to build human capital and achieve a higher purpose in these extraordinary times. Talent Disruption *is not just recommended reading, it is required."*—**Geoff Ballotti, President and CEO, Wyndham Hotels & Resorts; and recipient of the Arne Sorenson Social Impact Leadership Award**

"As large language models automate away busy work, building human capital is a monumental issue facing the healthcare industry. Alex Mirza's book provides a marvelous pragmatic road map to meritocracy, innovation and pay for performance in any service industry. A must read!"—**Jonathan Bush, CEO, Zus Health; and cofounder CEO, Athena Healthcare**

"My management colleagues and I understood thoroughly the first order differences in performance associated with variation across talent among property leaders, and the financial consequences of these differences. Likewise, we could measure the often tenfold difference in both productivity and service quality across talent among front line employees. The problem was what to do about it, at scale. In Mirza's path-breaking examination of how to create a data-driven marketplace for talent in the hospitality industry, he shows how to use emergent computational tools to build individualized profiles of talent at both ends of the hierarchy—from top management to front line—and allow the resultant transparency to lead to (1) better matching of talent to opportunity, and (2) stronger competition for improved performance among all stakeholders in the industry. One of the most encouraging results of this work is the opportunity for high performers, the Moguls, to receive the superior rewards that their talents richly deserve."—**Gary Loveman, Chairman and CEO, Well; former Chairman and CEO, Caesars Entertainment; and part owner, Boston Celtics**

"There is a huge need to update our traditional HR logic in the face of the dramatic changes that have befallen the hospitality industry. With Talent Disruption, *Alex Mirza has taken that step and advanced our understanding of how to use the new technology tools to address the considerable talent issues facing service firms. This is an absolute must read!"*—**Leonard A. Schlesinger, Baker Foundation Professor, Harvard Business School; and coauthor of landmark bestseller *The Service Profit Chain***

"With the world in flux and the hospitality industry at a crisis point, we are currently at the precipice of a new era of AI-driven upheaval and post-pandemic paranoia. Alex Mirza gives us a clear and concise road map to navigate these rough waters, with insights on how to harness the technological tools in our marketplace and to filter and analyze the vast amounts of data at our fingertips. Talent Disruption *is a must read for anyone who is interested in maximizing and optimizing talent development."*—**Wilburt Chang, Chairman and CEO, Greater China Hospitality**

"Provocative! Alex has done a masterful job of assembling data to help drive better decisions around human capital and rightly challenges old ways of thinking about talent. Whether you agree with all his conclusions or not, it is not debatable that employees must always be a top priority. Otherwise, your organization will struggle and never realize its full potential."—**Beverly K. Carmichael, independent board member and former Chief People Officer, Southwest Airlines, Ticketmaster, and Cracker Barrel Old Country Store**

"Our industry faces a foundational challenge in rethinking traditional business models to rebuild our talent pipeline and, once again, become an employer of choice. As one of hospitality's most innovative thought leaders, Alex's work comes at a pivotal time, providing much-needed, research-based answers to the most critical questions facing today's travel and tourism executives."
—**Adam Burke, CEO, LA Tourism Council & Convention Board**

"All of us in the hospitality industry know we are facing a crisis in recruiting and retention. Talent Disruption *goes beyond diagnosing the problem and charts a path forward using data- and AI-driven strategies to*

revolutionize human capital. Alex brings a fresh approach to solving talent discovery and empowerment in the service sector. A highly recommended read."
—**Harry Gross, real-estate developer and Chairman, G. Holdings LLC**

"If you are a CEO feverishly looking for Artificial Intelligence insights to revolutionize your business, look no further. Talent Disruption *equally educates and empowers you to embrace the change emerging within talent broadly and hospitality specifically. Decoding the intangible power of the immigrant experience is the byproduct of this fascinating journey led by Alex Mirza."*
—**Alex Dixon, CEO, nonprofit Q Casino; and former President and COO, MGM Circus Circus**

"Speaks to the alarming labor challenge confronting the hospitality industry and the imperative to change the model and innovate for how labor is engaged and retained within the sector."—**Douglas Tutt, CEO, HCareers, leading U.S. hospitality, senior living, and gig economy employment site**

"Alexander Mirza does what leaders do. He sees what is unseen, and in this book issues a rallying cry to accelerate the value of hospitality's main driver, the people who power it."—**Thomas Magnuson, CEO, Magnuson Hotels Worldwide**

*"*Talent Disruption *sheds light on an undeniable truth: hospitality is losing ground in the talent marketplace. Through in-depth research, Alex Mirza provides an applicable and disruptive roadmap for building a talent-centric culture that can drive innovation, growth, and competitive advantage in the industry."*—**Joe Rice, Managing Partner, JDI (JDI is twice ranked by** *Forbes* **as one of the Best Executive Recruiting Firms in America)**

"While Talent Disruption *focuses on the disconnects between talent management, compensation and value creation in the hotel industry, the insights are equally applicable to the restaurant and retail industries. As Mirza creatively and powerfully illustrates, talent is a highly leverageable and brandable differentiator, and companies should design compensation systems and marketing programs to fully leverage that power and value."*—**Rick Vanzura, CEO, Freight Farms; and former CEO, Wahlburgers and Panera Bread**

"Few people could do what Alex Mirza has done—written a book on Talent Management and Disruption that combines both hard data analysis with proven managerial insight. Building on his decades of experience and proven leadership in the hospitality industry, he has produced a rigorous and accessible book that should be required reading for anyone hoping to grapple with the modern talent management challenges this industry faces."
—**David Detomasi, Associate Professor, Smith School of Business, Queen's University, Kingston, Ontario, Canada**

"Talent Disruption by Alex Mirza is a game-changing exploration of the evolving service industry landscape. With its cutting-edge insights on AI-driven HR solutions and employee empowerment, this book paves the way for a revolutionary approach to talent management. Discover your blueprint for success in this indispensable read."—**Anita Gupta, Forbes 50 Over 50 Entrepreneur; Founder, KiwiTech**

"In Talent Disruption, *Alexander Mirza has dedicated some powerful research into the biggest concerns impacting global hotel operations today, with 85% of hotels currently understaffed in the USA alone, and others grappling to hold onto their employees. He identifies various new 'disruptors' such as Big Tech, that have evolved over the past decade which not only impact human resources in the traditional sense but the entire outlook on how you operate your hotel. It provides a very concerning outlook on the future of human capital, a strong focus on the value of cultural diversity and women in leadership roles. Including some very plausible solutions this book could well be a foundation upon which to start Hospitality's Great Reset. Don't rush through this, it's well worth the read, and should be on every hotelier's desktop."*—**Benedict Cummins, Publisher, HotelExecutive**

"It is not every day one comes across a book that manages to marry innovative and profound insights into the current state and future prospects of the global hospitality industry with a stimulating and creative discussion of recent debates in international relations theory. Yet this is exactly what author Alex Mirza has accomplished in his fascinating new study into the challenges facing the industry in an era increasingly being labeled by some scholars as

one of 'de-globalization.' Mirza wisely cautions that while it would be pre-mature to write off globalization, recent changes in the international arena brought on by pandemics and the return of great-power rivalry do require new thinking if executives are to adapt successfully in harvesting the full potential of their greatest productive asset, their talent pool."—**David G. Haglund, Professor of Political Studies, Queen's University, Canada**

Talent Is the #1 Issue Facing Hotel CEOs

"People do not view this as the easiest place to work, the best place to work necessarily. It was an issue before we came into this pandemic. We had a million unemployed coming into this pandemic. We fell to 4 million unemployed. It's been improving, but it's still our biggest issue."—**Geoff Ballotti, CEO, Wyndham Hotels & Resorts**

"The labor crisis is the number one issue facing the industry."—**Chris Nassetta, CEO, Hilton Worldwide**

"People always feel like you're going to abandon them in a crisis and there's no safety net."—**David Kong, Founder and Principal, DEI Advisor**

"To encourage people to return to the industry, we've got some heavy lifting to do."—**Anthony Capuano, CEO, Mariott International**

"Hyatt is committed to doubling Hyatt's Black representation in the next five years, period, end of story."—**Mark Hoplamazian, CEO, Hyatt Hotels Corp**

"We're all seeing our customer satisfaction scores in this industry, across the board, go down fundamentally, we just don't have enough people in the workforce."—**Keith Barr, CEO, InterContinental Hotels Group**

"We did what we shouldn't have done and went right back or are trying to go right back to how we did business before the pandemic when the customer has changed."—**Ted Darnall, CEO, HEI Hotels & Resorts**

Preface

The Future of Front-Line Work: What's Next?

As a double immigrant who worked his way through high school and university, I am a big believer in the lifelong benefits of working on the frontline. My first job was in frontline customer service at age 16 for Canada's largest sports store chain, Collegiate Sports (now Sport Chek), in a flagship mall in Toronto. I started as a salesclerk selling shoes, retail apparel, ski equipment, and stringing tennis racquets.

As a student athlete, I was fortunate to work in a large sports department store situated in a multicultural city and to serve all kinds of people across various ages and income groups. Our customers ranged from consummate "old stock Canadian" athletes, who were fanatical about every detail when ordering custom equipment, to wide-eyed gullible immigrants whose children were seeking to learn a new sport like ice hockey or snowboarding. It was a fast-paced atmosphere with dense traffic in the evenings and buzzing with energy on the weekends like a casino hotel on the Las Vegas strip.

It was also a very demanding job because it required being on your feet for eight hours per shift and being constantly "switched on" to anticipate customer needs. Employees engaged in their first frontline customer service role developed emotional intelligence through hundreds of daily interactions with customers. Over time, I learned how to read customers' non-verbal facial expressions and body language, which varied widely by their ethnicities, stage of life, and other factors.

The job required meticulous knowledge of every major sporting activity, current and incoming inventory, and prices for disparate product lines and brands while also including labor intensive tasks such as tagging the products, stocking the shelves, and cleaning the store after hours. Determining the best allocation of shelf space was a key decision. There were no "smart technologies" such as sensors, cameras, big data, and analytics used by retailers today to manage inventories and shelf-space. Hence arranging the optimal product assortment on the floor to generate traffic was an essential part of the job that required teamwork and an entrepreneurial mindset of experimentation through trial and error.

The store manager was a flamboyant French-Canadian named Guy who was a die-hard Montreal Canadiens fan with a profound sense of humor. Typical of 1980s Toronto, the staff was composed of up-and-comers, including many Asian, European, and Caribbean immigrants. Guy was great at motivating staff, casting people in the right departments, creating internal sales contests, and holding us accountable. He had a keen eye for talent and was adept at identifying and investing in adaptive learners who could conquer a multifaceted department such as ski equipment or hockey skates by efficiently conveying product knowledge to outsell others.

Guy's greatest skill was building an informal talent marketplace to grow the business in one of the world's most diverse cities. He understood that a high performing diverse team of employees who felt like the store was their own business would not just generate loyal customers but grow the sports retail business by engaging new communities. Under his leadership, the store became an incredibly diverse meritocracy of over 500 full time and part time employees: Caribbean kids rose from selling track shoes to managing winter sports and Asian women ascended from selling apparel to assistant manager roles overseeing budgets and purchasing. I remember training a Jamaican immigrant, who happened to be the best sprinter in Toronto, how to string tennis racquets at optimal tensions depending on the player's style, and she taught me about the subtle differences in track and field spikes depending on specific events and surfaces.

Like any store environment, it was not always pleasant. When the store missed its numbers by a wide margin, Guy scolded us for not being sufficiently productive. He would curse at us with Quebecois nouns, poke fun at our beloved Toronto Maple Leafs, and if revenues were under budget, walk us back to his office which doubled as "banc des pénalités" ("penalty box"). His diminutive office was adjacent to the boisterous warehouse receiving truck shipments, welding, and assembling equipment. Here Guy would shout out the disappointing financial results and present the dormant inventory and the blue-collar workers whose strenuous labor made it possible for us to sell these products on the floor. He reminded us that even the most talented players end up in the penalty box and cost their team when they fail to play together and trust their teammates.

Over the course of four years, this job taught me three things I would use in the rest of my career: First, the benefits of building a high-performing team of diverse colleagues who could teach each other through an apprenticeship model rather than formal training; second, how professional development is accelerated by highly demanding customers who make purchase decisions in a matter of seconds; and third, how the real world has a magical way of revealing where your greatest talents reside, even if it contradicts what your teachers and test scores suggest are your perceived strengths.

In my last year on the job, Guy got promoted to regional VP overseeing 100 stores in Eastern Canada. Still, he sought me out once every few months. In our last few meetings, he expressed his gratitude that I helped recruit tens of what he called "gens talentueux" or highly talented and diverse employees – mostly high school athletes and musicians - that drew waves of new customers into his stores and grew the business. The last few times we met, Guy tried to persuade me to become a store manager and retail executive like he was. As an Asian immigrant with Ivy League dreams, I was not ready to take the store manager career path.

However, years later after graduate school and a stint in management consulting, I joined the hospitality industry where I was able to harness this cross-cultural competence to achieve breakthrough results. And when I became an operating executive and eventually a hospitality CEO, it made an even bigger difference. Thanks to years on the frontline, I was able to swiftly unearth customer needs, connect deeply with frontline employees and build collaborative cross-cultural teams. My frontline experience was most helpful in relating to employees in emerging markets such as Shanghai where I had no prior work experience, did not speak the language, and had to motivate migrant workers, mostly mothers living apart from their children.

It was my years serving on the frontline in retail, sports, and health care that taught me to how to collaborate with colleagues, look customers in the eye and resolve their complaints, form teams to solve thorny problems, and meet the litmus test of becoming a leader by identifying and developing other people's talents.

The data and insights in this book validate that service industries are not just the largest employers: they are engines of human development for communities, cities, countries, and entire civilizations. From the United States to China and Saudi Arabia, business, and government leaders "get it" and are investing billions to rebuild human capital in hospitality centric service industries after the pandemic. These diverse stakeholders recognize the critical role of service industries in rebuilding their countries, diversifying their economies, and facilitating meritocracy for domestic and foreign employees of all ages, races, ethnicities, and genders.

Surprisingly, their efforts are increasingly lost on the workforce. Instead, a talent disruption, powered by innovative technologies such as generative AI, changing attitudes towards work-life balance, and a growing mistrust of capitalism and governments is changing the equation. Millions of Gen Xers and Millennials are choosing the gig economy or hybrid jobs where they can effortlessly circumvent human interaction and avoid the discomfort of face-to-face conflicts. Groundbreaking technologies such as generative AI are accelerating this talent disruption, further distancing employees and contract workers and hence brands from their customers.

Consequently, brands that achieved differentiation through personalized service may suffer from commoditization. What is more troubling are the long-term career development implications for individuals, especially Gen Xers and Millennials who are set to become the next generation of service managers and grew up performing these gig economy jobs. Driving around town and leaving bags at a front door with pictures, communicating via text confirmations, and receiving tips based on algorithms is not an equivalent experience to being on the frontline in a service operation. It may provide contractors with flexibility and income, but it comes at the cost of a lack of learning and customer contact that will serve to stunt their professional growth.

What is the solution here?

Solving the talent disruption requires more than just replacing labor intensive tasks with software and robotics. The industry needs a new factory that advances semi-autonomous hospitality and provides a platform for highly engaged employees to orchestrate service innovation. A new system must be spearheaded by elite talent ("the moguls") and employee-centric innovations including responsive workplace designs, profit-sharing compensation schemes and new standards for sustainability.

The ultimate goal of a semi-autonomous operating system is to transform employees from cheap labor to value-added human capital. The litmus test for a luxury hotel is not the aesthetics of its lobbies or the comfort of its guest rooms but rather the level of engagement demonstrated by its workforce that stands as brand ambassadors and community leaders. In the hospitality landscape of tomorrow, the fusion of human expertise and artificial intelligence (AI) will create the front-line of the future.

Foreword

More than 25 years ago, I joined the faculty at Cornell University's School of Hotel Administration. In those 25 years, there have been numerous changes at the hotel school and the industry. The hotel school has been renamed the Nolan School and is part of Cornell's College of Business. The hotel business which was once dominated by major brands that owned and operated their properties is now part of a complex structure where brands rarely own, sometimes manage, and mostly franchise and license. At that time, there was a new company called Expedia and the online travel agency was born. Soon, every brand had a website; business travelers stopped using travel agents and booked on their own. Technological changes are not limited to just bookings. Guests use their phones as room keys, text their questions to the concierge, and receive in room dining and other amenities from robots, and between lighting, outlets, and televisions, hotel rooms seemingly need an operating manual. Over this same time, the concept of revenue management went from an academic theory to accepted practice to the point that when people ask about a hotel stay the second question they ask is: what rate did you pay?

There are, however, four things that have not changed. First, the hospitality industry, despite the technological advances that reduced the need for certain services to be performed by employees, remains as the most labor-intensive industry in the world. Second, turnover in hospitality is higher than most, if not all, other industries. Third, hotel owners and operators are in a perpetual search for talent. Finally, despite the evaluation from personnel to human resource departments and despite the fact that HR has navigated from a secondary department to being part of the "C-suite" in most hotel companies, the prime duties of HR—finding, developing, and retaining talent—remain a mystery.

As the founding and current director of the Cornell Center for Innovative Hospitality Labor and Employment Relations (CIHLER) and the Nolan School's Ceriale Professor of Hospitality Human Resources and Professor of Law, I have had the privilege, along with my colleague

Professor Bruce Tracey, of developing the agenda for the National Human Resource in Hospitality Conference. In our 17 annual conferences and more than 70 roundtables, we have addressed numerous HR and Labor and Employment Law issues and, we believe, have provided creative solutions to the many problems our industry faces. One area we have not been able to truly solve is how to find and identify talent. We have had sessions on interviews, different industrial psychological tests, and numerous other methods that employers use to hire. One conclusion has permeated these discussions—nothing really works! Interviews have limited predictive values, psychological tests also have limited value and create adverse impact issues, job fairs simply provide numbers, and recommendations often create more internal problems than actually provide talent. The conclusion was simple: lots of options, but none that truly work. That was the fact until 2021.

At our 15th annual conference in San Diego, California, Alex Mirza approached us to discuss a new way to find talent. Alex's credentials were off the charts: he holds an MBA from Harvard, was awarded the Sasakawa Peace Fellowship for doctoral studies in international economics, York University, and held senior management positions, including leading corporate strategy, at industry stalwarts like Hilton, Starwood, and Caesars. His consulting career at Deloitte, a leading hospitality consulting group, resulted in him advising CEOs and high-level government officials. Even more impressive than his resume was his clear ability to communicate complex ideas in easily understandable language and peppered with relevant examples. After speaking to Alex for 30 minutes, I put him to work. We quickly created a conference roundtable for Alex to lead. The results were exactly what I expected: the participants at the roundtable were blown away by Alex's vision for identifying, developing, and retaining talent. Our conference speakers include CHROs, EVPs and SVPs of HR and Labor Relations, partners at major law firms, in-house counsel at major brands, owners, and high-level operators. At some level, it is a diverse group, in that there are very few sessions that all our stakeholders wish to attend. Alex's session was an anomaly: every profile of our attendees and speakers was completely enthralled by Alex's ideas. The only problem with Alex's presentation was that he only connected with 25 of our 350 attendees. Selfishly, I suggested a plenary session so that all our attendees could benefit from Alex's work. Realistically, I knew that Alex's work needed the broadest of distribution well beyond any conference in terms of reach and depth. Thus, I was thrilled when Alex notified me that he was writing a book. Two years later, I am honored to write this foreword.

Alex's book, *Talent Disruption, People Are The Brands,* is a groundbreaking work that incorporates the latest AI technology into the age-old search for talent. His technology creates a systematic method for identifying high-performing employees who have the right skill set and intangibles for the job. In addition, Alex applies his experience and knowledge into an AI model that provides guidance for employers who are determined to develop and retain those that have joined their organizations.

For 25 years, I have accepted the fact that employers simply cannot be certain that they have attracted the right applicant pool and that those hired will be high performers who can be long-term assets to the organization. Alex's work is the best method that I have ever seen to solve this problem. All employers, and especially hospitality employers, will be well served by not only reading this book but operationalizing the concepts and proscriptions in it. I, for one, am thankful for the content and look forward to our 2024 conference where Alex will blow us all away!

—David Sherwyn

John and Melissa Ceriale Professor of Hospitality Human Resources
and Professor of Law
Director, Cornell Center for Innovative Hospitality Labor and
Employment Relations
Stephen H. Weiss Presidential Fellow
Cornell University Nolan School of Hotel Administration
Cornell University SC Johnson College of Business

Acknowledgments

I cannot express enough gratitude to current and former colleagues at Mogul Hospitality for their hard work and dedication to this project even in the darkest moments of a global pandemic. I am grateful for the contributions of data scientists, business analysts, and hospitality experts who are recent graduates in their respective fields including Kristyn Wakimoto (CSU Fullerton), Ziyang Zhang (Columbia), Shujiang Tan (UC Irvine), Tu Lam (UC Irvine), Gajendra Choudhary (Texas A&M), Xue Li (USC), Shuhan Wang (USC), and Esther Chau (Cornell). Special recognition to our CTO, Sahar Cain (CSU Los Angeles), whose knowledge of AI and attention to detail significantly improved this book. This diverse and talented team collaborated on a number of fronts, from data science and writing algorithms to testing hypotheses and making predictions that made it possible to generate insights using big data gathered from numerous sources.

I am also grateful for the assistance of communications experts Taylor L. Cole (Dallas); Katherine Fleishman (Milan, Italy), Madeline Houk (Los Angeles); our brave economist Nadiia Kudriashova, PhD (Odessa, Ukraine); and finally long-time colleagues who have worked with me for the past decade including hotel operator Jessie Li (Shanghai, China), marketing leader Yvonne Choi (Los Angeles), finance leader Martin Key (Destin, Florida), designer Pauline Choo (Singapore), and international development expert Christian Johnson (Washington DC).

The completion of this project would not have been possible without the support of our investors including Kiwitech's CEO Rakesh Gupta, General Partner Randall Ussery (L37), Ziad Al-Hazmi (CEO, Lufthansa Technik), and the financial contributions of many family members, most notably my wife, Barbara Mirza (Partner, Cooley LLC Los Angeles).

Finally, to the many software clients of Mogul Hospitality around the globe who gave practical feedback on the algorithms and analytics that underpin hospitality's first AI-powered talent marketplace including hotel CEOs, CHROs, CIOs, hotel owners, and advisory board members of Mogul Hospitality, my heartfelt thanks.

CHAPTER 1

Introduction

Global Talent Disruption

If you're a service leader, an inquisitive consumer, or a student trying to make sense of the business world, this book is for you. It's the unvarnished truth about the current state of human capital in the world's largest service industries from the perspective of an expert insider who built hospitality's first AI-driven talent marketplace.

The buzzword "talent disruption," or lack thereof, is shaking up the service industry as we pick up the pieces postpandemic. With a crippling labor shortage in the United States, Canada, Europe, and the Middle East accelerated by the surge of the gig economy, it's become glaringly apparent that antiquated service factories need a revamp. Obstinate bureaucracy and a culture of financial re-engineering hinder the service industry from pioneering forward and competing with the booming and flexible freelance economy.

Harvard Business School professor Clay Christensen[1] coined the phrase "disruptive innovation," a process whereby a product or service takes root at the bottom of the market and relentlessly moves up, displacing established competitors. Until now, this is a predicament the hospitality industry had yet to experience—being a disruptor or being disrupted by a cost innovator, innovative technologies, or structural changes in the labor markets and global economy.

This book is about how a talent disruption is taking place in services with a focus on one of the world's largest and most powerful industries, accounting for 10 percent of global gross domestic product (GDP) and jobs (300 million people), and how these partially self-inflicted challenges due to a lack of strategy and leadership are spreading like a contagion across a decelerating globalizing economy.

During the global pandemic, hospitality companies laid off millions of Americans with 3 months of health care benefits, despite holding over $30 billion of capital reserves and lines of credit on their otherwise healthy balance sheets. Eighteen months later, they started asking the same people to return, but it was too late. Most chose to retool and move on to less physically demanding jobs, despite a cut in benefits, or leave the workforce altogether. As David Kong, the former CEO of BWH Hotel Group, remarked on a hotel conference panel after the pandemic, "People always feel like you're going to abandon them in a crisis and there's no safety net."

As we bounce back with skyrocketing demand for travel, hotel operators are struggling to make a comeback and suffering from a long losing streak in the labor market. According to the American Hotel Lodging Association (AHLA), 85 percent of hotels are understaffed and 22 percent are severely understaffed.[2] The U.S. hotel sector must hire 2.9 million people per year to reach equilibrium, including 1.3 million replacement hires.

Since the start of the pandemic, hotels have lost 20 percent of labor market share to the gig economy and other industries. The loss of top supervisory talent in the United States represents 100,000 people, half of whom are women and minorities trained over an average of 8 years by multiple hotel brands and management companies. Even with record hiring, increased immigration quotas, and an economic correction that could compel employees to return, it will take 12 years to rebuild this highly skilled talent pool. Regarding diversity, even if all qualified internal talent gets promoted, U.S. hotels need to source and develop over 8,000 minority general managers (GMs), an increase of 69 percent, to meet their own targets.

The issue is beyond just labor, an accounting term that connotes a "sweatshop" mentality: it's to build a high-quality base of talent in a compressed time frame across borders. Our research confirms that hospitality talent resembles sports and entertainment: the most talented performers outpace their peers by over 30 percent and are the hallmarks of their franchise. Without them, there is little prospect of building winning teams, attaining customer loyalty, and producing significant financial returns on invested capital.

What should hotel industry stakeholders do as the paradigm shift in the labor markets uproots their ability to recruit and retain talent? That's where this book comes in. Trapped in legacy HR technologies, the industry does not have a strong employee database, so it cannot properly market to hidden workers. Rather than continuing to treat the symptoms by advertising, social media, and embracing "big tech" job sites and applicant tracking system (ATS) platforms, there needs to be a complete shift to address the root cause. The hotel industry must transform itself through research and development and invest into partnerships that leverage AI and other human capital technologies to develop new talent pipelines in multiple regions of the world simultaneously.

Foundations: Christensen's Theory of Disruption Innovation

According to former Harvard Business School professor Clay Christensen, there are two primary types of disruption: low end and new market. Low-end disrupters address overserved customers by developing business models in lower profit markets, while incumbents typically respond by moving further upstream. Over time, fresh players migrate upstream to disrupt incumbents. Examples of this include Netflix (disruptor) versus Blockbuster (disruptee) or Quickbooks (disruptor) versus Accountants (disruptee) and more recently LegalZoom (disruptee). In travel and hospitality, discount airlines such as Southwest, Ryanair, Indigo Airlines, and Air Asia are examples of low-end disruptors that have grown to compete against incumbents by starting in tertiary routes and expanding to encroach on the most profitable routes. In contrast, over the last decade, attempts at low-end disruption in the hotel sector such as Oyo hotels—an India based start-up that operates "good enough" budget hotels without a lobby, restaurant, fitness center, or other amenities typically seen in economy hotels such as Motel 6—have failed to achieve operational success in the United States or other mature markets.

The other gamechanger is a new market disruption that offers products and services to underserved customers and competes primarily against nonconsumption. Incremental innovations include VRBO, which launched vacation rentals in 1995, offering standalone accommodations that provide an alternative to hotels, a model that was co-opted by hotel brands as timeshares. In contrast, Airbnb started as a new market disruption by serving leisure travelers who could only afford an air mattress or bed in an apartment or home and migrated rapidly upstream. While Airbnb has the potential to be a new market disruptor and incumbents such as Marriott have classically responded by establishing a super luxury home rental business, there is scant evidence that proves it has negatively impacted consumer demand for hotels in the United States, especially for business or even "staycation" travelers. Hence, the hotel industry has yet to be negatively impacted by a new market disruption except for new videoconferencing technologies accelerated by the pandemic such as Zoom that are contributing to reductions in business travel.

A New Theory of Talent Disruption

Professor Christensen's disruption theory focuses on technologies and product markets that address unmet customer needs. But there is a third type of disruption that is initiated by the unmet needs of labor markets that radically changes performance in the service industry: talent. A talent disruption is the process by which traditional labor ends and talent shifts from legacy full-time employment to higher paying, more flexible work, facilitated by technologies that empower individuals to build a personal brand. As disruption grows, talent ruthlessly migrates to the highest paying and most flexible sources of work, leapfrogging inefficiencies in hierarchies of legacy industries.

We developed a theory that predicts when talent disruption occurs along with a typology for its various forms, and most importantly, depending on their position, what incumbents can do to either mitigate or accelerate each type of disruption.

Talent Disruption Framework

The talent disruption framework has two dimensions: talent creation, or the ability of an organization to capture or lose share of elite talent;

and unit labor economics, or the total direct and indirect costs of talent divided by the unit of product or service. The slope of the disruption curve reflects the rate at which an economy or sector progresses on both dimensions simultaneously, and those industries or organizations along-side or to the right of the curve address unmet customer needs through an operating model that creates a talent disruption resulting in a long-term shift in the labor markets (see Figure 1.1).

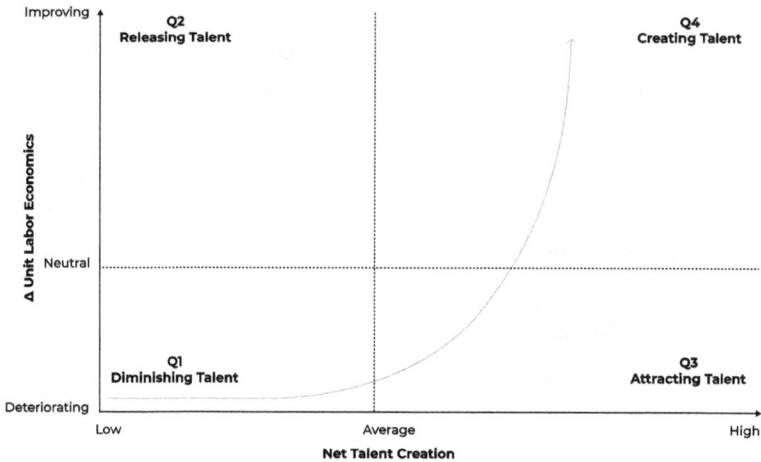

Figure 1.1 Talent disruption framework

On the horizontal X-axis, one can measure an organization's net talent creation in a market or a geographic hub. This is a measure of its employer brand equity that reflects its share of the industry's talent pool (either acquired or developed internally), less turnover, and backfill for promotions and internal mobility. Key performance indicators measure whether organizations, and specifically which functions and departments, are gaining market share of elite talent against other service industries including their direct and indirect competitors. Second, talent creation measures the velocity of upward mobility for these diverse elite talents as they rise from the front line to leadership positions such as GM or corporate executive.

At the low end of the talent creation continuum, rigid talent management practices require using executive search firms and job sites to recruit full-time permanent employees that have strict job definitions, multiple reporting layers, an established hierarchy, or pecking order supported by many standardized processes. At the extreme, they are unionized, with job-based pay scales and tenure-based criteria for advancement. An example is the U.S. public education system where teachers and administrators work in a highly formalized hierarchy that is usually unionized, which ensures their duties are well documented with established compensation models that are tenure rather than performance based. Other examples include unionized, full-service convention hotels or U.S. auto manufacturing plants prior to automation where factory workers earned wages and benefits 7 to 10 times the minimum wages at the time.

At the high end of the continuum are team-based organizations where much of the workforce wear many hats and perform multiple flexible jobs and a network of vetted part-time or gig workers may even be key contributors. Such organizations have what sports analysts refer to as "bench strength," and deep talent pipelines, that can withstand changes in demand by orchestrating faster or slower career mobility for its employees. The scope of employees' duties may vary radically by project, and they work in organizations that are flat with minimal bureaucracy and documented rules of engagement. An example is professional service firms such as investment banking, private equity, management consulting, or law firms where associates' assignments, types of work, and hours of engagement are project based, and the rules of engagement vary by the clients' demands and the managing partners in charge of the project or deal. Other examples include scientists or software developers at pioneering start-ups and elite military units such as the Navy Seals.

The vertical Y-axis measures change in unit labor economics, or the change in total compensation divided by a single unit or production or customers served. For example, in hospitals, unit labor economics can be calculated by dividing total compensation for full-time equivalents (including contracted labor such as nurses and technicians) by the number of patients discharged. In hotels or vacation rentals, occupied room nights and restaurant covers per seat are examples of the denominator used to measure unit economics. The extent to which an organization's unit labor economics improves or declines, for any reason such as an economic correction, process, or technology innovations, is charted over time, with a steeper positive slope of the curve implying positive gains.

The change in unit labor axis can also reflect different degrees of automation, starting with operational processes such as back-office and support functions, all the way to core customer-facing activities. At the low end of the continuum are highly inefficient organizations that continue to rely on labor-intensive processes such as luxury hotels in Asia that employ expensive expatriate managers, with fine dining restaurants that employ international culinary talent in roles such as prep, pastry, and pantry positions, which require certain certifications and training to produce haute cuisine. Another example is the factories and supply chains of luxury fashion brands such as Hermes and Richemont that contract with factories that hire sweatshop labor to perform stitching and embroidering in Italy, France, Portugal, and other European countries, including those who work at home. Finally, some of these companies that eschew technologies and are engaged in labor-intensive practices may have also outsourced or automated back-office functions, including the use of contract labor to perform activities that were once performed in-house. Consequently, their unit labor economics are deteriorating, and they lack the processes and technology tools to grow the talent pool other than through traditional methods which occur in low frequency. Examples include U.S. hospitals that experienced a 180 percent increase in costs per unit of service from 2019 to 2022, primarily due to a 258 percent increase in contract labor for nurses, technicians, and other roles over this 3 year period. Another example from hospitality is Marriott's assignment of all its property-level recruiting below the hotel GM level to a recruitment process outsourcing (RPO) firm that sources and screens tens of thousands of talents annually for their managed hotels. While RPO firms use certain automated marketing tools to source talent, they are still labor intensive and often result in equivalent turnover and a higher variable cost structure for service operators.

Talent Disruption in the Service Industry

We classified industries and organizations into one of four buckets to chart their historical performance and determine whether they are either facing a talent disruption or likely to confront one soon. It's also useful to chart the relative progress or decline of an organization's operational processes over time, including whether they are sustaining their model by relocating production to arbitrage differential currency, labor cost, and regulatory gains in the context of a global supply chain.

In the bottom left quadrant (Q1), industries and organizations experiencing "diminishing talent" are those whose talent pools are shrinking and experiencing increases in turnover, despite wage increases that outpace inflation. Full loaded labor costs, including benefits and overhead allocations, are growing faster than revenues. Typical tactics employed by participants who are experiencing diminishing talent include reducing product features and service levels, cutting back on labor, and, if possible, increasing prices and adding fees for customers despite potential backlash and regulatory risk. If organizations move too fast to unload risks and reduce costs, they render themselves vulnerable to further unionization, worker protests and strikes, and even government intervention and more regulation (see Figure 1.2).

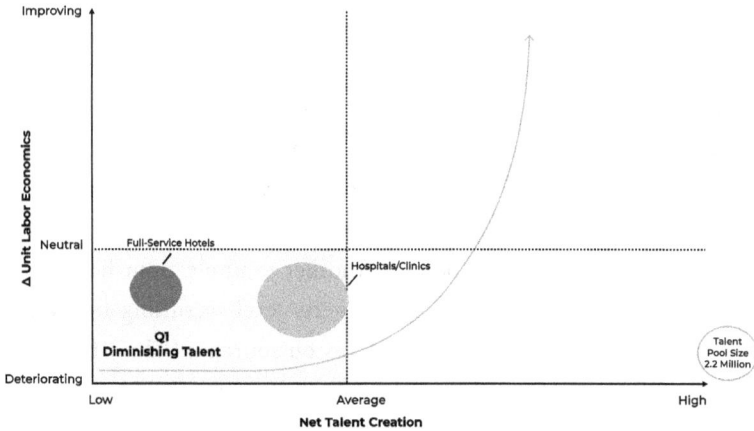

Figure 1.2 Talent disruption—diminishing talent (Q1)

As conditions deteriorate, less agile participants become even more rigid and bureaucratic, using executive search firms and job sites supported by undifferentiated employer brand marketing. They increasingly rely heavily on legacy ATS platforms and offer below-market wages and benefits that result in higher turnover and rising labor costs greater than 40 percent of the profit and loss statement. Hence, they are most likely to be facing a talent disruption with massive labor shortages and are vulnerable to their operating model being disrupted by a new competitor or a shift in the labor markets. Examples include most if not all hotel, restaurant, and hospital operators.

In the top left quadrant (Q2), organizations have favorable unit economics but are "releasing talent." Due to their strategic decisions in reducing the workforce, such as partial automation and outsourcing noncore functions and market conditions, their talent pool is shrinking. Costs are steadily decreasing as evidenced by store closures, the implementation of new customer self-service models, fewer entry-level positions for new graduates, and a shift in operating roles to warehouses or automated factories that bet on e-commerce (see Figure 1.3).

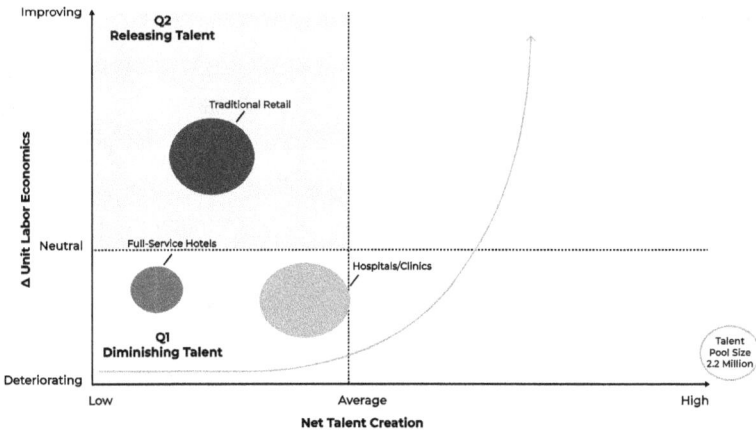

Figure 1.3 Talent disruption—releasing talent (Q2)

Often, these financially healthy organizations are still dependent on a finite number of talent pools such as animation and game developers and software engineers and an expensive and highly skilled full-time workforce with high unit labor costs. Companies in quadrant three have improved their unit labor economics with semiautomated workflows that scale at least some of their entire supply chains using machine learning and virtual training methods. Examples include traditional retailers such as Walmart and Costco, most U.S. auto manufacturers, including AI-driven EV technology companies such as Tesla, live entertainment, and content-centric companies such as Disney and Fox, and discount airlines such as Southwest, Ryanair, and Air Asia. The biggest challenge for these companies is growing the talent pool by redefining job descriptions to access noncandidates and upskilling talents and building an internal marketplace that includes experiential learning and development to improve the velocity of internal mobility. In the context of a labor shortage and immigration bottlenecks, only by reducing turnover to a healthy figure of 20 percent or less can these organizations increase the velocity of the internal upward mobility. For example, Tesla's store and mobile service units could chart a path from mechanic or engineer to regional service manager using an AI-enabled talent marketplace that includes online training and management simulations using AR and VR.

In the bottom right quadrant (Q3) are organizations "attracting talent," with flat organizations directly aimed at stealing elite and rising talents from their direct competitors and growing the talent pool of noncandidates, including from other industries. These often-promising organizations are often private (such as family office, venture, sovereign fund, or government backed) and have the capacity to outspend their rivals, at least in the short term, to acquire talent but have yet to establish processes or the managerial quality required to scale their workforce at lower marginal costs. However, their weak talent pipelines render them vulnerable to an economic downturn or shift in the capital markets that may cut short their path to a successful talent disruption (see Figure 1.4). Historical examples of organizations that successfully attracted talent on

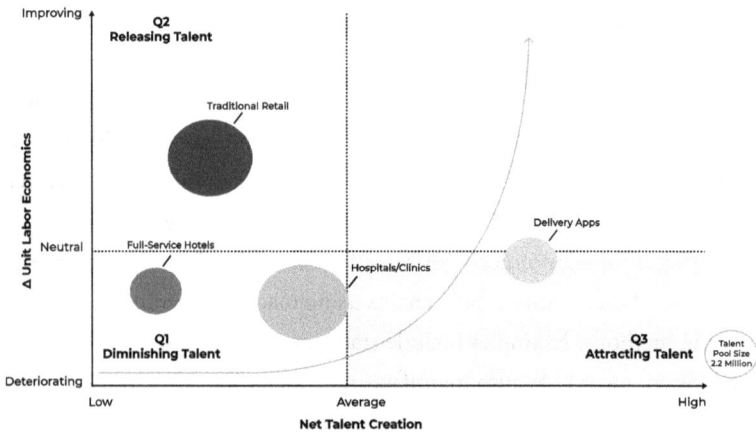

Figure 1.4 Talent disruption—attracting talent (Q3)

a large scale to disrupt incumbents, in a brief period, include low-cost air-lines that started as domestic or regional players such as Ryanair and Air Asia as well as luxury airlines such as Emirates and Qatar Airways. Less favorable well- documented examples include the co-working start-up WeWork or Oyo hotels, which failed to scale as its marginal labor costs outpaced the revenues associated with its aggressive unit growth as well as many otherwise successful U.S.- and European-based start-ups, finance, and professional service firms in China such as Airbnb, the Vanguard Group, and Royal Bank of Scotland.

In the top right quadrant (Q4) are organizations "creating talent" and making a step function leap in unit economics compared to incumbents. These winners are usually new entrants that accelerate their competitive advantage in talent acquisition by using targeted talent marketing invest-ments that establish an employer brand with a deep purpose. Their busi-ness models scale deep learning to broaden their talent pool by leveraging adjacent skills and race to the front of the marathon by using internal talent marketplaces supported by employee ownership models that create a culture of perceived meritocracy. They are investing in artificial intelli-gence, automated marketing, and robotics to achieve higher degrees of automation in their workflows. Their hybrid workforce often includes full-time marketing and service teams who work alongside highly skilled part-time workers and freelancers who are well compensated for perfor-mance by both employers and consumers. Employers in quadrant four also generate elite talent at two to three times the rate of their competi-tors by attracting a global talent pool and investing disproportionately in experiential training and development to enable hybrid and remote work (see Figure 1.5). This fourth quadrant includes professional sports leagues such as the NBA; category-leading consulting, law, banking, and private equity firms; digital music; biotech firms; online travel and retail firms; and category-leading social media companies. These companies are grow-ing the talent pool for their industries by attracting noncandidates regard-less of their formal education and gaining talent. In addition to stealing talent from their competitors, these magnets for talent are also gaining market share of talent both nationally and globally from other industries from their traditional Fortune 500 brick and mortar counterparts. They

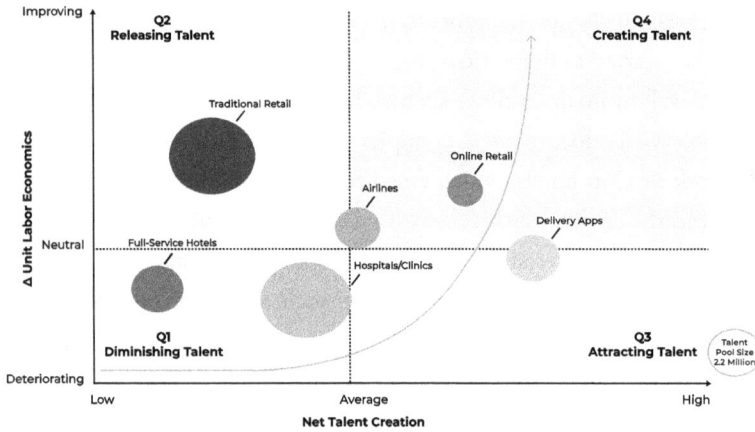

Figure 1.5 Talent disruption—creating talent (Q4)

are adept at acquiring undervalued, demographically diverse rising talents and converting them from acquired companies, developing them at a reasonable cost, and either promoting or recycling them with a high velocity of internal mobility and "up or out" pay for performance models whose equilibrium is turnovers of 25 to 40 percent. Given their growth, the challenge for organizations in this quadrant is growing the talent pool outside traditional channels, such as college and high school teams for the NBA. For example, the NBA has not just aggressively recruited from Europe but has created the Black African League (BAL), a separate league based in Africa, with the objective of sourcing and developing prospects outside the system in Angola, Egypt, Tunisia, Morocco (in 2021), Nigeria, Rwanda (since 2022), and Senegal. American teams send scouts to attend the final matches. Outstanding players from Africa are given a chance to showcase their talent in the NBA Summer League in the United States where they have a chance of securing a contract.

Accelerating and Combating the Talent Disruption in Service Industries, 2019 to 2023

Organizations evolve not just in response to changes in their external environment but also due to changes in leadership and labor. Former Harvard Business professor Christensen's initial work focused on the computer hardware industry, which was a fertile ground for research given its short product cycles and relentless pace of technological innovation. Similarly, the immediate pre- and post-COVID-19 pandemic period from 2019 to 2023 provides a superlative window into the performance of service industries, especially hospitality, retail, and health care, as either the disappearance or surge of demand for their services forced management to seek and implement labor market efficiencies, as well as changes to the operating model, in a short period of time, on a scale that may have otherwise taken several decades to be implemented.

We used AI and machine learning to analyze and chart the human capital performance of over 1,000 internally managed properties at over 100 publicly traded companies in the hotel, hospital, retail, and delivery sectors. A case in point is the health care industry, which is facing significant challenges, including rising costs, a labor shortage, and declining operating margins. The United States is projected to face a shortage of more than 200,000 registered nurses and more than 50,000 physicians in the next 3 years. The turnover rate for nurses is 20 percent, double the industry average, and a key bottleneck is the lack of seats to meet the demand: U.S. nursing schools turned down over 80,000 applicants and are suffering from a shortage of nurse educators, inadequate campus facilities, and equipment. In the coming years, health care leaders expect a drop in margins of between 25 and 75 percent, which could place even more workload for an already stressed workforce and necessitate hospital closures and layoffs.

Furthermore, the industry is seeking improvements in diversity, equity, and inclusion (DEI). Nurses with associate degrees are mostly minorities without a clear path to becoming a registered nurse, which limits their income potential and professional growth. While 28 percent of physicians are immigrants, only 6 percent of Hispanics and 5 percent of black people identify as physicians; 75 percent of general practice doctors are men.

However, innovative models are being adopted that shift the industry from hospital-based care to lower acuity sites and home-based care, enabled by innovative technologies; $1 trillion of productivity improvements are being ushered in by telehealth, virtual testing, and remote patient monitoring. Furthermore, the industry is responding to improve transparency and data sharing, including price transparency, data interoperability, and data access. The integration of price and quality-rating information across health care providers will help consumers make better decisions about where to go for care. Furthermore, the regional expansion of academic medical centers through mergers and acquisitions into distribution networks such as UCLA Health, that include doctors' offices and clinics, is resulting in burgeoning talent pools for nurses, technicians, and residents and reductions in admission costs per patient. R&D has grown to over $200 billion, or 6 percent of revenue, including over $20 billion invested in building AI-driven "hospitals of the future," and the industry has attracted over $50 billion of capital since 2021 focused on creating workflow efficiencies and using data for clinical decision support.

Therefore, as health care becomes less expensive and automated, less invasive, and more precise and customers have access to their data, unit labor costs for hospitals and most health care providers will decline sharply. Public–private partnerships in health care are investing in technologies such as remote monitored robotic surgeries that are changing the nature of work, and further investments in hospitals from private equity will create more cost efficiencies that mitigate the labor shortage.

The retail industry is expected to close 50,000 stores in 2022 alone and continue investing in e-commerce automation. Given the restructuring of commercial real estate, retail may permanently shrink as an employer. However, new roles in fulfillment, logistics, and AI will be created, and retailers will increasingly compete for talent with traditional manufacturing, logistics, and other businesses.

In contrast, absent significant innovation, the labor productivity in U.S. hotels will continue to diminish. Even taking into consideration an economic recession, changes in U.S. immigration policies, and departures from legacy brand standards that result in lower levels of service and further investment in talent marketing and employer branding, the industry will continue to have 2.4 million job openings annually. Hotels will continue losing talent share to other industries and experience growing labor costs buttressed by the expansionist agenda of labor unions and the intensifying talent shift to the gig economy (see Figure 1.6).

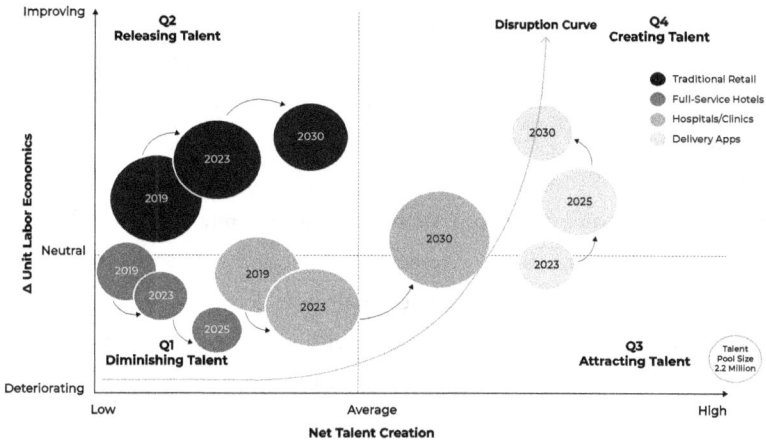

Figure 1.6 *Talent disruption—industry case studies*

Talent Disruption in a Turbulent World Economy

Despite economic uncertainty, rising geopolitical tensions, and upheaval in the financial markets, repatriated talents in the service industry have lost faith in free market capitalism and are embracing organized labor, which is gaining traction not just in hospitality, but in health care, retail, education, delivery, logistics, and other industries. In this context, Starbucks founder and chairperson Howard Shultz recently bemoaned that young people have become disillusioned:

> It's my belief that the efforts of unionization in America are in many ways a manifestation of a much bigger problem. There is a macro issue here that is much, much bigger than Starbucks. I was shocked, stunned to hear the loneliness, the anxiety, the fracturing of trust in government, fracturing of trust in companies, fracturing of trust in families, the lack of hope in terms of opportunity.

At the top level, this book is made for the consumer—the most powerful stakeholder, whose pent-up demand for hospitality and travel reflects its importance as an essential life experience and avenue for human growth and development. Consumers deserve full transparency to know who (not just what) they are getting when they fly, check in to a hotel, or dine at a restaurant. They also deserve to know where their money goes and how profits are distributed among stakeholders so that they can also play a role in ensuring hospitality and travel regenerates for future generations.

Consumers are voting with their wallets and choosing experiences that are quite different from traditional hotels, retailers, and doctors' offices, which are in turn accelerating the talent disruption. Consumers want one-on-one engagement with their service providers, customized experiences, two-way reviews, and the opportunity to tip them if they deserve. From hospitality hosts, accountants, lawyers, digital marketers, software developers, and graphic designers to drivers, electricians, and dog walkers, a new generation of service leaders are earning their income and building their personal brand on category apps. Apps such as Airbnb, Uber, DoorDash, Upwork, 99designs, Fiverr, Instacart, TaskRabbit, Peloton, Rover, and Wag are capturing the lion's share of consumer spending and talent in the form of contractors who set their own work rules, who they do business with, and their compensation.

In 2023, the *Wall Street Journal* reported that Uber drivers in the United States are making over $35 an hour—the average wage on gig platforms after the apps take their fees from both the talents and the users— versus $22 an hour for hotel workers, even after recent pay increases. While these apps have quickly become household names, the real brands are the talents that provide the goods and services and earn either part or all their living on the app, which is leveraged across social media, such as TikTok or Instagram, to showcase their skills, accomplishments, and services (see Figure 1.7).

From a user's perspective, talents and small business providers across the world can be searched, scheduled, and messaged within the app. In the case of Upwork, users can choose to set milestones and payment terms for their projects, which could range from short term to long term. These applications can be seen on a continuum, from those who have talent tiers as expert and rising, based on the number of projects successfully completed, customer reviews, spend, and engagement on the app at one end to those who simply match talents with projects on the user's behalf based on geography, availability, and other factors in their algorithm (see Figure 1.8).

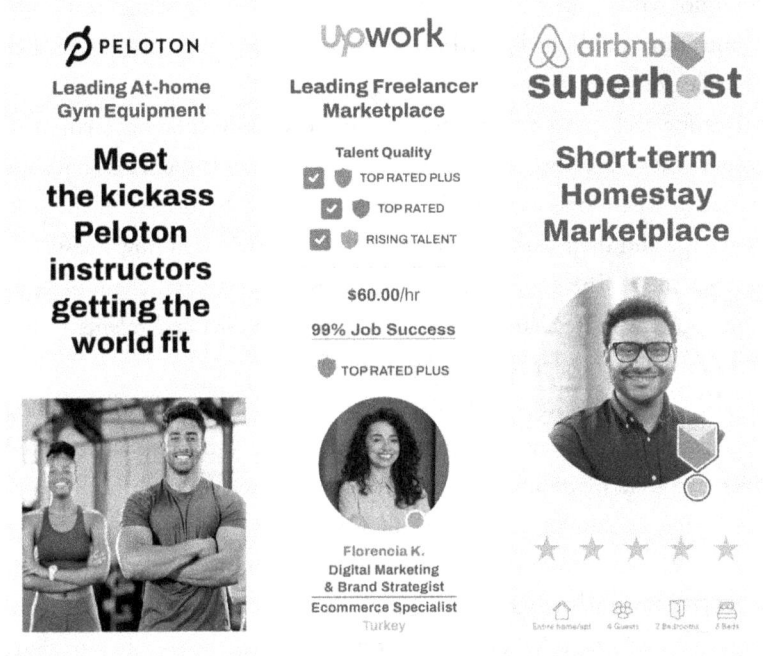

Figure 1.7 Gig platforms: talents build their brands

Figure 1.8 Continuum of user experiences on gig platforms

People Are the Brands: Entrepreneurship Finds a Platform on the New Media

These new, disruptive talent marketplaces are a stark contrast to the way hotel and restaurant chains market their services and recruit and compensate their talents. The hotel industry operates with a deeply held belief or orthodoxy that talent is best kept under the radar and that direct communication should be limited to on-site messaging. At most, brands like Four Seasons sometimes provide biographies of their top five hotel executives for each property on their corporate website (but no method to contact them directly), and InterContinental Hotels launched a concierge initiative where one can see the biographies and headshots of the lead concierge and their team members, with information on how guests can contact them. There are very few examples where a hotel chain or boutique hotel website shares information about its GM and talents in key positions with travelers or even frequent guests.

To further investigate this orthodoxy, we used CrowdRiff, a leading aggregator of user-generated content in the travel business. We reviewed over two years of photoshoots developed by hotel brands and property marketing executives, including 100,000 pieces of content. We found that less than 1 percent of this content featured employees or named their accomplishments such as catering a Hollywood award event, making an exquisite wedding cake, or orchestrating a magnificent social event. Furthermore, while some hotels celebrate individual talents who get positive mentions on TripAdvisor (which may only include their first name and position), they don't see talent marketing as a revenue-generating opportunity. The hospitality industry continues to adopt a real-estate mindset—focusing on maximizing earnings on every square foot of real estate, for example, by selling poolside cabanas at $250 a day—rather than experiment with an Airbnb Superhost type of model to generate price premiums or higher occupancies.

One of the lessons of platforms that make talent the brand is that they are scalable through algorithms and provide value to users through service innovations such as pricing by talent tiers. For example, Airbnb's "Superhost" status is earned with review scores of 4.8 and over at least 10 stays and generates 5.9 percent more revenue; Upwork's "Top Rated Plus" is the top 3 percent with at least $10,000 of annual spend; and TaskRabbit's "Elite Taskers" must score 4.9 out of 5 and earn on average $6,554 a month. Our research suggests that holding all other factors constant, each talent tier commands a 30 percent price premium above the lower tier. Top-rated talents on Upwork, who reside in over 120 countries, are also eligible for faster payments, discounts on fees, and premium customer support from the app. Similar applications are gaining traction in health care, among nurses, lawyers, and other professional services.

Celebrating elite talents and encouraging them to leave to further advance their earnings or careers is in the best interest of the business. Hotels and casinos in the United States have an established track record of generating outsized marketing returns by investing in celebrity chefs, whose success drives traffic and generates disproportionate public relations media, loyalty program sign-ups, room bookings, and events and casino gaming spending, not just in Las Vegas but nationally. The most successful celebrity chefs earn $5 million a year on average, with a net worth of $50 million to $100 million based on recurring revenue streams such as restaurant licensing, equipment, merchandising, television, and social media where they have an average of 500,000 followers. However, the reality is that few celebrity chefs have proven to be successful operators in hotels—they typically earn licensing and appearance fees off the top and add food and labor costs to a restaurant, bar, or lounge and decrease its profitability by 20 to 30 percent. In contrast, chefs trained by hotels that may include shared kitchens and profitable banquet and catering operations and working in union operations are far more likely to succeed across a hotel portfolio. Given that most celebrity chefs are also European men, including those represented by talent agencies such as CAA, it also represents a significant opportunity for hotels to lead advance DEI. That said, of 40 full-service hotels we surveyed in Los Angeles, only 13 (mostly boutique hotels and small luxury brands) even mentioned one of their chefs in their property website, press releases, and social media. Few hotel marketing teams and brand managers have prioritized making stars out of their hotel chefs or allocating marketing budgets to help them write cookbooks or develop cobranded products that could be an additional source of revenue for the hotel and their chefs. In a world where 25 million U.S.-based small businesses, including many chefs and restaurants, rely on social media platforms such as TikTok, Instagram, YouTube, and Facebook, including dedicated channels and shops, and independent film producers are being discovered by audiences on Amazon and Netflix, hotel chains have allocated few resources to talent-centric marketing that celebrates their culinary teams.

Few businesses have more contact points for making talents the brands, and in the process, creating ancillary revenue and higher employee engagement than hospitality, including event planners and catering, spas and fitness, restaurants, concierge, and leisure activities at resorts. These are fertile opportunities where locals and travelers seeking unique experiences could be educated, be entertained, and provide valuable feedback to the hotel or resort.

Skeptics may contend that turnover, the risk of employees poaching customers, and increases in compensation render a talent-branding approach too risky compared to other marketing investments. Such concerns are shortsighted and not data centric. If anything, hoteliers should help their most successful chefs get contracts to be represented by leading artist management companies such as CAA, which has a practice dedicated to up-and-coming culinary talent. Hotel brand managers should provide talent representation referrals and establish a list of preferred agents and agencies for elite talent in their properties, regardless of whether they are owned, managed, or franchised. Unlike apps, hotels have real-estate and operating systems that provide a platform for talent to develop a personal brand. If a star is born, new aspiring stars will be much easier to recruit to the same platform, including from other industries.

There is another reason the hospitality industry should change its mindset and begin to experiment with new forms of talent marketing across its leisure business: establishing a new revenue management model that is more sustainable than additional resort fees and nickel and diming guests. As the postpandemic recovery has demonstrated, enthusiasts, such as spa-goers, golfers, and foodies, are willing to pay a premium for their experiences to be curated and hosted by elite talent, only available as direct bookings on the company's website.

The data received from these experiences, including customer reviews, can feed into an internal talent marketplace, which can provide operators the ranking, worth, and promotion readiness of each employee and gig worker. Over time, these data, along with financial data that evaluate the profitability of the hosted experience, can be used as a variable in revenue management, setting price guidelines and amenities. This information can be stored either in the property management system or on the cloud and support a new technical architecture where people are the brands.

This book lays out far-reaching solutions that can be implemented in a turbulent multipolar world to combat the talent disruption, including dynamic talent marketplaces, employee profit-sharing and ownership, and talent sharing between hospitality companies and across industries. For example, leading private equity firms are pioneering employee ownership in many sectors and, after decades of positive impact on the airline industry, the time has come for its adoption in hotels. The franchising business model also requires an overhaul as the labor shortage grows and immigration remains contentious as we migrate from globalization to "the clash of civilizations." The next decade will be marked by a restructuring of supply chains, digital firewalls, and diminished cross-border capital and talent flows. In a multipolar world, hospitality brands must return to playing a strategic role in human capital management, including reinvesting some of their program fees and marketing funds into providing owners and third-party operators with talent solutions.

Without this strategic transformation, the hospitality industry, one of the world's greatest engines of human meritocracy, is at risk of contraction and relative decline as an employer. Moreover, the prospects for filling the talent gaps and improving diversity, including hiring and promoting women, minorities, refugees, and members of other economically disadvantaged communities and eventually building a larger pool of diverse entrepreneurs including hotel owners, are otherwise bleak. Labor unions will continue to grow, and government taxes and regulations will increase, thwarting the possibilities of innovation and threatening the prospects of market-based solutions that can be extended across borders.

CHAPTER 2

The Brutal Facts

Rebuilding the Service Profit Chain

Across the globe, hundreds of millions of people are required to join the service industry workforce—from health care to hotels and restaurants—amidst what labor economists are calling "the Great Resignation." Inflation, high interest rates, and economic and geopolitical turbulence not seen for decades are creating new cost pressures and uncertainties, making it more challenging for the service industry to forecast its operating requirements. Meanwhile, remote workers and distributed teams armed with powerful collaboration tools are bucking the notion that career ascension requires working for a single employer or that only secure innovation blossoms in the office. These long-term trends are contributing toward a discontinuity or permanent structural shift from labor as we know it to a new era of distributed talent management.

In 2019, the top three global service sectors—hospitality, health care, and retail—accounted for 707 million jobs or 23.5 percent of worldwide employment. Due to the growing demand for their services, these figures are projected to grow to 965 million or 30 percent of global employment, primarily due to the growth of health care facilities, job openings associated with record hotel development pipeline prior to the pandemic, and to a lesser extent the growth of retail stores internationally in regions such as Asia and the Middle East.

In this context, hotel, restaurants, and leisure, representing a 300-million-person workforce, 10 percent of employment, and a staggering 10 percent of global GDP, are a bellwether for the global economy. The hospitality industry is embarking on hiring an additional 60 million people by 2024 as it prepares to satisfy pent-up demand for travel and open a record hotel pipeline over the next 5 years in the United States, China, the Middle East, Germany, and elsewhere (see Figure 2.1).

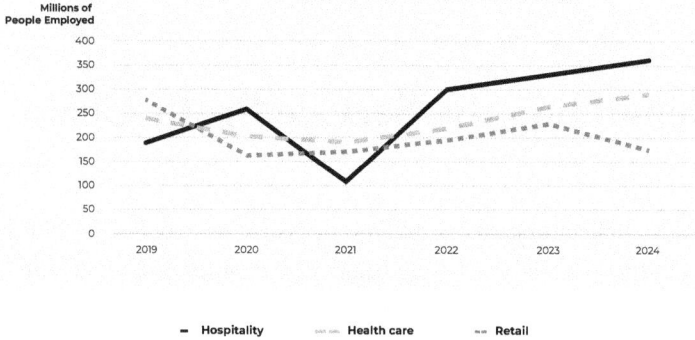

Figure 2.1 Global employment—hospitality, health care, and retail

Retail, health care, and hospitality are also among the largest employers in the United States, together accounting for 31.3 million full-time jobs in 2023. However, they are also experiencing record high turnover rates that require filling another 15.4 million full-time positions to sustain current operations plus another 4.4 million new positions due to support growth (see Figure 2.2).

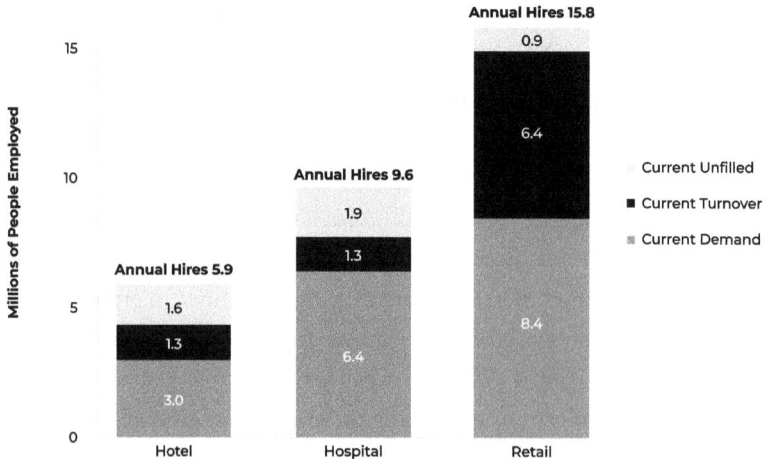

Figure 2.2 U.S. employment—hotels, hospitals, and retail

Furthermore, there will be an additional 50 million hires required in U.S. retail, health care, and hospitality due to 60 to 100 percent turnover and relatively high quit rates. While hospitality has always suffered from turnover rates much higher than the broader economy, the number of U.S. job openings nationally now exceeds 10 million and its quit rates are now 2.5 to 3.0 times that of the broader economy.

The root cause of this turnover and labor shortage is an overall increased workload for frontline employees: for example, postpandemic operational decisions to memorialize cost reductions by allocating managers across multiple properties and reducing service levels for housekeeping, restaurants, and other departments, thereby increasing workloads across markets.

The hospitality, health care, and retail industries in the United States experienced significant increases in workload per employee between 2019 and 2021 (see Figure 2.3). The 20 percent increased workload in the health care industry has had several negative consequences. Health care workers have reported feeling stressed, burned out, and undervalued. The increased workload put a strain on health care budgets, as turnover among nurses and hospitals raised wages, incurred high contract labor costs, and paid more overtime.

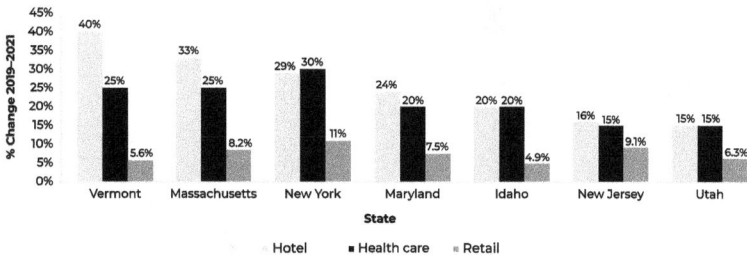

Figure 2.3 Increased workload—U.S. hotels, health care, and retail

To a lesser extent, the retail industry also experienced a 7.5 percent increase in workload per employee between 2021 and 2019. This is due to several factors, including the COVID-19 pandemic and the rise of online shopping, which resulted in a shortage of retail workers tasked with fulfilling orders and processing returns.

The hotel industry's 30 percent increase in workload was the result of millions of layoffs during the pandemic followed by changes to the operating model including a reduction in services such as restaurants and daily housekeeping. The increased workload per employee, such as housekeepers, amidst an acceleration of pent-up consumer demand with leisure occupancy levels returning to 2019 levels earlier than expected, further increased workloads for a smaller workforce. Like hospitals, hotels became addicted to contract labor for functions such as laundry, housekeeping, security, engineering and maintenance, and other functions. Overtime and contract expenses rose further in 2022 in part due to diminished capability of hotel managers to predict travel patterns as booking windows for many customer types shrunk to less than a week.

In addition, wage pressures and increased unionization are negatively impacting hotel profitability and outpacing revenues in the United States and most European markets. According to the Bureau of Labor Statistics, many hotel operators are paying wages of $20.10 an hour, well above the minimum wage, but still 25 to 33 percent less than the hourly earnings of Uber drivers. Percentage changes in average hourly wages and benefits such as health care costs have also skyrocketed with labor per occupied room climbing seven dollars higher than 2019, equivalent to a 3.7 percent compounded monthly growth rate outpacing other service industries (see Figure 2.4).

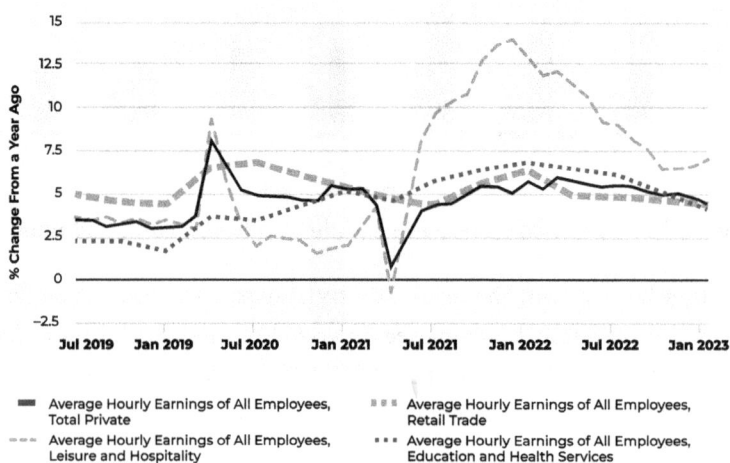

Figure 2.4 *Increase in wages—U.S. service industries*

Source: Bureau of Labor Statistics via FRED.

According to *CoStar*,[1] gross operating profits in U.S. hotels were $74.8 billion, but labor costs were a record high of $70.9 billion, despite less frequent housekeeping, reduced food and beverage offerings, and a growing reliance on contract labor to reduce benefits costs.

Customer satisfaction in service industries has reached its lowest point in decades, according to the American Customer Satisfaction Index (ACSI). Hotels have suffered the most, with an 8 percent drop in their ACSI score from 2017 to 2022. Health care also saw a significant decline in its ACSI score by 5 percent to historic lows while retail service scores also declined 3 percent (see Figure 2.5).

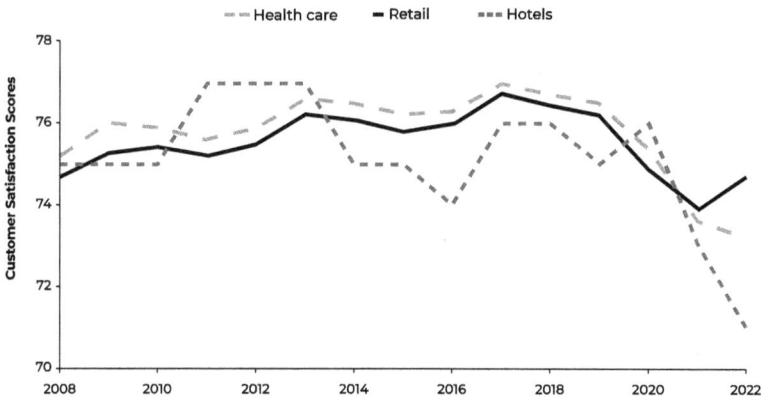

Figure 2.5 *Customer satisfaction—U.S. hotels, health care, and retail*

Source: Statista Research Department.

Given these trends, it is not surprising that despite pent-up demand, customer service scores are also at record lows. North American hotel guests aren't satisfied anymore, according to the ASCI, which has dropped to the lowest levels in 14 years.

JD Power's 2022 North America Hotel Guest Satisfaction Index (NAGSI)[2] study identifies the root causes of growing customer dissatisfaction: prices have increased by an average of 34 percent, and travelers are not satisfied with the costs and fees they are paying, especially given the reduction in service levels and lack of transparency. Satisfaction with hotel costs and fees dropped by 18 points. More specifically, satisfaction with guest rooms—highlighting the labor shortage in housekeeping—also declined by 10 points in 2022, despite a wave of renovations and new hotel openings, contributing to the overall decrease.

What's not apparent in these figures is that hospitality's labor shortage is symptomatic of a much bigger problem: a reputational problem, resulting in the inability to attract new talent on a meaningful scale to replace the highly skilled, experienced supervisors who left the industry. With fewer high-quality supervisors, department heads, and general managers, frontline employees lack qualified mentors, a sense of purpose, and a rewarding career path. Meanwhile, customers paying higher rates with lower real incomes are airing their grievances upon an understaffed and underpaid workforce, ill-equipped to meet their expectations. The industry's hastened franchising, bureaucratic hierarchy, and growing unionization are compounding the problem.

Initial Research Questions to Address in the Discovery Process

At this decisive moment for service industries, our research team spent 2 years pouring over data from numerous sources and in the field interviewing and observing hospitality operations across the postpandemic United States. MogulRecruiter's team formulated three key research questions that kicked off our discovery process to gather facts prior to developing a software platform that facilitates a new talent management system for hospitality and other service industries:

- What are the root causes of the talent problem in service industries, starting with hospitality?
- What are the relevant talent segments and what is the employee's worth to the business?
- How significant is the diversity gap and where do the biggest opportunities exist?

But before we delve into data-driven insights and prospective solutions, it's important to place our work within a governing framework known as the service profit chain. This theoretical framework enables us to diagnose the problem and quantify the return on investment in talent management.

Governing Framework: Hospitality as a Service Profit Chain Business That Requires an Employee Value Proposition

The service profit chain confirms the interrelationships between employee engagement, customer loyalty, revenues, and profitability. It leverages big data and algorithms to quantify these relationships and determine the level of investment in the workforce required to achieve greater levels of profitability. In hospitality and service businesses, its foundation is customer data (such as current spend, lifetime value, and customer reviews), employee satisfaction and engagement, financial, and other transactional data that inform marketing and human capital reinvestments required to grow revenues and improve market share and profitability. It also provides insights that enable management teams to determine the type and level of capital investments required to generate higher profit margins and establish key performance indicators or achieve operational metrics. It is through investments in acquiring, training, and adequately compensating employees that the chain of service profits is set in motion. The service profit chain model enables operators to not just optimize investments in their workforce, but determine how to do so for each respective customer segment in every part of the operation, from the front line to the back office. Professors Schlesinger, Heskett, and Sasser[3] refer to a "high retention strategy in services," when economic value for stakeholders is created in the form of price premiums and reasonable profit margins sustained by well-compensated, well-trained, motivated, and productive employees whose contributions are valued by loyal customers who refer new business (see Figure 2.6).

Conversely, in the case of a "low retention strategy," any weakness along the entire chain reverberates in both directions and, ultimately, affects the bottom line. For example, while cutbacks in training and relatively low compensation may result in labor productivity and improve short-term profits, they increase turnover and employee dissatisfaction, resulting in customer defection and higher marketing costs. Over time, if an industry adopts such practices and they become the new orthodoxy, they may reduce the customer's willingness to pay and

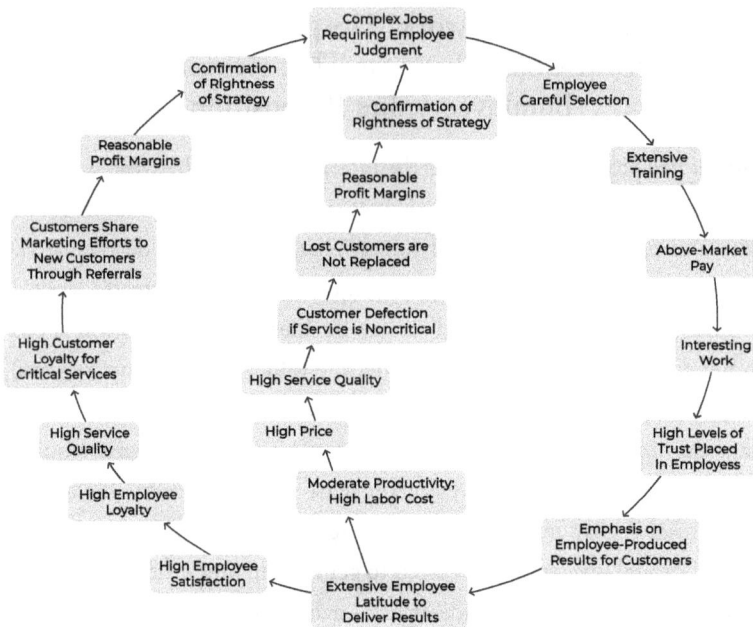

Figure 2.6 The logic of a high retention strategy in services

Source: What Great Service Leaders Know and Do: Creating Breakthroughs in Service Firms (by James L. Heskett, W. Earl Sasser, Jr., and Leonard A. Schlesinger)

thereby create an opening for substitute products and disruptive innovation (see Figure 2.7).

The linkages in the service profit chain have been repeatedly validated in the hotel, restaurant, and casino gaming business, not just in the United States, but globally across brand segments, and in every department of the business. Studies found that, on average, a 1 percent increase in employee satisfaction generates a 1 percent increase in customer satisfaction and a 0.5 percent increase in revenue per available room (RevPAR) and its REVPAR index, a widely used measure of market share gains against a local competitive set. More specifically, the following linkages exist in the hotel service profit chain: a 25 percent correlation between changes in employee satisfaction and retention; a 30 percent correlation between changes in employee satisfaction and customer satisfaction; and a 35 percent correlation between changes in customer loyalty and revenues (see Figure 2.8).

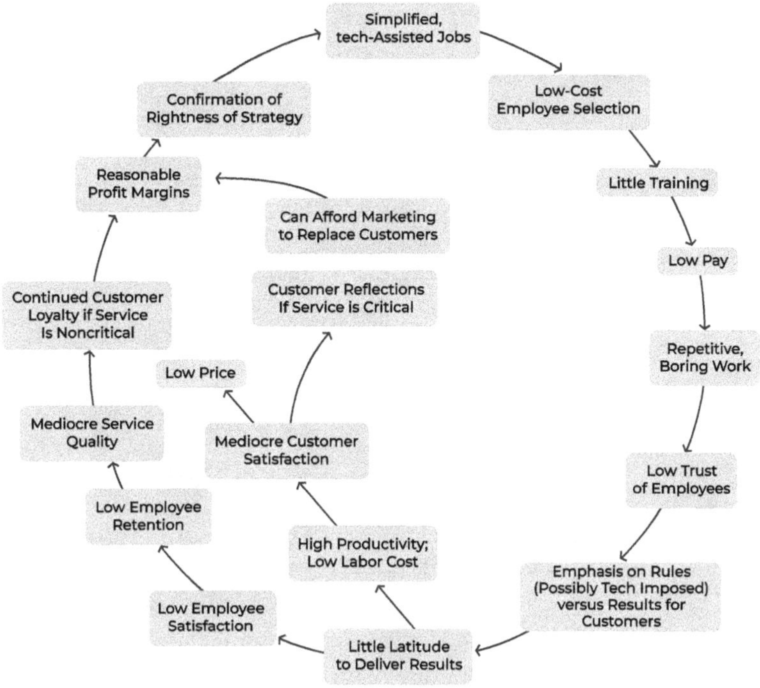

Figure 2.7 The logic of a low retention strategy in service

Source: What Great Service Leaders Know and Do: Creating Breakthroughs in ServiceFirms (by James L. Heskett, W. Earl Sasser, Jr., and Leonard A. Schlesinger)

How Big HR Tech Distorts the Service Profit Chain

The talent disruption has been accelerated by the unintended consequences of big tech, specifically big HR tech companies that are seeking to establish what game theorists call a "choke point" around employee databases. As a standard operating procedure-driven culture, the hospitality industry likes to standardize and replicate technology, especially with respect to labor management. More than 90 percent of hotel operators that manage more than 10 properties in the United States have implemented a recruiting management or marketing system (RMS) that complements their applicant tracking system (ATS), which automates the recruiting process from job description templates to resume parsing, candidate scoring, messaging, and communications including engagement with job sites.

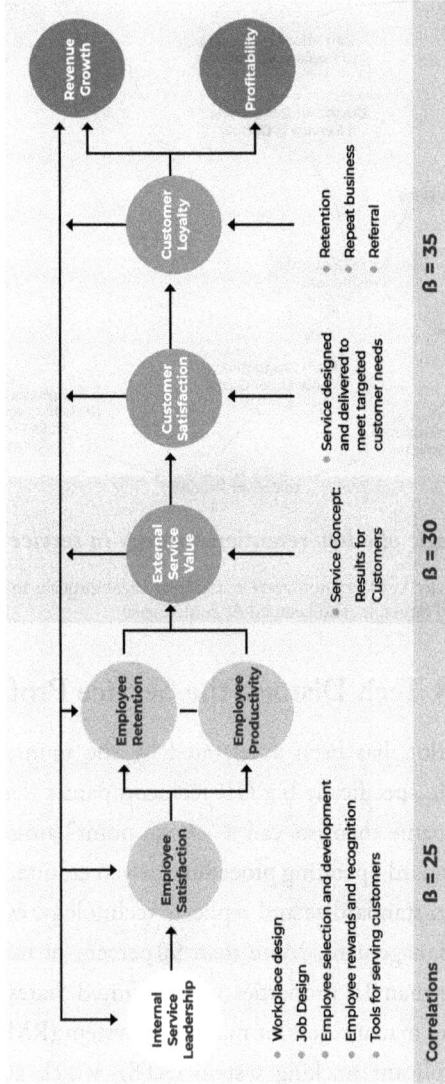

Figure 2.8 The service profit chain and service delivery system

Source: The Service Profit Chain: How Leading Companies Link Profit and Growth to Loyalty, Satisfaction and Value (by James L. Heskett, W. Earl Sasser, Jr., and Leonard A. Schlesinger)

This "big HR tech," which enables the collection and processing of data on cloud-based HR systems, provides hospitality companies the foundation for building fully automated, intelligent HR processes based on machine learning. This enables an even higher level of efficiency. In theory, these applications can be used to reduce staff turnover, assess employee sentiment, measure changes in the perception of the employer's brand, and determine the type of employee that is most effective in a given company, in a given position, and for a given region. The features and capabilities of ATS platforms have evolved along the lines of customer relationship management software in its early stages, but their legitimacy hinges on their ability to provide a single user interface for recruiting and predicting talent matches with job opportunities. As a result, work gets done faster, and human resources have time for more strategic and creative tasks. For example, on average, a recruiter invites only 5 out of 250 applicants screened on their behalf by the automated system to the interview stage.

Big HR tech is gaining traction across service industries. For example, in 2018, SAP created a smart recruiting system based on machine learning for a large bank. When recruiting employees, it automatically analyzes resumes and opens profiles of job seekers on social networks. Then, it compares them with data about people who have already been selected for a similar position and are successfully working in the company. If the job seeker's profile is similar to that of a successful employee, the system recommends hiring him or her and explains the reasons for choosing him or her. A smart system developed by SAP analyzes the experience, skills, and appraisal results of each individual employee and then finds the most suitable positions for career growth. It tells everyone what skills need to be improved in order to increase the chances of a new position, and independently appoints the necessary refresher courses for this. Having prepared in advance, a person, with a high probability, can move up the career ladder as soon as a vacancy appears and immediately successfully start work. Transparent growth conditions within the company increase employee motivation, and managers always have a pool of internal candidates for important vacancies.

We tested and benchmarked over 30 ATSs, including the top 10 most widely used in hospitality, such as Workday, SAP, and Oracle. We also tested the top hospitality job sites from a talent perspective of providing potential job matches to resumes and preferences. We found these systems have radically different levels of user-friendliness and are generic and inflexible. For example, they are inflexibly configured and generate candidates using very specific parameters. Their acceleration, in response to pressures to generate cost savings, has exacerbated hospitality's shortage and created blind spots with their filters that most HR executives are not even aware exist. Worse, independent research from Deloitte, BCG, and other consulting firms suggests that the ecosystem of big HR tech has discouraged women and immigrants from applying for positions where they don't "check all the boxes." Research confirms that ballooning job descriptions also affect the behavior of the talent pool by intimidating applicants, especially women and economically disadvantaged groups. Too often, these systems automate a flawed hiring process and add skills and qualifications on top of old job description templates used in resume parsing software on job sites (see Figure 2.9).

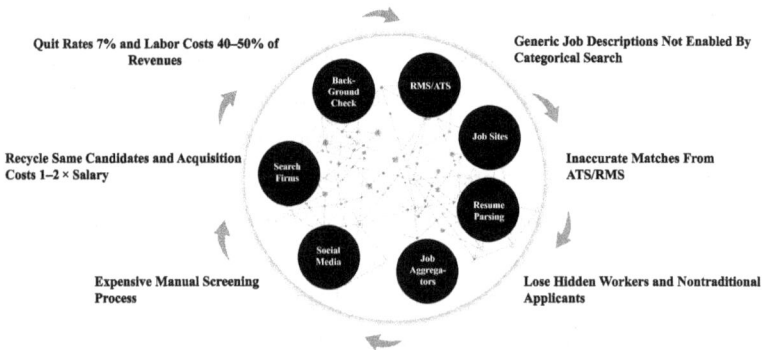

Figure 2.9 Talent death cycle in service industries

Big HR tech's resume parsing excludes from consideration thousands of viable or semiqualified candidates for every job post. A comprehensive, multiyear study by Harvard Business School and Accenture found that over 27 million "hidden workers,"[4] including those with employment gaps of more than 6 months, immigrants, caregivers, relocating partners and spouses, veterans, and those with physical disabilities, were excluded from consideration. We estimate that if hotel operators reformed their approach to talent acquisition, it could immediately open the industry to at least two million semiqualified hires capable of performing jobs in both the frontline and early supervisor levels of hotel properties. Ironically, many HR executives seem to acknowledge these blind spots and blockages in surveys but have done little to address the root causes.

Research also suggests these "hidden workers" are a good bet: when employers reform their talent acquisition process and hire these semiqualified workers filtered out by big HR tech, two-thirds of them perform significantly better at a cheaper cost and are more loyal.

Few hospitality operators have dedicated resources in their corporate HR or technology divisions focused on HR technologies or cross-functional initiatives in place to broaden their visibility and options outside existing solutions. Making matters worse, rather than experiment with new models for a segment or region or conduct experiments with control groups, most HR executives screen potential breakthrough solutions and alternatives based on whether they integrate into legacy ATS platforms on day one.

Building Employer Brands: From Fake News to Truths

But what about the positive attributes of the Internet, such as employers and hotel review sites and social media as a source of talent and information about employer brand quality? What insights do existing job sites and HR tech solutions provide for talent either aspiring to work in the business or to move up the ranks?

Let's consider the quality of information available to current and prospective employees about hospitality employers. In 2022, *Fortune* Magazine named Marriott #23 and Hyatt #70 among the Top 100 Best Places to Work in America.[5] The celebrated *Fortune* rankings can be useful for current and prospective corporate-level employees, but what—if any— insights do they provide for people working in the properties of a largely franchised business not operated by these same hotel chains?

For example, as of 2022, 74.9 percent of Marriott's 8175 U.S. hotels are franchised. Does the *Fortune* ranking suggest that if hotel employees had a choice, they should consider working in a property carrying one of 30 Marriott flags more than one carrying a flag of a Hyatt brand? The answer is a resounding "no." Our research shows that the brand does not determine the quality of the employer; instead, it is largely determined by the quality of the property's general manager (r^2 = 35 percent).

For a hospitality talent marketplace to be accurate and truly efficient, the workforce must know the reputation of the company operating the hotel, the owner's track record of funding operations and capital improvements, and what, if any, advantages exist in working for the brand.

Unfortunately, talent searching for jobs won't be able to find useful insights on their actual prospective employers on Glassdoor, Yelp, or Tripadvisor. Furthermore, a *Wall Street Journal* study proved that Glassdoor's employer reviews are already widely discredited and corrupted, resulting in massive grade inflation (see Figure 2.10).

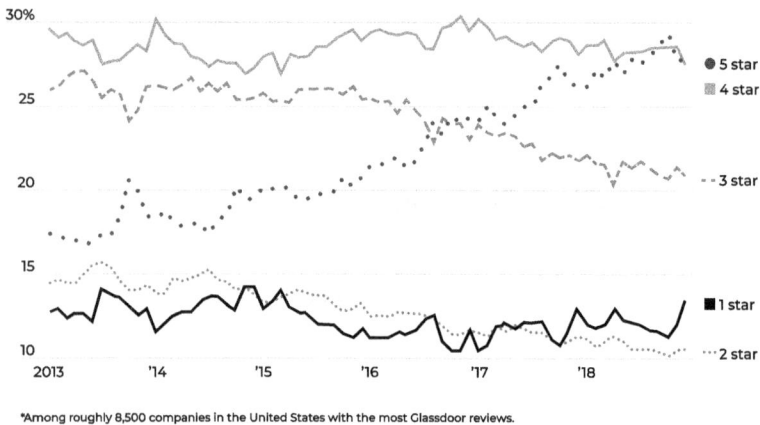

*Among roughly 8,500 companies in the United States with the most Glassdoor reviews.

Figure 2.10 Share of Glassdoor reviews by star rating

Source: The Wall Street Journal, January 2019.

At the corporate level, once employers catch on that their reputation is at stake, they compel employees to write positive reviews. For example, the standard deviation in Glassdoor scores among the top 25 hotel brands and operators is 0.02 or extremely negligible. Furthermore, Glassdoor doesn't confirm whether an employee even worked at a company they review. It was created to review corporate offices, prior to the company evolving into a job board. In hospitality, Glassdoor often gets the employer wrong, and their sample size alone renders their property-level reviews invalid: most individual hotel properties have under 20 mentions.

Let's review a mini case study. Say you're considering applying for a front desk agent job at the Marriott Syracuse Downtown Hotel. On the surface, it looks insightful; there are 1119 reviews, with Marriott International's CEO Anthony Capuano featured on the page where he has an impressive 88 percent approval rating by employees, with the hotel's overall score of 4, ranging from 3.5 to 4.0 out of 5 on attributes such as culture and benefits. On Glassdoor, more than half of current or former employees (or fake reviews) complain at length about being underpaid, working long hours, and lack of training for housekeepers. The problem is Marriott doesn't manage the hotel: it's franchised and managed by Crestline Hotels & Resorts, a third-party operator that manages 125 properties and has a total of 226 reviews across all their hotels (see Figure 2.11).

Marriott Syracuse Downtown 4.0 ★
Front Desk Agent AYS - FULL TIME (Front Desk Staff)
Syracuse, NYC

✓ Employer Provided Salary: $16.48 Per Hour ⓘ

⚡ Easy Apply   ♡ Save

Marriott Syracuse Downtown Ratings

4.0 ★★★★

77%	88%	
Recommend to a friend	Approve of CEO	Anthony Capuano
		1119 Ratings

Career Opportunities	★★★★	4.0
Comp & Benefits	★★★★	3.7
Culture & Values	★★★★	4.0
Senior Management	★★★★	3.7
Work/Life Balance	★★★	3.5

Figure 2.11 Glassdoor case study: hotel employer review (part one)

Source: www.Glassdoor.com, March 2023.

Back to the aspiring hotel employee in Syracuse who wants a job near downtown. Perhaps Indeed.com, the world's largest job aggregator, which features employers' reviews, could solve the problem. At first glance it seems promising. Indeed has over 23,000 reviews from current and former employees who worked at Marriott branded hotels in the United States.

However, Indeed.com has no property-specific reviews for the Marriott Syracuse Hotel. It has reviews for all hotel positions across Marriott International properties nationally and shares market locations, not by hotel names. Like Glassdoor, Indeed.com fails to identify the specific property or management company.

Furthermore, Indeed's employer reviews are organized by the brand, which is grossly misleading (see Figure 2.12).

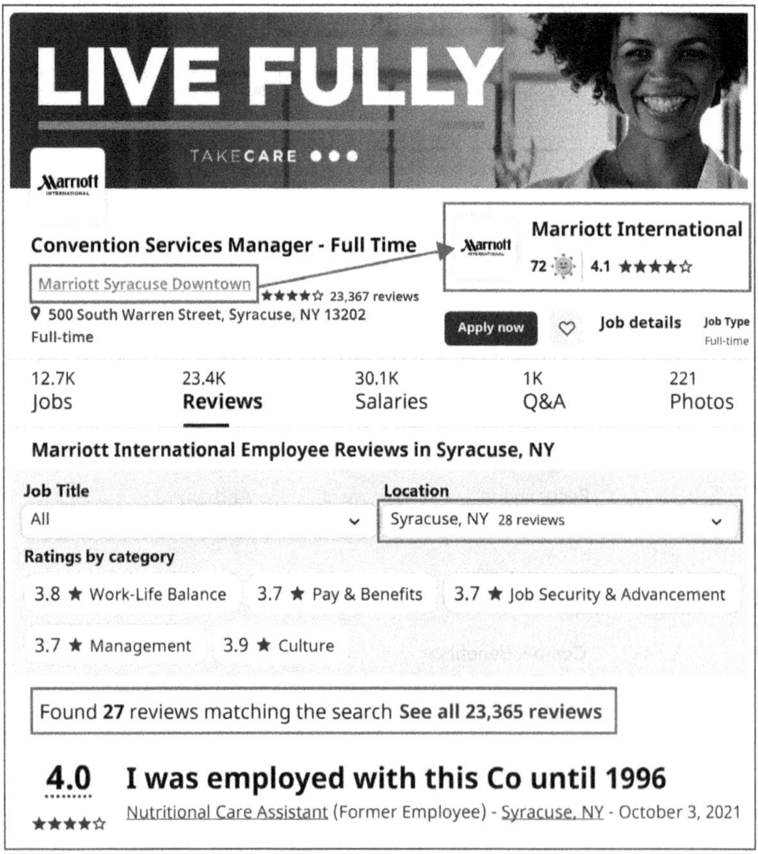

Figure 2.12 Indeed case study: hotel employer review (part two)

Source: www.Indeed.com, March 10, 2023.

It is not surprising that hotel brands have not shared management and owner reviews for potential employees. After all, Marriott began to share customer reviews on their booking sites a decade after Tripadvisor and other online travel agencies. Marriott's reviews do enable customers to see reviews by loyalty tier, but it's unclear whether their overall customer review scores are adjusted for customer worth.

Few other hotel brands share customer reviews on their booking sites, despite Google's aggressive marketing of hotel bookings and their rise to becoming the #1 hotel review site.

Rebuilding the Service Profit Chain with Data Integrity and Science

To kickstart the discovery process, MogulRecruiter's data science team and industry experts, with over 50 years of C-suite experience in hospitality, analyzed the performance of over 500,000 hotel managers in the United States and 10,200 hotels across 50 Metropolitan Statistical Areas (MSAs). We also analyzed the top 150 U.S. hotel operators covering 5 years of data, from 2018 through 2022, from various sources including STR, JD Power, HVS, CBRE, JLL, and Mercer. Our team proceeded to organize the datasets into tables, wrote scripts, and developed algorithms that mapped over two million data points generating insights that were reviewed with senior management at hospitality companies, brands, and owners.

The following variables are used to score and rank talent:

- *Service score*: This variable measures change in a hotel's department-specific performance over the past 24 months indexed against its competitive set. We acquired data from the leading third-party customer review firms such as Google and online travel agencies to analyze the change in each hotel's department scores, including subcategories that provide insights on how hotels are performing in specific areas and services. How these scores are weighted depends on a candidate's position.

- *Brand score*: This variable measures the quality of brands in a candidate's experience using datasets from JD Power and STR. It's not simply an indication of experience at category-leading or prestigious brands. For example, we give more credit to talents for improving an underperforming brand with an inferior product than a category-leading brand that may provide talent at a higher quality hotel to manage.
- *Market score*: This variable measures the difficulty of operating in each market. We use data from HVS, CBRE, and others to analyze the supply and demand of hotels in each market.
- *Experience score*: This variable measures tenure, with a threshold of at least 2 years in a position to qualify as an elite talent in a specific role.
- *Stability score*: This variable measures the infrequency of changing employers. A higher stability score means that the person has stayed with the same employer for a longer period of time, while a lower stability score means that the person has changed employers more frequently.
- *Quality of the employer*: This variable is measured using internal data plus the employer rankings from the *Wall Street Journal*, Fortune Forbes, and other sources. Our proprietary employer ranking includes the top 120 hotel operators benchmarked by directors and department heads for the hotel segments in which they operate. Employers are also ranked for diversity, women, and minorities across their managed GMs, directors, and department heads.

The algorithm sets different benchmarks for performance based on hotel segment and product quality: it gives credit to talented managers who improve hotels with inferior product quality and lesser ranked brands in inferior locations compared to their peers.

We proceeded to create talent tiers of these talents: the equivalent of customer worth segments for elite talent. The top 1 percent of talents are called *Super Moguls*, the next 10 percent are called *Mega Moguls*, and the following 20 percent whose scores are increasing at two to three times their peers are called *Rising Moguls*.

We synthesized our findings into the "top 10 insights," organized along the lines of the two principal participants in the talent marketplace: talent (the property-level workforce from the front line to general managers) and employers (hospitality operators, including brands, management companies, or owner operators). The next section is dedicated to elucidating the following "top 10 insights" and sharing some of the potential approaches to reversing hospitality's talent drain:

Talent

1. *The top 100 GMs are way ahead of the pack but their impact is not appropriately recognized.*
2. *Elite talent outperforms by a wide margin that grows over time.*
3. *The current model does not compensate elite talents for performance.*
4. *The talent pipeline is insufficient to meet diversity targets in the United States.*
5. *The path to hotel GM is over a decade and must be shortened.*

Employers

6. *Luxury and lifestyle brands lead the way for building human capital.*
7. *Scale is not an advantage with respect to talent in hospitality.*
8. *Publicly traded chains lead with respect to diverse elite talents.*
9. *Bigger doesn't mean more diverse below GM.*
10. *Food and beverage is a bright spot for developing diverse, elite talent.*

CHAPTER 3

Asset Right

Building Human Capital in an Era of High Finance

The hospitality industry has become a "high-finance" real-estate business. From quick service restaurant chains such as McDonald's to coffee shops such as Starbucks who own and lease billions of dollars in real estate on one end of the spectrum to single asset billion-dollar branded resorts, timeshares, and residences such as Ritz Carlton on the other, the industry uses high amounts of debt, including from nontraditional sources and cutting-edge financial engineering innovations, to monetize assets and create wealth for equity and debt investors.

The game differs by geography but remains a real-estate business at its core. In the United States, hotels can be highly leveraged up to 70 percent or greater with various tranches of collateralized and securitized debt. Usually, the bet pays off as hotels generate huge cyclical cash flows and benefit from real-estate appreciation. For example, the U.S. hotel industry experienced 12 consecutive years of record operating profits over $80 billion prior to 2020. In other regions of the world, particularly in China, metropolitan hotels may be largely unprofitable; however, incorporating 5-star hotel brands into development projects can offer ancillary benefits to developers, such as obtaining government permits, securing access to government-supported bank loans, and boosting residential, commercial, and retail rental rates by 30 to 40 percent.

Creating Shareholder Value

The sole governing objective of many U.S.-based corporations, including hospitality chains, is to create shareholder value. Since 2018, the lion's share of the equity market capitalization has been captured by search engines and online travel agencies (OTAs), led by Google Travel, Airbnb, and Booking.com. As of March 31, 2023, Booking.com's equity market capitalization is more than that of the three biggest U.S.-based hotel chains (Marriott, Hilton, and Wyndham) combined (see Figure 3.1). This suggests that the market ascribes a far greater value to agnostic technology platforms despite their lack of inventory ownership, established loyalty programs, and management capabilities that enable hotels to generate 30 to 50 percent additional revenue streams.

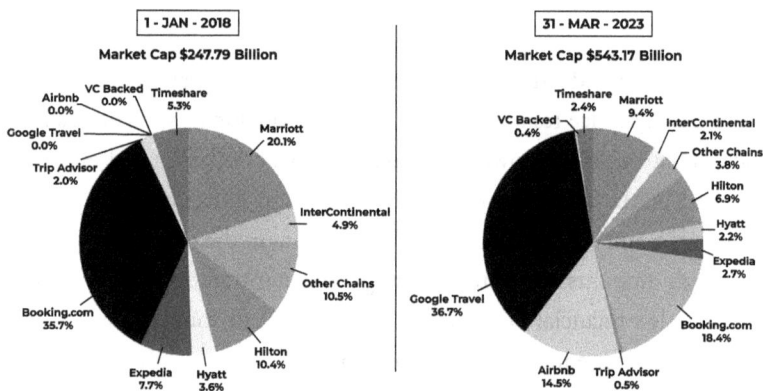

1 - JAN - 2018

Market Cap $247.79 Billion

Airbnb 0.0%
VC Backed 0.0%
Timeshare 5.3%
Google Travel 0.0%
Trip Advisor 2.0%
Marriott 20.1%
InterContinental 4.9%
Other Chains 10.5%
Booking.com 35.7%
Hilton 10.4%
Expedia 7.7%
Hyatt 3.6%

31 - MAR - 2023

Market Cap $543.17 Billion

Timeshare 2.4%
Marriott 9.4%
VC Backed 0.4%
InterContinental 2.1%
Other Chains 3.8%
Hilton 6.9%
Hyatt 2.2%
Expedia 2.7%
Google Travel 36.7%
Booking.com 18.4%
Airbnb 14.5%
Trip Advisor 0.5%

Figure 3.1 Value migration in hotels and online travel

Furthermore, despite decades of mergers and acquisitions and unprecedented brand growth, there is no clear-cut winner among global hotel chains. The top five global hotel chains—Marriott, Hilton, Accor, IHG, and Wyndham—collectively account for 21 percent of equity market capitalization. Marriott, the largest global hotel chain by number of properties, leads the race with 9.4 percent of total value created and trades in line with its peers. However, Hilton, which grew its market cap by 46 percent versus only 3 percent for Marriott in the same 5 year period (2018 through 2023) but represents only 6.9 percent of the economic pie. The economic rationale for the gap in trading multiples between the two rivals is that Hilton generates over 70 percent of its revenues from franchising less economically sensitive limited-service hotels primarily in the United States, while Marriott generates the majority of its fees through more cyclical management and incentive fees from full-service hotels with greater exposure to international markets such as China. Another interesting difference between the two is that in the 15 year period between 2008 and 2023, Hilton grew organically by adding limited-service and economy-franchised brands without acquiring any other brands or companies and divested its relatively capital-intensive timeshare business. In contrast, Marriott acquired Starwood, whose focus was operating high-end union hotels, including large convention and group properties in gateway cities such as New York, and spent many years integrating its operations and loyalty program and realigning its brand architecture. Meanwhile, branded timeshare companies, VC-backed start-up brands, and membership business models such as Sonder, Oyo, and Soho House represent less than 1 percent of the total equity market capitalization.

Building Stakeholder Alignment

Today, hospitality brands also compete in various arenas to satisfy the interests of a burgeoning ecosystem of stakeholders. The five major stakeholders include equity shareholders; hotel owners and lenders; state, county, and city governments; individual and group customers; and talent, including employees and contracted labor. At the intersection of this ecosystem of stakeholders, each of whom has its own food chains, is the ultimate long-term objective: building brand equity. To succeed, these brands must generate economic profits via returns on invested capital that exceed their weighted average cost of capital for their shareholders, achieve millions of dollars in lifetime customer value for their highest worth individual and group customers, and garner and sustain a disproportionate share of elite talent (see Figure 3.2).

These stakeholders include state, county, city governments, and tourism improvement districts whose interests are to build the brand equity of their respective jurisdictions as travel destinations. These government entities levy occupancy taxes of 5 to 20 percent of room revenue typically for transient stays under 30 days. These taxes on room revenues are expected to generate a record $46 billion windfall in tax revenue in 2023, up 13 percent from the prepandemic peak year of 2019.

Shareholders/Investors
. Equity/stock price
  appreciation with less risk

• Strong ROIC with compelling same
  store and unit growth

• Confidence in management

Brand Equity:
• **Return on Invested Capital**
• **Lifetime Customer Value**
• **Share of Elite Talent**

Customers
• High satisfaction with
  products and services

• Value for money

• "Emotional" rewards
  with brands

Real State Owners
• Operating cash flows

• Asset appreciation/returns

• New investment opportunities

Employees
• Purpose - strong and
  positive culture

• Well remunerated,
  long-term incentives

• Interesting job with
  career path

Governments
• Economic development

• Tax revenues - state, city

• Employment and
  wage growth

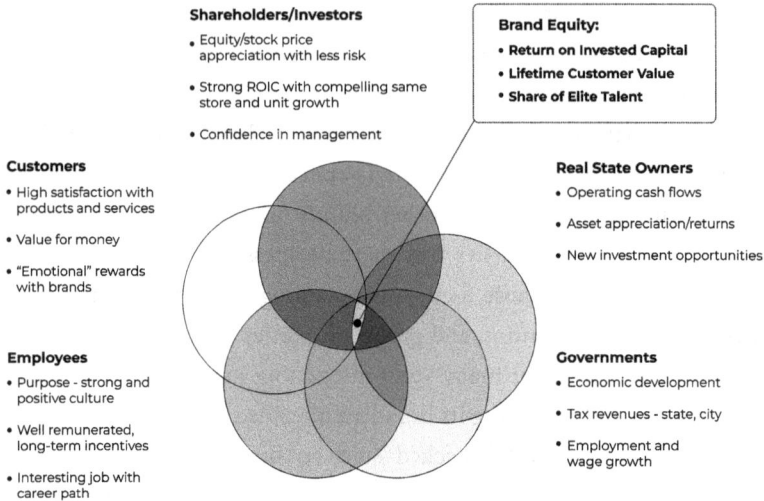

Figure 3.2 Key stakeholders in hospitality management

Hotel Brand Fees and the Franchise Model

Hotel taxes pale in comparison to the 15 to 20 percent of ongoing revenue franchise fees, including royalties, advertising or marketing contribution fees, sales/reservation/loyalty program fees, and miscellaneous fees charged by the brands. These fees have grown at 8 percent compounded annual growth since 2013, far exceeding same store revenue gains in the same time period. While each hotel chain and brands have slightly different formulas, these fees continue to grow and, in the case of full-service brands, often include food and beverage revenues. These annual fees, including loyalty programs, soft brands, independent collections, and residential branding, exceed $120 billion globally. These funds cover the corporate overheads of the brand teams and loyalty programs as well as other corporate initiatives.

While owners' councils may review the allocation of the funds, Uniform Franchise Offering Circulars (UFOCs) provide brands with extremely broad discretion in how they are used. Historically, brands have steered clear of using their funds to support franchisees in any human capital-related matters, such as recruiting, learning and development, performance reviews, compensation practices, work rules, diversity, equity, and inclusion often citing potential legal liabilities as the reason to draw this line. MogulRecruiter's survey of 100 UFOC agreements found an average of only two paragraphs in a 200-page agreement dedicated to human capital management—a few scant references to half-day mandatory general manager and assistant general manager training in brand standards. With respect to architectural and design brand standards, our research across 100 brands and surveys with owners found few guidelines addressing the "back of the house" or "heart of the house," as some luxury brands call dedicated employee workplaces, with no minimum requirements for lockers, cafeterias, or even employee entrances.

The U.S. capital markets have memorialized the value of asset-light franchising, valuing hospitality brands inversely to their capital and management intensity. For the trailing 12 months ending in April 2023, publicly traded hotel chains created $760 million of economic value with a weighted average returns on invested capital (ROIC) of 11.5 percent. The largest valuations are ascribed to high-growth, franchise-driven, global brands at 12 × to 15 × EBITDA, such as those of Hilton and Marriott whose ROIC exceed their cost of capital during most of the industry cycle. At the other end of the spectrum, asset-heavy hotel chains such as Hyatt and Accor failed to create economic value during much of the last industry cycle. Except for Host Hotels and Ryman, Hotel REITS (which own real estate, not brands) also struggled to typically generate attractive yields or create economic value. None of the third-party management companies that manage properties without their own brands have been publicly traded since Interstate hotels, which was acquired by Aimbridge Hospitality. During its tenure as a publicly traded management company that did not own any brands, Interstate, a pure management company, traded between 5 × and 8 × EBITDA, well below that of hotel chains and more in line with REITS. Holding all factors equal, the market also ascribes two to three basis points higher EBITDA multiples to franchise-driven brands with high ROICs and internally managed lifestyle and luxury brands on the other hand, which command long-term contracts 25 years or longer and have residential branding fees of 5 to 10 percent of revenue—a proxy for the value they create for real-estate developers. Hence, when it was publicly traded, Four Seasons hotels had a multiple of 25 × to 40 × EBITDA (or greater with frequent negative earnings when it was publicly traded) and many relatively small luxury brands have sold for 15 × to 20 × EBITDA despite having a relatively small footprint (see Table 3.1).

Table 3.1 *Valuation of global hotel chains and OTAs—March 2023*

Managed/Franchised

Company	Ticker Symbol	ROIC	Value Creation ($M)	TEV/EBITDA	Market Cap. ($M)	Weight	% of Profit From Hotels Owned/Leased
Marriott	MAR	10.50%	$387	15.0×	$51,287	42%	8%
InterContinental	IHg	17.60%	$107	19.1×	$11,707	10%	3%
Wyndham	WH	9.80%	$89	13.2×	$5849	5%	0%
Choice	CHH	28.80%	$315	13.6×	$5982	5%	0%
Hilton	HLT	10.60%	$289	19.2×	$37,535	31%	4%

Owned/Leased

Company	Ticker Symbol	ROIC	Value Creation ($M)	TEV/EBITDA	Market Cap. ($M)		% of Adj. EBITDA From Hotels Owned/Leased
Hyatt	H	2.50%	($368)	16.2×	$11,878		34%

OTA

Company	Ticker Symbol	ROIC	Value Creation ($M)	TEV/ EBITDA	Market Cap. ($M)	Weight	Price/Book (Current)
Expedia	EXPE	4.30%	($283)	13.3×	$14,879	8%	7.1×
Booking.com	BKNg	31.50%	$3841	17.6×	$99,859	51%	29.2×
Tripadvisor	TRIP	−0.3%	($136)	19.5×	$2800	1%	3.6×
Airbnb	ABNB	94.40%	$6844	36.9×	$78,537	40%	13.0×
Weighted average		54.20%	$10,266	25.0×	$196,075	100%	20.7×

REITs

Company	Ticker Symbol	ROIC	Value Creation ($M)	TEV/ EBITDA	Market Cap. ($M)	Weight	Price/Book (Current)
Ryman Hospitality	RHP	12.40%	$197	12.8×	$4892	19%	74.9×
HOST	HST	12.50%	$675	10.3×	$11,765	45%	1.8×
Apple Hospitality REIT	APLE	8.10%	$71	11.8×	$3560	14%	1.2×
Park	PK	5.10%	($70)	10.4×	$2743	10%	0.7×
Xenia	XHR	6.40%	$4	10.0×	$1459	6%	1.1×
Pebblebrook Hotel Trust	PEB	4.90%	($66)	13.1×	$1769	7%	0.6×
Weighted average		10.30%	$811	11.2×	$26,188	100%	15.4×

However, the valuations of hotel chains pale in comparison to the category-leading OTAs such as Booking.com and Airbnb, which created over $10 billion of economic value with ROICs ranging from 30 to 94 percent during the same period.

Given the brutal efficiency of the capital markets that ascribes more value to franchising, and the ever-shrinking holding periods of U.S. stock market or public market equity investors to under a year, it's not surprising that hospitality executives, whose long-term compensation is tied to share price performance, are predisposed to franchising rather than management. Hence, hotel franchising has witnessed explosive growth with 3000 new properties added to its business model from 2017 to 2022 and six out of seven employees work for franchisees as opposed to brands, the opposite ratio that existed in 1995. The franchising business model continues to experience double-digit growth in both the United States and China (see Figure 3.3).

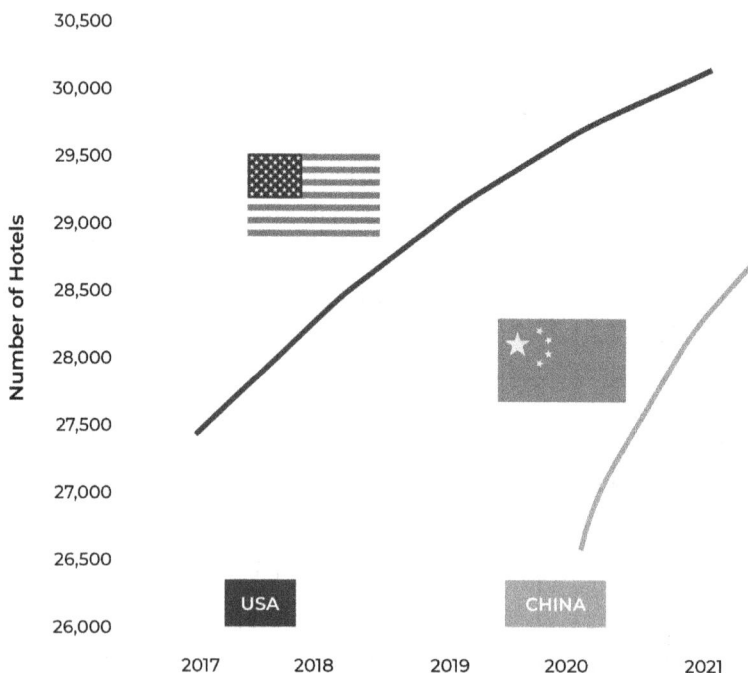

Figure 3.3 Growth of franchising business model since 2017

Source: FRANdata 2020, the companies, Statista.

Downside of Franchising: Brand Dilution

While hotel brands and operators like to say their greatest asset is their talent, evidence suggests investments in people and HR processes are usually addressed on a leftover basis as needed, typically in the context of property or corporate mergers and acquisitions.

The contradiction is that franchising has not been proven to work at the high end of the business, with only a few exceptions in the highest growth international markets. While the capital markets have their perspective, with respect to employees—the focus of this book—research performed by numerous independent consulting firms and internally by several hotel and restaurant chains demonstrates that an employee's engagement is greatly impacted by the general manager (r^2 = 35 percent) and the culture of the management company (r^2 = 20 percent) far above real-estate factors such as product quality (r^2 = 12 percent) and location (r^2 = 15 percent). But if the research about these interdependencies is so clear, why couldn't the brands adjust their business model to help their operators protect their brands? Put differently, how did real-estate owners and lenders extract record profits at the expense of other stakeholders, exposing one of the world's biggest industries to a historic talent disruption?

Real Estate/Management Split: Financial Returns with a Human Cost

Americans are familiar with the blockbuster movie hit *The Founder*, which tells the story of how a milkshake machine salesman named Ray Kroc became CEO of McDonald's and built a real-estate company that earns most of its profits and valuation from owning 45 percent of the land and 70 percent of the buildings at their 36,000 plus locations. Former McDonald's CFO Harry J. Sonneborn said,

> We are not technically in the food business. We are in the real estate business. The only reason we sell fifteen-cent hamburgers is because they are the greatest producer of revenue from which our tenants can pay us our rent.

This is reminiscent of the U.S. hotel industry, which started with an asset-heavy business model that attracted real-estate developers. For example, in the 1990s, Hilton owned over 200 hotels in the United States and made one-third to half its income during economic boom periods from recapitalizations, refinancing, and financial engineering. As recently as 2005, Marriott had billions of off-balance sheet debt, with the most complex financial statements and disclosures of any Fortune 500 company at the time. The upshot was they also invested in hospitality schools, managed most or all their full-service hotels, and even leveraged their HR infrastructure and brands to manage assisted living facilities, timeshares, and casino resorts. Hotel brands were winning awards for service quality across sectors and employees knew who they worked for and how they could build a rising and relatively stable career.

This changed in the late 1990s and 2000s. Financial engineers led by former Marriott and Disney CFO Steve Bollenbach (who later became Hilton CEO for over a decade whose administration I worked in for 3 years as head of corporate development) capitalized on market inefficiencies and spun out hotel real estate into tax-efficient REITs starting with Marriott. Marriott later split into Host Hotels, the largest hotel REIT, and Marriott International, the largest hotel chain, and later Marriott divested its assisted living and vacation ownership businesses. At the time, Marriott mostly managed hotels and had just started scaling the franchising of the one-time category killer Courtyard by Marriott. This "prop-co/op-co split" caught on and hotel chains referred to the goal of their strategic plan to be "asset right," which required owning the right real-estate assets in the right market at the right time, including balancing cities and resorts and creating an optimal portfolio that included noncyclical or countercyclical cash flows optimal. In the context of this industry transformation, hotel REITs were eclipsed by private equity, family office, and sovereign real-estate funds and dedicated hotel equity and debt funds became highly specialized by investment stage, hotel segment, product type, and market and geography. By 2019, private equity, in its various forms, increased its ownership of U.S. hotel rooms to 59 percent, up from only 12 percent in 2003, while REITs dropped from 67 percent to only 33 percent. High net worth individuals, including family offices, account for the majority of the remaining

% of Rooms

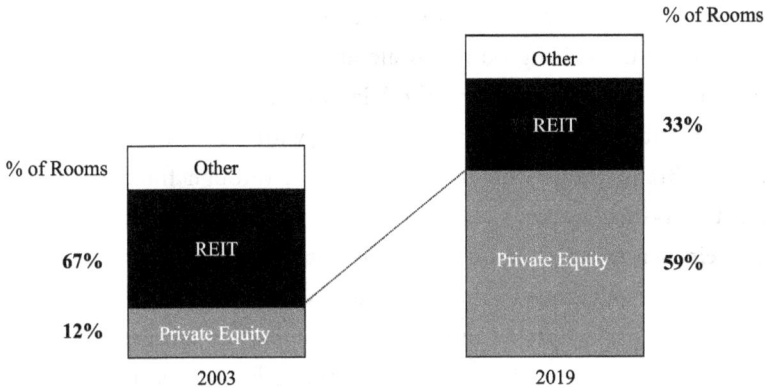

Figure 3.4 Evolution of hotel ownership in the United States, 2003 to 2019

hotel investors, 6 percent of ownership in 2019, with the remaining 2 percent represented by sovereign funds and state-owned enterprises (see Figure 3.4).

Therefore, unlike McDonald's and Starbucks, who play the checkers version of a real-estate game, hotel investing is a more strategic game of chess that is difficult to predict precisely and model. As a trading business, hotel investment is often a full-blown drama resembling a home-flipping reality television show as new owners come and go on average every 5.5 years. To maximize real-estate investor returns and ensure assets are unencumbered, most owners do their best to separate the brands from less-expensive and more flexible management companies, who are themselves put on a short leash with an average of 90 day termination rights, sometimes as short as 30 days. The drama unfolds as owners, led by private equity, minimize their equity investments, convert senior debt and mezzanine loans to equity, borrow to reposition assets, lease restaurants to reduce union labor, and, if necessary, change management companies and brands or even create new brands of their own.

Hotel Chains: Doubling Down on Opportunism

Hotel brands have also adjusted their tactics to create value for their shareholders and ensure their survival in the real-estate game. As the industry evolved through mergers and acquisitions, a short-term mindset prevailed as brands adopted highly complex business models by owning hotels that were cash cows, managing most high-end properties and widely franchising both upscale and limited-service hotels. Over time, brands deteriorated, and the mix of business models became ripe with potential conflicts of interest, starting with "turf wars" inside hotel chains. Brand teams who preferred to scale through franchising and third-party management came into direct conflict with the executives of their own management company as hotel chain operators sought to sustain their relevance to the real-estate capital markets. Furthermore, inside asset-heavy hotel chains, real-estate and asset management teams sought to monetize underutilized assets and refinance and recycle hotel investments based on their "privileged insights" rather than invest small amounts of equity, debt, or key money to buy management or franchising deals. The few full-service brands that achieved stakeholder alignment and consistently achieved revenue premiums and higher fees—for example, Westin, which became a category killer in the upper upscale segment, charged owners 3 to 5 percent of revenue more than its peers—did so by masterfully managing a portfolio of owned and managed hotels churning over 50 percent in less than a decade. Other brands such as Sheraton, Crowne Plaza, Howard Johnson, DoubleTree, and Holiday Inn became tired, inconsistent, and lost relevance with consumers and employees.

When All Else Fails, Create New Brands

As upscale or full-service hotel assets age and go through renovations, whether new build or conversion, they become dissimilar to the consumer, which creates another play: reflagging into another brand. But this ideal outcome is unusual—most of the time, owners and lenders forgo this risk. It's extremely rare for a hotel to be removed from the system of a hotel chain altogether, no matter how poorly it performed. What's even more rare—unlike other consumer-facing industries such as packaged goods or automobiles (in 2004, Oldsmobile, a 106-year-old automobile brand, was retired by General Motors)—is the elimination of a hotel brand due to poor performance or redundant characteristics. Hotel brands have almost never been phased out even when a similar brand was acquired or developed. The complication for hotel chains has become a consistently incoherent portfolio, where a lower priced brand with fewer services often can have a superior offering in a certain market and charge more than a higher-end brand which may only be a few decades old. Over time, this discrepancy undermines direct bookings and drives up marketing and cost of sales as consumers flock to meta review sites and OTAs such as Booking.com, Expedia, and Tripadvisor for impartial and timely information on their purchase decisions rather than relying on the brand's reputation to tell them what to expect.

Instead of prudently managing a portfolio of brands like other consumer businesses, hotel chains have risked cannibalization by introducing new brands, attempting to create microsegments similar to what Toyota has done in the automobile business with over 35 brands. Multi-unit hotel chains created over 120 new brands between 2003 and 2018 (see Figure 3.5).

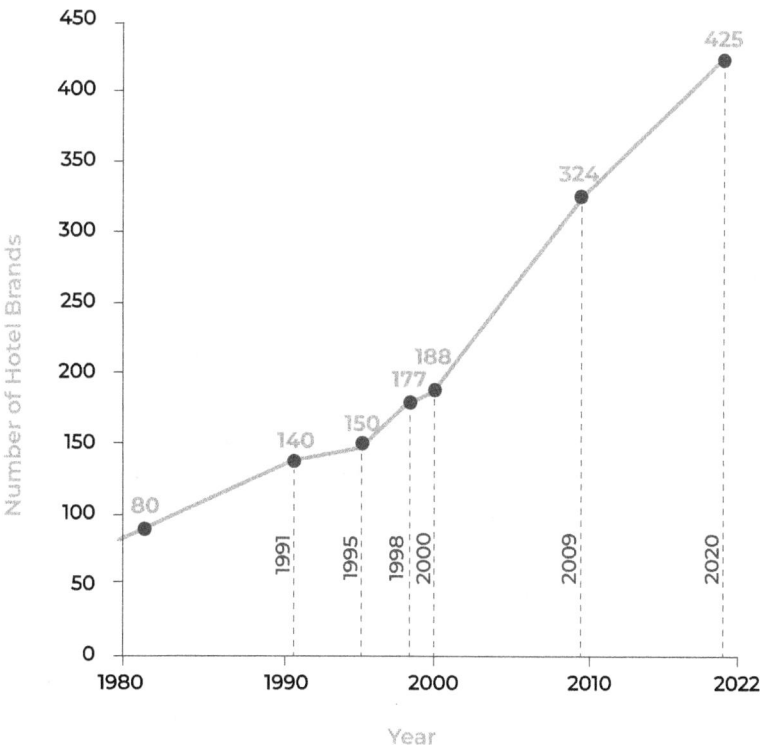

Figure 3.5 Growth in number of global hotel brands

Source: Bear Steams 2001, STR 2001, PriceWaterHouse Coopers 2001, American Hotel and Lodging Association 2001. (M&A's—Mergers and Acquisition).

During the same period, the five major U.S. hotel chains increased their brand portfolios by 35 percent through a combination of organic development and acquisitions. Mergers and acquisitions have further compounded the issue of brand portfolios that lack coherence (see Figure 3.6).

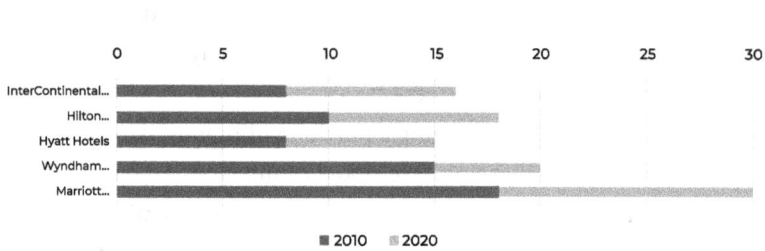

Figure 3.6 New brands launched by global hotel chains, 2010 to 2020

In theory, most hotel chains have capital or finance committees that assess "impact," or cannibalization, of a new hotel against others when deciding to approve whether it goes forward as proposed by either the franchising, management or real-estate team, depending on the internal sponsor. But franchise deals seldom get rejected by hotel chains due to cannibalization of its existing hotels, including the ones owned or managed by the chain. The net present value of a full-service hotel, $15 million to $25 million in fees or greater depending on its size and brand segment, is simply too good to give up.

The industry extended the reach of its franchising distribution platform to attract independent, largely nonunion, boutique and luxury hotel owners through the creation of "soft brands," a long-term pattern in hotel branding often associated with "Leading Hotels of the World" and started in chains by Starwood's luxury collection—an affiliation network of distinctive luxury boutique properties that leverage the chains' booking engine, reward program, and other sales platforms.

The bigger issue is that the brand portfolios of the hotel chains no longer make sense to consumers because their features and services are not aligned with their relative prices. Few consumers can tell most brands apart or describe their distinctive features, let alone soft brand collections. As a case in point, we examined the 14 hotel choices on www.marriott.com for a 3-star to 5-star hotel two-night stay in Times

Square, New York, on weekdays in April 2023. What's striking is the average daily rates are actually higher for the 3-star tier, limited-service branded hotels such as Courtyard, Fairfield, and Four Points than most full-service brands such as Westin, W, Renaissance, and Marriott. Even the full-service Sheraton brand is priced less than its limited-service spin-off, Four Points by Sheraton. To be fair, these higher priced limited-service hotels are relatively new, opening over the past 7 years or earlier, but they offer fewer amenities and lower service levels (see Figure 3.7).

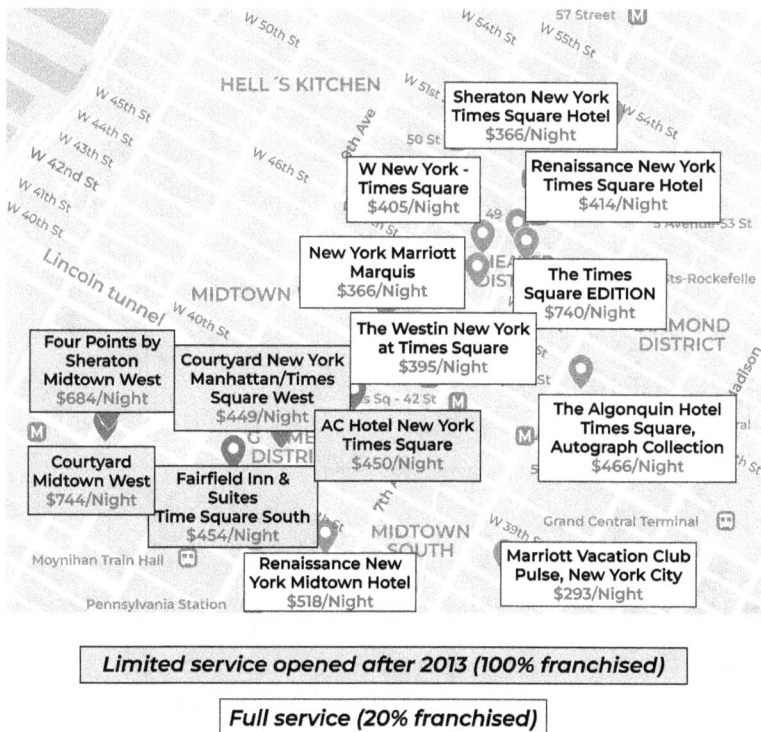

Figure 3.7 Marriott branded hotels in Times Square, New York City

Furthermore, when we analyze the ownership and management of these 14 hotels—facts that are not disclosed to consumers on any website, not even review sites or OTAs—there are nine different management companies and 12 different owners. Regarding the limited-service hotels, each one has a different owner, and three are owner-operated (see Table 3.2).

Table 3.2 *Ownership and management of Marriott hotels in Times Square, New York City*

	Marriott Midtown Manhattan—Full-Service Hotels					
Property	Management Company	Owner	Address	Nightly Rate	Stars	Year Opened
The Algonquin Hotel Times Square	HEI Hotels & Resorts	Cornerstone Real Estate Advisors	59 West 44th Street	$466	4	1902
W New York—Times Square	Marriott International	Marriott International	1567 Broadway	$405	4	2001
New York Marriott Marquis	Marriott International	Host Hotels & Resorts	1535 Broadway	$366	4	1985
Renaissance New York Times Square Hotel	Marriott International	Marriott International	714 Seventh Avenue	$414	4	1992
Marriott Vacation Club Pulse, New York City	Marriott Vacation Ownership	Marriott Vacation Ownership	33 West 37th Street	$293	4	2009
The Westin New York at Times Square	Marriott International	Tishman Realty and Construction	270 West 43rd Street	$395	4	2002
Renaissance New York Midtown Hotel	Marriott International	Stonebridge Companies	218 West 35th Street	$518	4	2015
Sheraton New York Times Square Hotel	MCR Hotels	MCR Hotels & Island Capital group	811 7th Avenue 53rd Street	$366	4	1962
The Times Square EDITION	Marriott International	Natixis	701 7th Avenue	$740	5	2021

Marriott Midtown Manhattan—Limited-Service Hotels

Property	Management Company	Owner	Address	Nightly Rate	Stars	Year Opened
AC Hotel New York Times Square	OTO Development, LLC	OTO Development	260 West 40th Street	$450	4	2018
Courtyard New York Manhattan/Midtown West	Endeavor Hospitality group	Endeavor Hospitality group	461 West 34th Street	$744	3	2019
Courtyard New York Manhattan/Times Square West	Stonebridge Companies	Stonebridge Companies	307 West 37th Street	$449	3	2013
Fairfield Inn & Suites/Times Square South	Real Hospitality group	gehr group	338 West 36th Street	$454	4	2019
Four Points by Sheraton—Midtown West	Real Hospitality group	Joy Construction	444 10th Avenue	$684	4	2016

Source: Marriott.com.

Marriott manages five of the full-service hotels that are unionized and owns two of them outright. While all employees wear Marriott uniforms, only the managed hotels receive human capital-related services from Marriott, including recruiting, training, development, and career paths. In other words, Marriott's own management company may compete with its franchisees for talent. Rather than franchise territories like other businesses do, it has created an ecosystem where multiple owners and management companies compete for the same customer and talent pool. This is not an uncommon predicament isolated to New York—the highly fragmented ownership and management of hotels, the inconsistency of brands, and potential conflicts of interest can be found in all major markets for hotel chains across the country.

The Employer Brand Equity Problem: Implications for a Talent Disruption

So how do the inconsistencies and lack of coherence in hotel branding impact current and prospective employees and set the stage for a talent disruption, the subject matter of this book? With all the internal contradictions and broken brand promises to guests, the owned/managed/franchised business model of hotel chains is damaging when it comes to attracting and developing talent. A brand is a key pillar in attracting talent to work in a hotel property, especially given the relatively low brand awareness that third-party management companies have in the labor market.

Put differently, a consumer-facing brand is also the employer brand. Our research suggests that today only 18 percent of employees below the executive team of the hotel understood the basic facts about their actual employer—where they are based, how many hotels they manage, and the name of the CEO. In fact, according to our research, 35 percent of hotel frontline workers and supervisors can't recall who they worked for in three of their last four jobs. They work in a Marriott hotel and wear a Marriott uniform but are hired by a third-party management company, and their paycheck comes from a third entity. Many are also surprised to learn that the brand whose uniform they wear competes against them directly by managing other hotels, either with the same brand nearby or another brand whose rates and amenities are strikingly similar.

The online recruiting presence of the industry is also confusing to talent. For example, some hotel chains advertise franchise jobs on their job sites as "franchised hotel" (they don't name the third-party operator), and others don't, citing exposure to potential employment litigation associated with recruiting for third parties. Jobs are also advertised by third-party management companies on their websites often using the hotel brand as the leading name.

As a result of their short-sighted, incoherent, and opportunistic business model, hotel chains rendered themselves and the entire ecosystem of owners, franchisees, and other stakeholders including employees highly vulnerable to a talent disruption. Organized labor seized the day to offer employees some form of representation, even where they lack the ability to garner higher wages, strict work rules, and indexed increases to their health care benefits. Prior to the pandemic, there were one million unfilled positions in the hotel sector as employees started to question the quality of their supervisors and absence of training, which often resulted in not meeting brand standards amid the daily pressures associated with meeting budgets so financial investors could pay back their lenders and generate sufficient short-term returns. Decades of financial engineering, outsourcing management, and harvesting brands have squeezed the passion out of the most zealous hospitality students who increasingly sought roles on the real-estate and technology sides of the business. Industry stakeholders seeking to help the industry return to its roots could start by redefining the phrase "asset-right" to go beyond real-estate factors and include the right human capital assets as well as operating the right hotels in the highest performing markets.

Asset-Right Model Gains Traction Across the Service Industry

The "asset-light" model that was generated after decades of financial engineering, mergers, and acquisitions by the hotel industry is being adopted by other service industries, including casino gaming, health care, and retail. Higher interest rates and the turmoil in commercial real estate in big cities are accelerating this transformation to asset-light or at least asset-right, with fewer core-owned properties. Tactics include sale lease-back of assets (HCA), REIT spin-offs (Casino hotels), and horizontal and vertical consolidation (hospitals, clinics, and doctors' offices) to increase ROIC and reduce capital intensity by leveraging brands (Mayo Clinic, UCLA Health, Nike, and Walgreens e-commerce) to new service formats and online.

In this context, the market share pie charts of health care, retail, and other service industries are beginning to look like hospitality and travel. Value is increasingly migrating to technology companies who are capturing the lion's share of economic value (such as online health care apps, telemedicine in health care, or warehouse operators in retail). These new players will be AI driven, automated, and more amenable to hybrid or gig economy workforce models.

One fast follower is the casino gaming industry. From 2019 to 2023, the gaming industry added about $96 billion to its market cap. However, the traditional casino gaming sector lost about 22 percent of its equity market capitalization share of the pie, falling from 84 to 63 percent. MGM and Las Vegas Sands sold many of their properties to REIT called Vici Properties, a relatively new entity created by the restructuring of Caesars Entertainment. The REIT category also increased its market share from 8 to 17 percent, with Vici Properties Inc. leading the way with 11.7 percent of the market share. The top three players in the traditional gaming sector also changed to Las Vegas Sands Corp, Galaxy Entertainment Group, and Sands China Ltd, with 15.6, 10.5, and 10 percent equity market share, respectively. Moreover, the online and digital gaming sector gained 12 percent of the market share, rising from 6 to 18 percent led by Fluffer Entertainment Plc and DraftKings Inc. DraftKings became a public company in 2020 after merging with SBTech and Diamond Eagle Acquisition Corp. The services category maintained its market share at around 2 percent. Meanwhile, traditional casino gaming companies such as Wynn continue to evaluate spinning off their online divisions. The gaming industry is evolving similar to the hotel industry, with category-leading brands divesting their real estate, managing in key markets like Las Vegas and licensing in new formats and (subject to regulatory approvals) spinning off their online divisions (see Figure 3.8).

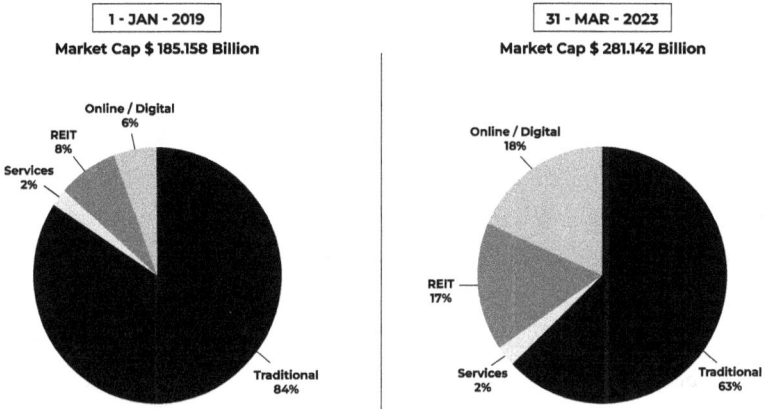

Figure 3.8 Value migration in casinos and online gaming

In retail, over the past decade, online players such as Amazon and Alibaba have captured most of the economic pie as traditional brick and mortar retailers, such as Walmart, Costco, and Walgreens, have battled back with significant investments to increase their e-commerce revenues from 10 to 30 percent closing thousands of stores in the process (see Figure 3.9).

For example, Walmart, who owns 70 percent of its land and buildings worth an estimated $230 billion, has started to sell land and buildings to a REIT and then lease them back to raise capital and remain focused on their core business. They also have a real-estate arm, Walmart Realty, that

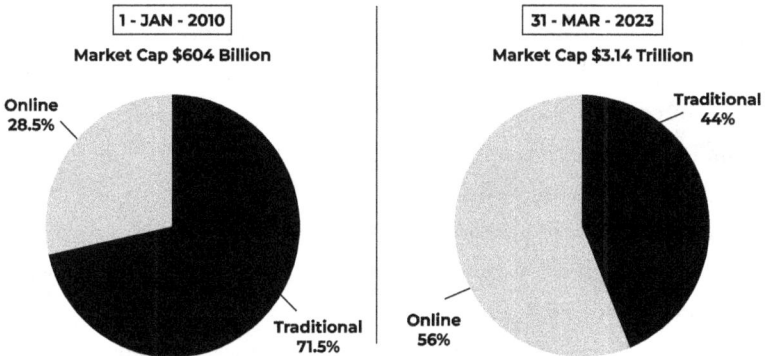

Figure 3.9 Value migration in retail and e-commerce

owns and manages distribution centers and parking lots, which could be spun out at a later time. Home Depot and Costco also own the vast majority of their real estate, which has a combined value of $250 billion.

In the coming decade, retailers may exit more real estate to private equity, REITS, and other restructures. This will set the stage for the mega store retail brands to consolidate through merger and acquisition and become asset-light e-commerce platforms and to distribute their products in new formats. Absent government intervention, such as bailouts that saved the U.S. auto and airline industry, the only traditional retail incumbents that will survive are those who invest in AI and automation to significantly improve their unit labor costs, minimize unionization, and capture market share of elite talent in key roles.

The health care industry is also struggling with capital intensity, which has enormous implications for what type of activities for-profit companies choose to perform and their ability to combat perhaps the most significant talent disruption of any industry. The United States is expected to face a shortage of 200,000 registered nurses and 50,000 physicians in the next 3 years. While industry revenues are growing in line with inflation and payer and services segments generating healthy free cash flows, hospitals are experiencing skyrocketing labor costs resulting in operating margins compressing 25 to 75 percent, implying they are burning cash like a high-risk technology start-up.

Health care companies have increased their market cap from $1.4 trillion to $4.7 trillion in 13 years. However, pharmaceutical companies have seen their market share decline, from 69 to 51 percent, with Johnson & Johnson and Eli Lilly holding large shares of 8.5 and 6.9 percent, respectively. In contrast, biotechnology companies have improved their share, from 14 to 25 percent, with Novo Nordisk and Thermo Fisher Scientific gaining market share from Amgen and Gilead Sciences with 7.5 and 4.7 percent total market share each. Payments category also showed significant growth, from 9 to 17 percent, with UnitedHealth Group being the top player with 9.3 percent share (see Figure 3.10).

In the early years, biotechnology companies faced a number of challenges, including high costs, regulatory hurdles, and competition from pharmaceutical companies. However, the industry has grown rapidly in recent years, and biotechnology companies are now developing a wide

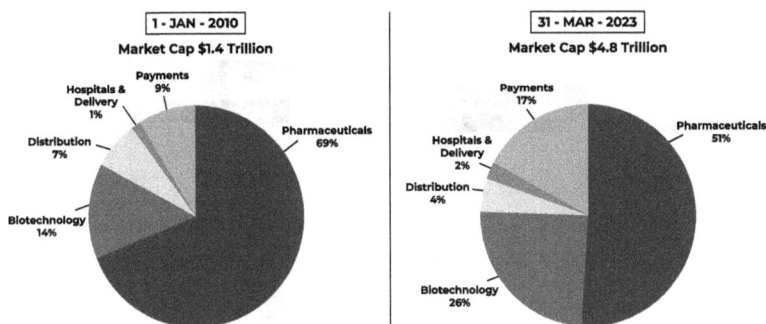

Figure 3.10 Value migration in health care

range of products, including drugs for cancer, heart disease, and other diseases. The growth of biotech companies is partly driven by the emergence
of venture capital firms and the expansion of the pharmaceutical industry
with a market cap increase of 1.4 trillion over the past 13 years. One
remarkable finding is that despite a relatively healthy EBITDA multiple
over 9×, hospitals and health care delivery went from 1.3 percent to only
2.5 percent of the economic pie.

Today, 64 percent of U.S. hospitals are either nonprofits (including
leading research hospitals) or state or local government owned. In addition, similar to hospitality and casino gaming, private equity is stepping
up to acquire more hospitals and doctors' offices along with REITs—
together they account for 9.5 percent of ownership in 2023, up from zero
in 2010 (see Figure 3.11).

Furthermore, despite the trends supporting clinics, telemedicine, and
home care, many of these nonprofit hospitals such as Ohio State, UPenn,
and Indiana University are using donor and taxpayer money to build billion-dollar hospitals of the future that leverage AI, robotics, autonomous
vehicles, and genomics and share information across networks to enable
remote monitoring (see Figure 3.11).

Globally, over $50 billion is being invested in new construction hos-
pitals of the future, from the UAE and Taiwan to Hangzhou, through
public–private partnerships that are the envy of other industries.

Furthermore, between 2013 and 2016, private equity acquired 355
physician practices focusing on those with a particular specialty, taking
control and adding value by streamlining administration, negotiating
higher rates with insurance companies to boost physician incomes. Today,

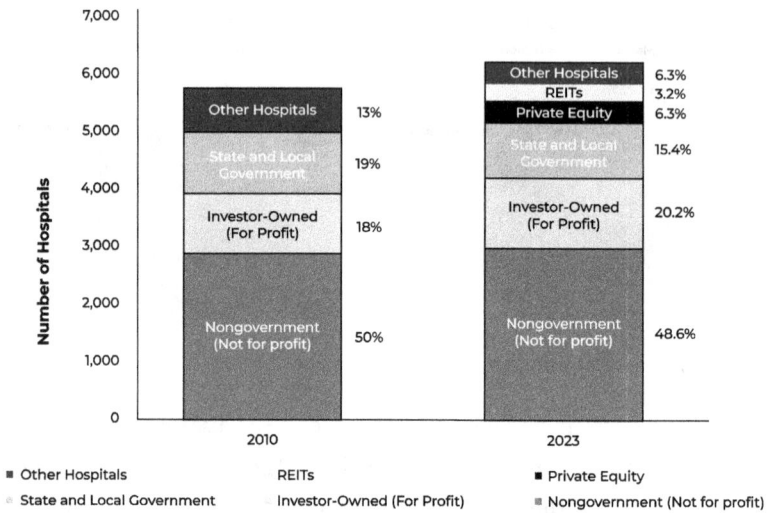

Figure 3.11 Evolution of hospital ownership in the United States, 2010 to 2023

25 to 40 percent of emergency rooms in hospitals are also staffed by private equity-backed companies.

HCA, the leader of the pack in terms of value creation among publicly traded hospitals, appears to be playing a hotel real-estate-type of game, focusing on targeted acquisitions and divestitures of smaller hospitals and clinics to achieve an "asset-right," positioning its 182 hospitals and invest in building networks of postacute, outpatient, and home-based services that can leverage its additional 2300 facilities.

Deja Vu: "Asset-Light" Branding and Licensing Comes to Health Care

The health care industry is rapidly evolving through consolidation, brand expansion, and patient information networks in ways very similar to the hotel and online travel industry's evolution in the 1990s and early 2000s. Hospital chains are engaging in acquisitions and joint ventures and creating brand extensions; high-end academic clinics are establishing geo-clusters with specialty health care centers to win talent and licensing their brands with value-added technology services globally; brick and mortar pharmacy retailers are providing outpatient care services launched during COVID; and pure play technology intermediaries are trying to win the customer by capturing them with online and virtual solutions, including affiliations that have committed networks of doctors and nurse practitioners.

In health care, brand equity translates to a loyal patient base, stronger negotiating leverage with insurers and suppliers, and the ability to acquire and retain human capital including top-quality physicians and clinical staff. In the last decade, major health care systems have invested significant capital in growth through acquisitions, conversions, joint ventures, franchising, and licensing agreements. This is essential given the intensifying competition for individual customers and employer accounts with brick and mortar retail players such as CVS and Walgreens and well-capitalized technology companies such as Amazon, Teladoc, MDLive, and Doctor on Demand.

The focus on achieving horizontal scale in core markets is also the strategy of UCLA Health, a nonprofit owned by the California Regents, that has leveraged the brand equity of its four world class research hospitals such as Ronald Reagan UCLA Medical Center with 260 clinics offering primary care and specialty services such as pediatrics and outpatient services that employ over 33,000 people in Southern California. Its sophisticated career site features over 1,500 openings with dedicated job pathways for nurses, research, information technology, new graduates, residencies, and internships.

A hybrid model is being pioneered by One Medical, who was acquired by Amazon for $3.9 billion in February 2023. One Medical has over 200 offices across 19 markets with dedicated doctors and nurses under management and an app that serves over 815,000 paid members with on-demand virtual care services, 24/7 video chats, and in-app messaging. One Medical also pioneered a health information exchange (HIE), a network of clinically integrated organizations that share information based on patient consent, resulting in better care coordination for members across a continuum of settings. Amazon's acquisition of the business enables it to leverage big data, prescription delivery, and Whole Foods.

Mayo Clinic Health Systems have expanded to 86 clinics, mostly in the Midwest region, and expanded internationally into 12 countries with cobranding services in their network including comprehensive health assessments, specialty consultations, second opinions, and diagnostic services. Similarly, University of Utah Health developed an affiliate network that includes 22 regional partners with cobranding, so hospitals and providers access the clinical expertise, research, and resources to serve patients in their communities. Cobranded facilities such as University of Texas MD Cancer Network establish standards of care and treatment plans so that partner hospitals fully integrate their clinical cancer operations with MD Anderson and report to their medical directors. In another case study, the University of Michigan Health System (UMHS) established a new affiliate business model that includes an ownership earn-out of up to 20 percent of partners such as Mid-Michigan Health. Traditional players like Emory health care and HCA are also consolidating their footprint and integrating branded primary and urgent care facilities with their hospitals in regions such as the southeast.

"Asset-light" models are the future of health care. Industry consolidation across service formats and the evolution from operators to branding companies that establish high-quality networks are reminiscent of hotel franchising, which was built on the premise of booking engines, cross-selling within a family of brands, and various levels of CRM. The implications are reduced unit labor costs for the industry and a shift in the talent markets, from traditional hospitals and clinics to hybrid or virtual models. This will result in more flexible work arrangements for nurses and physicians, less turnover, and massive savings in health care administration. It may even render the projected labor shortage of nurses and doctors moot, especially if virtual service models begin to go global.

In the coming years, health care industry structure may evolve to become similar to hospitality:

- Incumbents like HCA and UCLA Health continue to divest noncore hospitals and expand through mergers and acquisitions, in the process capturing a high share of medical practices and regional hospitals and gaining leverage in their negotiations with insurance companies and other payers.
- REITS and private equity own a large number of hospitals as incumbents unload real estate in exchange for triple net leases to pay down debt and access cash for expansion.

- Online disruptors such as Amazon leverage One Medical to provide virtual care to prime members, using big data and AI to accelerate the home care models.
- Leading academic health centers franchise their brands and establish networks in the United States and license their brands internationally.
- Pharmaceutical-centric retailers like CVS and Walgreen shift their model to e-commerce and partner with online disruptors and hospital networks to reduce brick and mortar units to those who provide value-added diagnostic services such as vaccination.

CHAPTER 4

Talent Valuation

Bringing Moneyball to Hospitality

Insight #1

The Top 100 GMs Are Way Ahead of the Pack but Their Impact Is Not Appropriately Recognized

MogulRecruiter's data science team used big data and machine learning and developed proprietary algorithms to rank property-level talent in the U.S. hotel industry. Being able to identify and put an elite GM in-place could have a substantial impact on the ability of hotel investors to improve operations and realize higher asset values. A next-level calculation to quantify the value of elite talent to a hotel asset would be to identify the contribution of, for example, an elite GM to the value of a hotel asset versus an average or "replacement-level" GM. Since hotel

GMs contribute to both revenue management and cost management, the contribution of the elite GM to the hotel asset could be the net operating income realized by the elite GM minus the net operating income that would be realized by an average performing GM. The incremental net operating income generated by the elite GM could then be divided by the current hotel asset market cap rate to calculate the contribution of asset value by having an elite GM versus an average GM. For example, if an elite GM can generate a net operating income of $1 million at a particular hotel while an average GM, all else equal, can only generate a net operating income of $800,000, and the current cap rate for hotel assets in the market is 8 percent, then the asset value generated by an elite GM in this case would be $200,000/8 percent = $2,500,000. The implications of understanding and correctly valuing elite talent in the hotel industry could therefore be immense.

Contrary to conventional wisdom, hotel management is an elite talent business, similar to music and sports, where the top 1 percent outperforms their peers by wide margins. The top 100 (top 1 percent or 99th percentile) hotel general managers outperform their peers by 30 percent and the next 100 GMs (top 2 percent or 98th percentile) by 12 percent (see Figure 4.1).

We started by developing the rankings for the top 100 hotel general managers in the United States. On the surface, the professional backgrounds of the top 100 GM Super Moguls in the United States are not surprising: they are highly experienced individuals, with an average of 10 years of

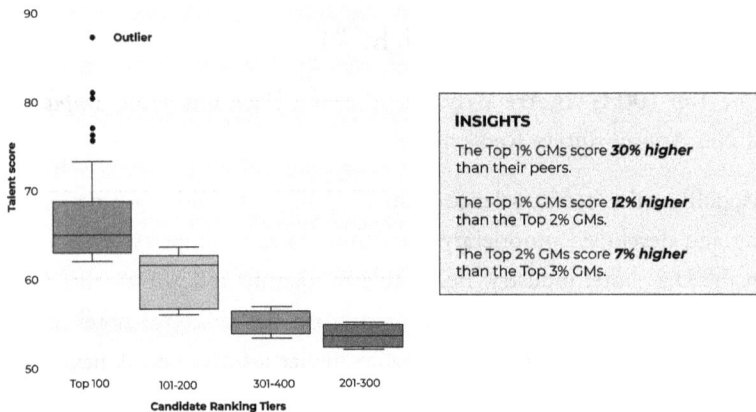

Figure 4.1   *U.S. hotel GM ranking score distribution by talent tier, 2018 to 2022*

experience as a general manager. What defies conventional wisdom is the type of properties they manage, their locations, and employers. For example, 40 percent of the top 100 hotel general managers led limited-service hotels and 59 percent worked in franchised operations, including branded and independent hotel properties, equally spread across gateway cities and small markets; 60 percent of the top 100 GMs managed hotel properties in highly competitive markets defined by STR index spreads for RevPAR index of under 3 percent, supply growth that exceeded demand growth and greater proportion of new build hotel competition, such as New York, Miami, Houston, and Orlando. There was a slightly positive correlation between property size and relative performance, but two-thirds managed properties less than 400 rooms (see Figure 4.2).

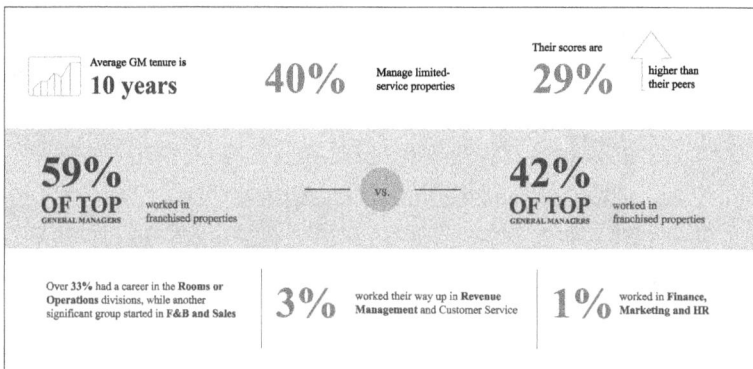

Figure 4.2   Top 100 U.S. general manager insights

DNA of Top 100 GMs

- Many of these elite GMs were not trained from the front line up from the best-known hotel chains. In fact, many came from small towns and started their careers as schoolteachers, department store clerks, banquet captains, and in military service.
- The pathway to becoming an elite GM varies, but 43 percent rose through the rooms or operations departments while 33 percent "cut their teeth" in food and beverage as well as sales and marketing roles.
- A total of 12 percent are generalists who didn't major in a particular function prior to becoming a GM.

- Only 3 percent were from highly analytical functions with less customer contact such as revenue management, digital marketing, and finance and only 1 percent come from a human resources background. Instead, these more technical property-level directors largely bypassed the GM role and remained in their functional silos, either leaving the industry after an average of 5 years or seeking higher paying roles in regional operations, the corporate office, or other industries.
- Only 8 percent came directly from outside the industry—a remarkably low number compared to other service industries, such as retail, where 25 percent of GMs come directly from another industry.
- The demographics of the top 100 U.S. hotel GMs were even more astonishing: approximately 50 percent of the top 100 are women, 30 percent are minorities, and most are high school educated who moved up the ranks in operating limited-service hotels in relatively small markets (see Figure 4.3). For the list of the top 50 U.S. hotel general managers and their worth, see Appendix II.

Top Hotel General Managers

Figure 4.3   Top Hotel General Managers

Insight #2

Elite Talent Outperforms by a Wide Margin That Grows Over Time

We subsequently used machine learning to scale the process and apply our ranking algorithm to levels below and above the GM, including supervisors such as front office managers and regional hotel general managers who oversee a portfolio of properties in a region and other service industries including restaurants, retail, delivery, and logistics.

Our data scientists captured findings in a ranking score distribution chart with box plots that represent the 25th to the 75th percentile with a median score for each position. Two major findings emerged. First, regardless of level in the organization, the outliers or highest performers (the dots) are prevalent for all positions, with wider score differentials for customer-facing supervisor positions such as guest relations. Second, the talent differentials between median performers and the highest performing outliers grow as we move up the organization to regional heads of operations who oversee a portfolio of properties or stores. Starting not just with hotels, but also in restaurants, retail, and other service sectors, there are significant outliers in each position's performance range, and the spread grows as one moves up in title and position (see Figure 4.4).

How Much Are Elite Talents Worth?

We wrote predictive algorithms and used machine learning to determine the present economic value that individual talents create for the hotel and their respective organization. We call this "Mogul Worth": the employee equivalent of the present value of lifetime customers' value to the business, typically used to segment customers into tiers to receive differentiated marketing offers and service levels. Mogul Worth predictive algorithms were trained on Mercer's compensation dataset and estimate the worth of each talent based on various dimensions such as talent tier, score, difficulty of the market, brand segment, and

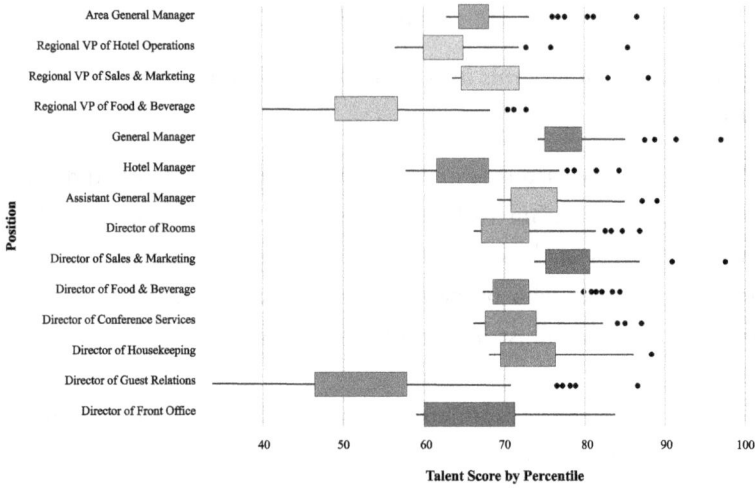

Talent Score by Percentile

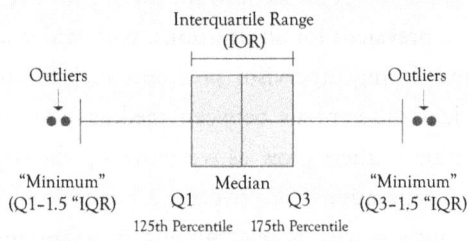

Box Plot provides a visual representation of statistical
data based on the minimum, first quartile,
median, third quartile, and maximum. Outliers can
be plotted on Box Plots as individual points.

Figure 4.4   Talent ranking scores for hotel positions

property size. Mogul Worth does not convey how much the individual
talent is earning today or the current market value of the position. It
is a measure of how much value talents create for the organization and
can be used as a guideline for employers when setting compensation
and other benefits.

We proceeded to predict the worth of all supervisors and above elite
talents in our database and compared the results to the reports shared by
executive search firms that benchmark the actual compensation ranges
for hotel GMs including JDI, Aethos, job sites, and other sources. The
results of our top 50 U.S. hotel general managers in 2022 can be seen in
Appendix II.

Insight #3

The Current Model Does Not Compensate Elite Talents for Performance

After estimating their true worth, we analyzed the current compensation ranges for elite talent versus their peers, starting with hotel general managers in New York, Los Angeles, Atlanta, San Francisco, and Dallas. The data clearly suggest the hotel industry compensates general managers in a linear, hierarchical model like government civil servants, with minimal consideration of property cash flows or value they create for hotel assets as a real-estate investment.

These findings are reminiscent of Michael Lewis' bestselling book,[1] *Moneyball: The Art of Winning an Unfair Game*, where independent analysts from outside baseball discovered the mispricing of talent and capitalized on the informal market inefficiencies:

> There was but one question he left unasked, and it vibrated between his lines: if gross miscalculations of a person's value could occur on a baseball field, before a live audience of thirty thousand, and a television audience of millions more, what did that say about the measurement of performance in other lines of work? If professional baseball players could be over or undervalued, who couldn't?

We analyzed the Average Annual Value (AAV) of over 4,500 players[2] in four major league sports based in the United States: football (NFL), basketball (NBA), baseball (MLB), and hockey (NHL) in 2023. We used a violin plot chart to analyze the distribution of income for each league, including the median and mean incomes earned by the average player against the highest paid elite talents (see Figure 4.5).

There are two major insights. First, professional sports teams such as the NBA use analytics to assess key drivers of revenue production such as attendance, sponsorship, content and advertising, and playoff optionality to generate the net present value or worth of a player. Each player's value is situational and determined based on the context of a specific team, considering a player's marketability and leadership role in developing talent. A player's worth can be compared to his or her replacement value and

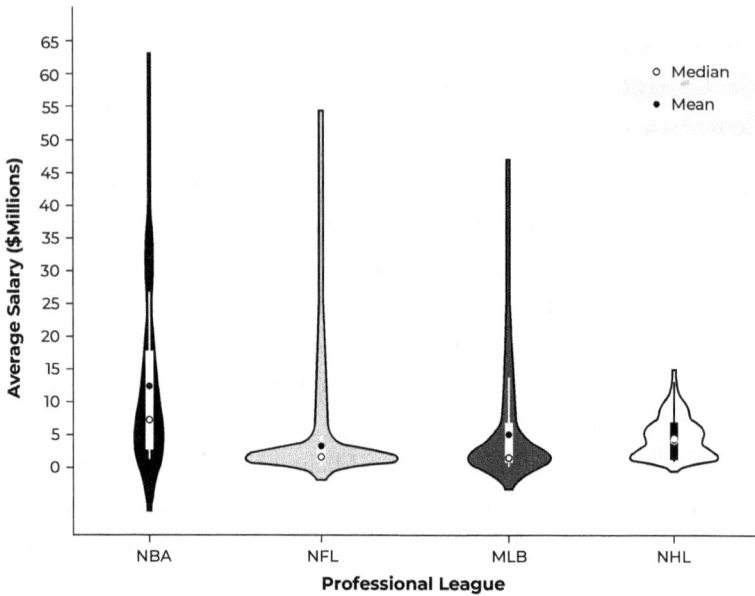

Figure 4.5   Salary distribution in U.S. professional sports

Source: Average Anual Value data from www.spotrac.com.

adjusted for injury risk. In the last several years, fantasy sports websites enable fans to compute an athlete's value above replacement and convert the score into betting dollars.

Generally speaking, professional sports leagues have agreed to pay their players 45 to 50 percent of team revenues as part of collective bargaining agreements. Since 2015, median salaries have been growing 25 percent in the NHL and NFL, 50 percent in the NBA, but down 30 percent in MLB.

In the NBA, the top 10 players, such as Nikola Jokic, Stephen Curry, Joel Embiid, Bradley Beal, and Lebron James earn more than $49 million while more than 65 percent of NBA players earn lower than the $11.9 million average. The top 10 highest compensated players change every 7 years by 60 percent and every decade by 90 percent.

In contrast, the NHL displays the smallest gap between its mean and median average AAV: 251 (45 percent) players make AAV between $0 and $3 million, 180 players (32 percent) make AAV between $3 million and $6 million, and only 125 players such as Nathan MacKinnon, Connor McDavid, Auston Matthews, and Drew Doughty (22 percent) make above $6 million with the top 10 players earning between $10.5 million and $12.6 million.

Similarly, in the NFL, around 2472 (nearly 87 percent) players make between $0 and $5 million, with salaries highly concentrated around the median; and the highest, including Lamar Jackson, Jalen Hurts, Aaron Rodgers, Russel Wildon and Kyler Murray earn more than $46 million. However, unlike the NHL, the NFL pays its super elite talent extremely well. The top 10 NFL players earn 14.5 × the league average and two players—Lamar Jackson and Jalen Hurts—earn more than more than $50 million.

Second, plotting player compensation by league in a Lorenz curve provides a graphical representation of the economic inequality model with the population percentile on the X-axis and the cumulative wealth on the Y-axis (see Figure 4.6). League-imposed salary caps of $123 million per team in the NBA, $224.8 million per team in the NFL, and $82.5 million in the NHL have "leveled the playing field" between teams and also reduced income inequality among players: the top 10 NHL players earn only 3 × the average player. As the only league without a salary cap,

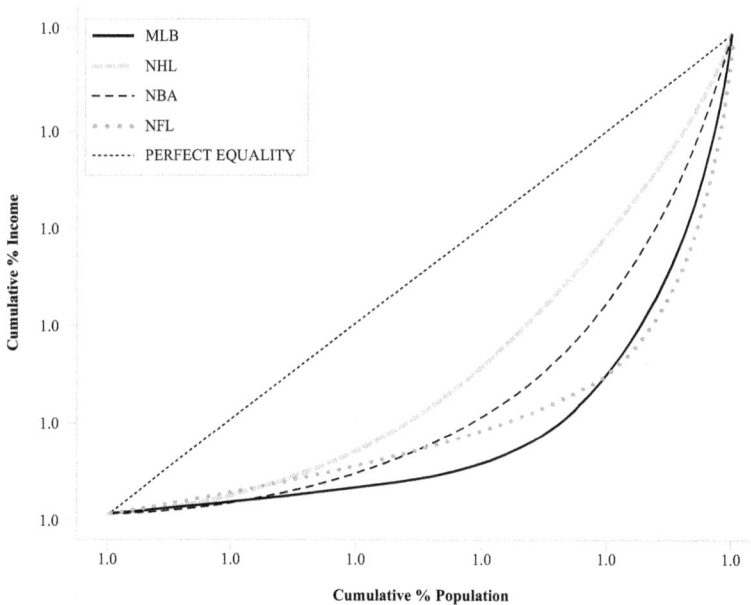

Figure 4.6   Salary distribution by population in U.S. professional sports

Source: Average Anual Value data from www.spotrac.com.

MLB has the most unequal distribution of income across its players, with
the top 10 players earning above $32.5 million, which is 7.8 × the average
compensation per player.

Few service industries use analytics and data science to determine
the relative compensation of their best operators. In hotels, our research
uncovered that geographic market and hotel product segments primarily
determine GM compensation, followed by brand prestige and other non-
financial product characteristics, which are used as a proxy for operational
complexity. For example, less tenured GMs whose scores were consistently 20 percent higher than their peers were paid 20 percent less in cash
compensation, even in the same markets (see Figure 4.7).

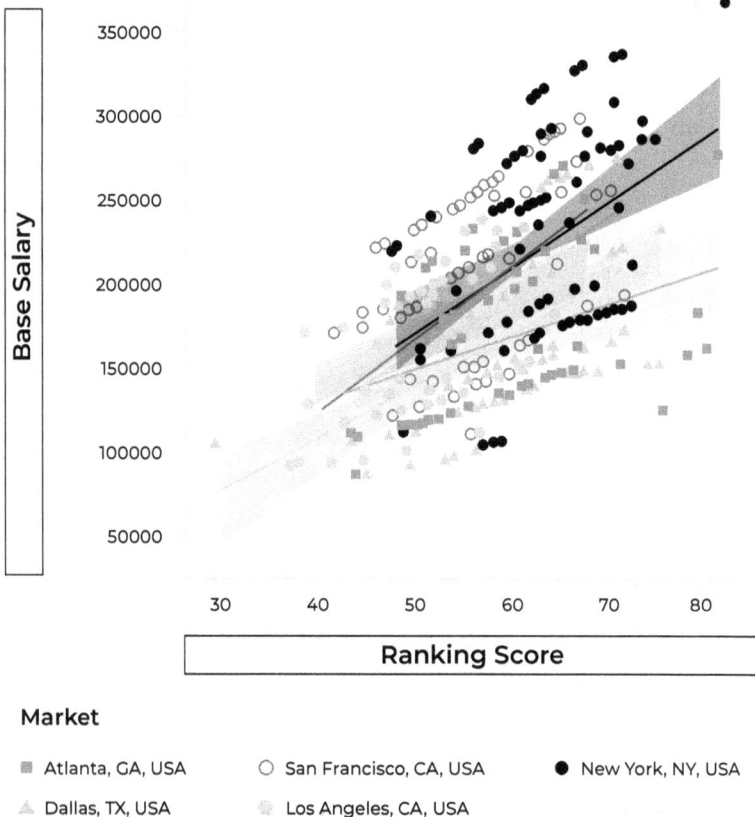

Market

▦ Atlanta, GA, USA	○ San Francisco, CA, USA	● New York, NY, USA
▲ Dallas, TX, USA	Los Angeles, CA, USA	

Figure 4.7   General managers' salary by score in top five U.S. markets

Surveys with CHROs, hotel operators, and owners confirmed that relatively small changes in fixed and variable compensation bands exist in today's market. A case study of compensation for Los Angeles hotel GMs by talent scores illustrates that many long-tenured mediocre GMs are overpaid, and elite talent, especially rising stars, are underpaid compared to their peers and the value they create for hotel assets. Also, mediocre GMs at luxury and upper upscale hotels were paid more than elite performers, who managed less prestigious properties whose unit economics were far more profitable (see Figure 4.8).

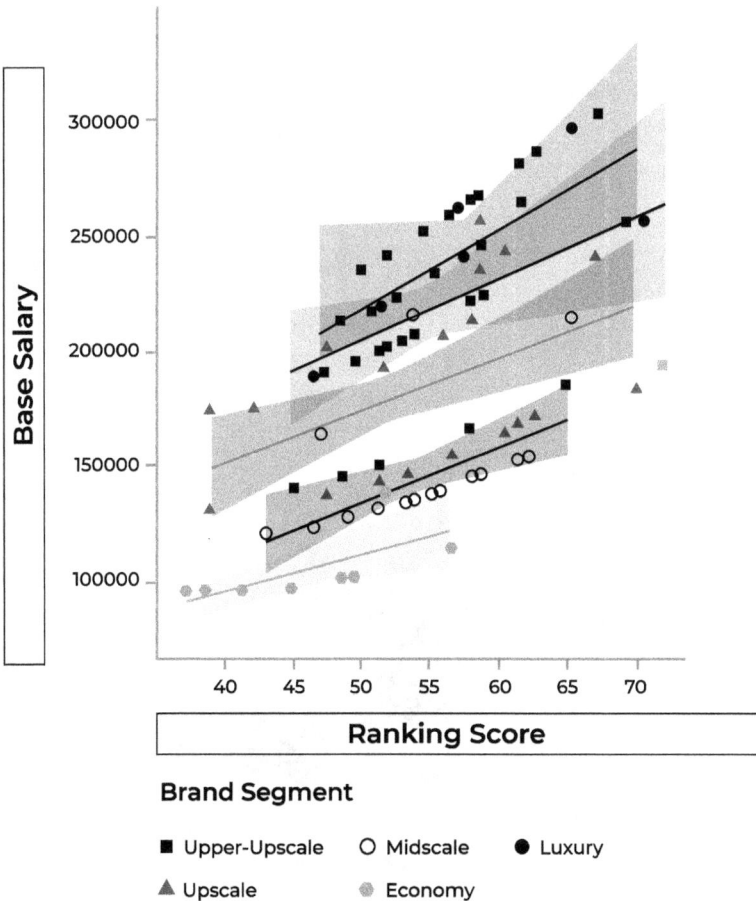

Figure 4.8   *General managers' salary by score in Los Angeles, California*

Insight #4

The Talent Pipeline Is Insufficient to Meet Diversity Targets in the United States

According to our research, women and minorities comprise 60 and 40 percent, respectively, of the U.S. hotel front line. However, only 20 percent of U.S. hotel general managers are women and only 10 percent are visible minorities (people of color). Black people represent 15 percent of the front line and only 1 percent of hotel general managers (see Figure 4.9).

Overall, significant innovation is required to close the diversity gap in the property or store level. While public disclosures from the hotel chains confirm that ethnic minorities represent from 62 to 68 percent of their workforce and significant strides have been made in the corporate office, diversity has remained stagnant over the past 15 years in terms of supervisor and above roles, except for more white women rising to general manager.

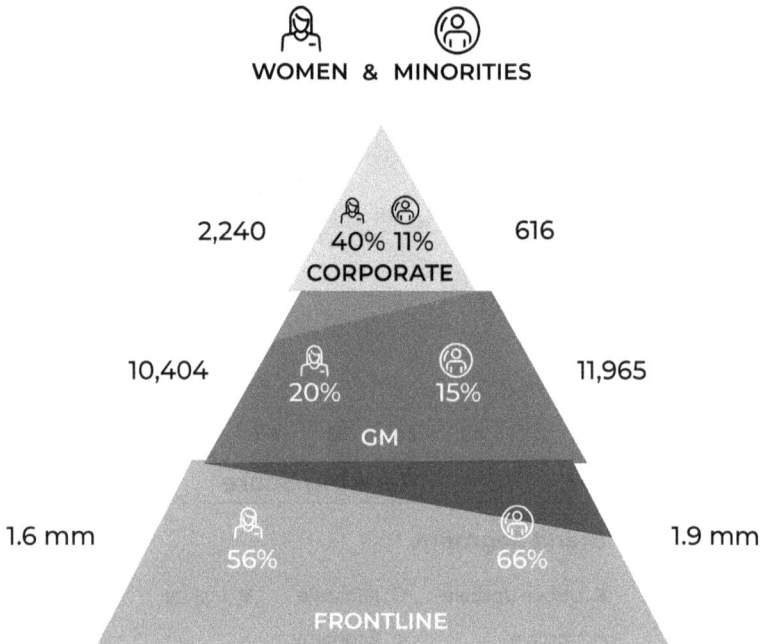

WOMEN & MINORITIES

2,240   40% 11%   616
CORPORATE

10,404   20%   15%   11,965
GM

1.6 mm   56%   66%   1.9 mm
FRONTLINE

Figure 4.9   U.S. hotel industry demographics by organizational level

Also, while CEOs of hotel chains often praise their company's track record in increasing the number of women in the corporate office to 40 percent, similar improvements have not occurred at the regional or property levels, where most employees are employed. For example, according to their ESG and human capital disclosures, while Hilton has 45 percent women in corporate executive roles, only 22 percent of general managers are women. In their ESG reports, Hilton, Marriott, and other hotel chains have set broad goals to increase Black, Indigenous and People of Color (BIPOC) to 25 percent in corporate director and above roles in the next 5 to 10 years while little has been detailed with respect to BIPOC targets for GMs (see Figure 4.10).

With respect to meeting its espoused diversity targets, the first question that comes to mind is: how much progress is likely in the next decade if hotel brands and operators do a better job of developing and promoting the talent that already exists, one level below the corporate office and one or two levels below the hotel GM?

We analyzed the demographics of the workforce at the property levels in great depth. Gender and ethnic/racial diversity vary at the property level, including general manager, assistant general manager, hotel manager, all director-level positions, restaurant managers, and executive chef roles. Assuming 35 percent retention, promoting female talents in GM-ready positions will reduce the gender gap to 32 percent (total gain of 12,216 talents). In the same way, promoting minority individuals who are prepared for GM positions can reduce the minority gap to 69 percent (total gain of 6066 talents).

WOMEN				MINORITIES		
CURRENT	TARGET	GAP		CURRENT	TARGET	GAP
2,240	2,800	25%	CORPORATE	616	1,848	200%
10,404	26,010	150%	GM	11,965	26,323	120%
1.6 mm	1.4 mm	-	FRONTLINE	1.9 mm	950,000	-

Figure 4.10   Hotel industry—U.S. diversity gap (2023)

Therefore, the U.S. hotel industry must recruit and develop 3,390 women GMs and 1911 minority GMs from outside the industry or country to meet its targets in the next decade. For a detailed breakdown of diversity by position for regional and property levels, and the gaps after internal promotions, refer to Appendix III.

Insight #5

The Path to Hotel GM Is Over a Decade and Must Be Shortened

It takes an average of 11 years working in the hospitality industry to become a hotel general manager and 15 years for a full-service lifestyle or luxury property, regardless of whether it's managed by a brand, third party, or owner operated. Even for limited-service hotels in small markets, which are usually nonunion and lack food and beverage, spa, and other managerial responsibilities, it takes an average of 9 years to rise from front line to general manager (see Figure 4.11).

In this context, Cornell University Hotel Professor of Human Resource Management Bruce Tracey recently compared the number of years to become a hotel general manager to being a physician specializing

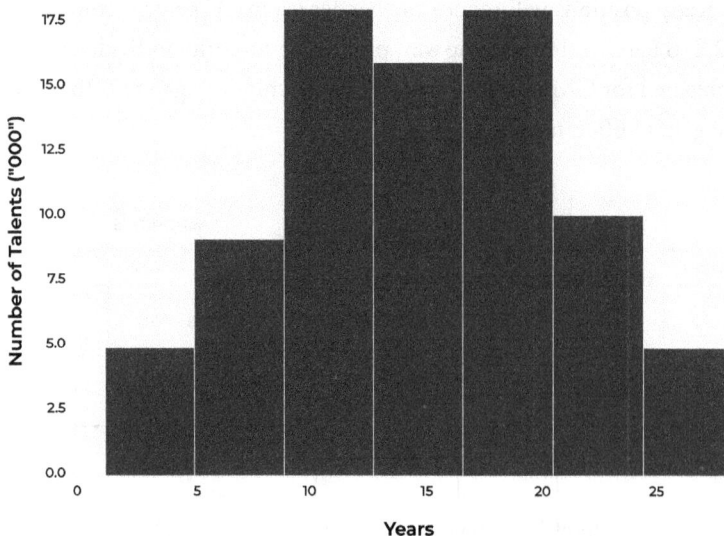

Figure 4.11   Years of experience to become a hotel GM

Number of Years of Experience in Hospitality

Figure 4.12   Number of years of GM's work in hospitality

in neurosurgery: "How long does it take for people to train up to be a brain surgeon?"

Today, most hotel GMs based in the United States have 20 to 30 years of hospitality experience and are an aging population. The relatively small talent pool of GMs with under 10 years of experience reflects the absence of a home-grown talent pipeline in the industry and its employee turnover of 90 to 115 percent (see Figure 4.12).

Insight #6

Luxury and Lifestyle Brands Lead the Way for Building Human Capital

Next, we turn our attention to determining the quality of hospitality managers. We benchmarked over 100 U.S. hotel operators who manage at least five hotels in five distinct markets, by their share of elite talent and diversity, over a 5 year period, from 2018 to 2022. We also indexed their share of elite talent (top 10 percent) against their peers: talent pools at hotel chains, brands, full-service, and limited-service management companies were compared against each other for general managers, rooms, housekeeping, sales and marketing, and food and beverage functions. It was an arduous undertaking: over 80 percent of the U.S. hotel industry is franchised, with hundreds of management companies investing in building employer brands to attract and retain talent.

Today, approximately six out of seven U.S. hotel industry employees work for third-party management companies as opposed to hotel GMs (see Figure 4.13).

However, properties operated by luxury and lifestyle brands continue to lead the way for talent and have the highest proportion of elite GMs. In fact, the top 14 hotel operators in terms of proportion of elite talent are brands, starting with privately owned luxury and lifestyle pure-play brands Rosewood (#1), Four Seasons (#2), and Accor (#3) (see Table 4.1).

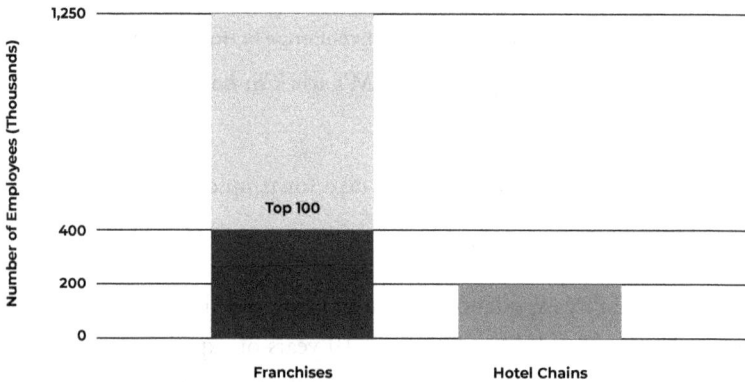

Figure 4.13   U.S. hotel workforce by employer type

Source: Top 100 hotel management companies—hotel business magazine.

Table 4.1   Top U.S. hotel employers with highest talent score

Rank	Employer	Properties	Score	Category
1	Rosewood Hotels & Resorts	29	99.0	Hotel brands
2	Four Seasons Hotels & Resorts	115	97.9	Hotel brands
3	Accor	269	97.7	Hotel chains
4	Marriott International, Inc.	636	97.7	Hotel chains
5	Radisson Hotel Group	44	97.1	Hotel chains
6	InterContinental Hotels Group (IHG)	178	96.7	Hotel chains
7	Wyndham Worldwide Corporation	228	96.2	Hotel chains

Rank	Employer	Properties	Score	Category
8	Loews Hotels	21	96.1	Hotel brands
9	Hyatt Hotels Corporation	182	96.0	Hotel chains
10	Omni Hotels & Resorts	51	95.8	Hotel brands
11	Hilton	246	95.6	Hotel chains
12	Sage Hospitality Group	64	94.2	Full service
13	Highgate Hotels	409	92.5	Full service
14	Crescent Hotels & Resorts	118	92.5	Full service
15	Dimension Development Company	85	91.1	Full service
16	HEI Hotels & Resorts	80	90.2	Full service

Top U.S. Hotel Employers with Highest Talent Score

The top operators have a 10 to 15 points lead in elite talent at the hotel general manager level and have department-level talent indexes of 125 to 130, compared to their peers who average 100. It should be noted that Accor Group, the largest ranking chain, grew in North America almost entirely through the acquisition of luxury and lifestyle brands, including Fairmont and SBE Entertainment Group. After Accor, the #4 to #11 top operators are large chains, Marriott, Radisson, IHG, Wyndham, Loews, Omni, Hyatt, and Hilton, most of which are publicly traded. It isn't until #12 that third-party management companies emerge, starting with Sage and Highgate Hotels.

We summarized our findings in the talent share matrix chart in Figure 4.14. The chart shows a company's share of elite talent on the X-axis and the number of properties managed on the Y-axis. The talent scores are measured for each property over a 5 year period, 2018 to 2022. We classified the best hotel operators into two buckets: high potential (talent scores above the median, high growth, and below-average portfolio size and growth) and stars (talent scores above the median, high growth, and above-average portfolio size and growth).

We found that three legacy hotel chains that manage a substantial proportion of their full-service and luxury hotels—Marriott, Accor, Hilton, and Hyatt—are *stars* that stand above the rest alongside a few noteworthy,

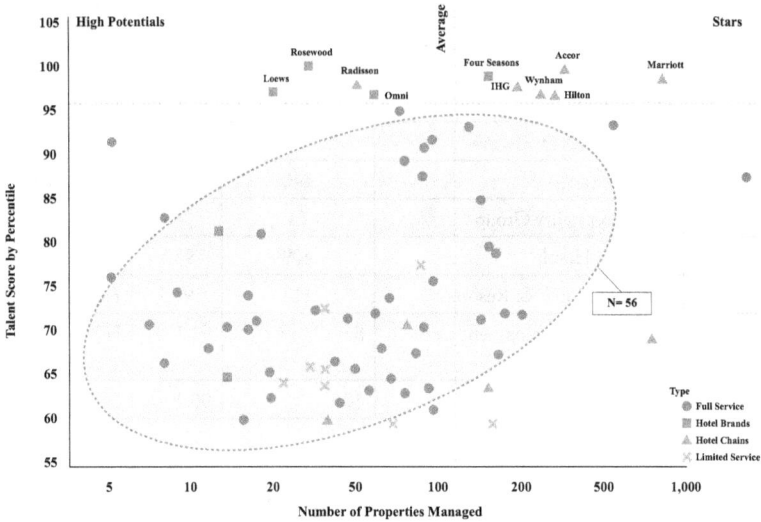

Figure 4.14   Top employers in U.S. hotel industry by size

small hotel management companies. There are also some high-performing mid-size luxury brands such as Four Seasons and Loews (but very
few hotel management companies) that are *high potential*, whose future
success depends on their ability to scale their elite talent as they grow.

Insight #7

Scale Is Not an Advantage with Respect to Talent in Hospitality

There is negative correlation between the size of the employer and talent
scores: talent scores decrease by small amounts as the size of the employer
increases. Therefore, there is minimal evidence that supports the claim
that larger employer and management companies have an advantage in
attracting and developing talents (see Figure 4.15).

How do third-party management companies fare? The top three,
namely Sage (#15), Highgate (#16), and Crescent (#17), are well represented in terms of elite talent relative to their peers. Until Highgate's
recent M&A spree, all were "mid-size" in scale under 100 hotels. After
that, the next wave includes large players like HEI (#19), White Lodging (#21), and Aimbridge (#23) as well as smaller niche players such as
Dimension (#17), Landry's (#18), and Hospitality Ventures (#20).

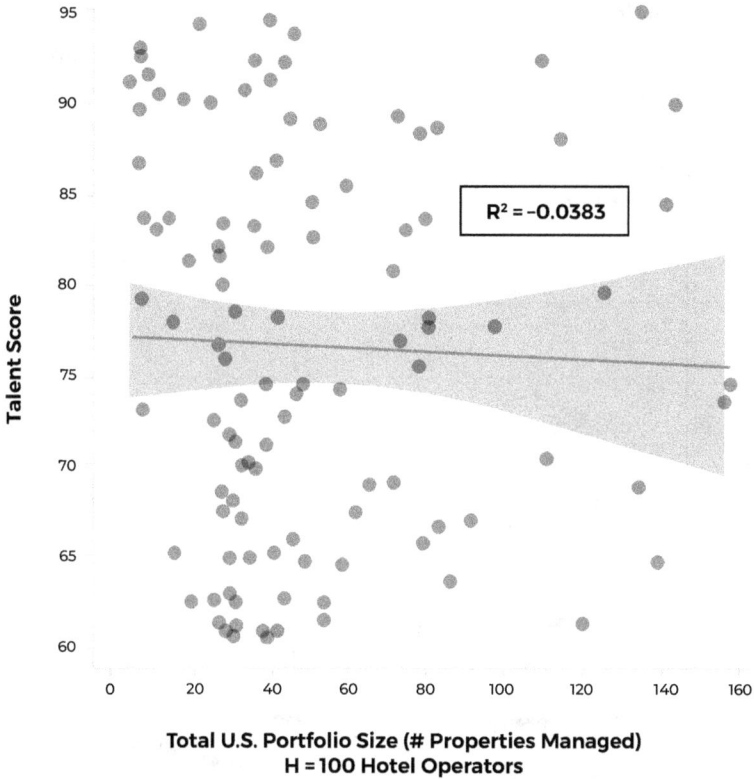

$R^2 = -0.0383$

Figure 4.15   Correlation between employer size and quality of talent

On the surface, these findings appear to mirror the overall results: there is little evidence that the number of properties under management or operational scale nationally or regionally creates advantages in terms of attracting or building a high-quality talent pool.

Insight #8

Publicly Traded Chains Lead with Respect to Diverse Elite Talents

Those in the top quartile, including a few third-party operators, are in a class of their own regarding minorities and women in their hotel management ranks. That said, according to the data, few hotel operators have scaled the acquisition and development of "diverse, elite talent" as an organizational capability.

Our findings are captured in a U.S. diversity share matrix that shows a company's share of diverse elite talent on the X-axis and the number of properties managed on the Y-axis (see Figure 4.16).

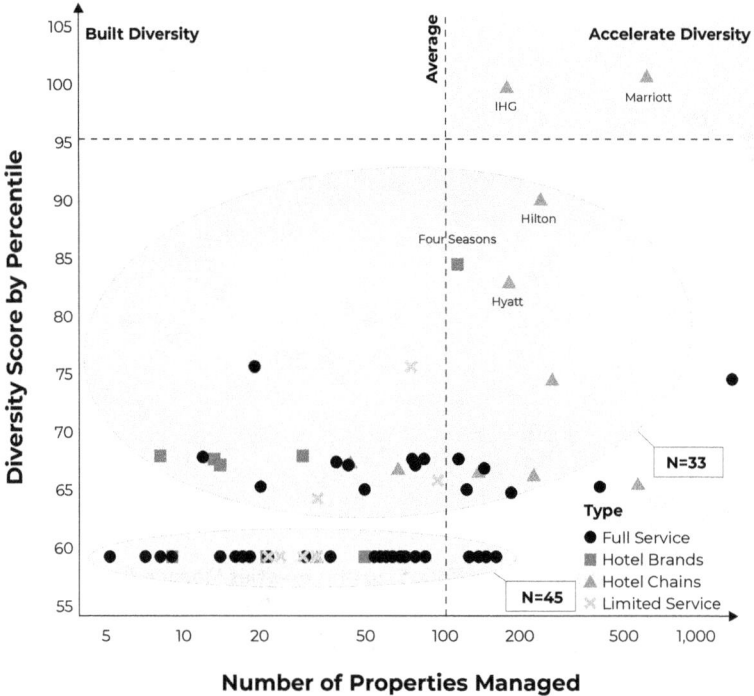

Figure 4.16   Top U.S. hotel employers for diversity

The diversity data are measured over a 5 year period from 2018 to 2022. We classified the best 100 operators into two buckets: building diversity (high diversity scores and below-average portfolio size) and accelerating diversity (high diversity scores and above-average portfolio size and growth).

There is strong evidence that elite talent and diversity go hand-in-hand. There is a 92 percent correlation between a change in the company's quality of talent score and its diversity talent score (see Figure 4.3). Among the top-ranked companies, Marriott, IHG, and Hilton followed by Hyatt have greater market shares of hotel management diversity across the board—from general managers, rooms, food and beverage, and

Table 4.2   Top employers in U.S. hotel industry for diversity

Rank	Employer	Properties Managed	Talent Score	Category
1	Marriott International, Inc.	636	100.0	Hotel Chains
2	InterContinental Hotels Group (IHP)	178	99.1	Hotel Chains
3	Hilton	246	89.8	Hotel Chains
4	Four Seasons Hotels & Resorts	115	84.1	Hotel Brands
5	Hyatt Hotels Corporation	182	82.8	Hotel Chains

housekeeping to sales and marketing, finance, and human resources (see Table 4.2). The top brands, Fairmont and Four Seasons, are also in this elite class. A few management companies, led by Aimbridge and Crescent, are also leaders in their category and emerging leaders nationally. However, below the top 20, most hotel managers and brands, including lifestyle and luxury, have major gaps and lack bench strength and depth in diversity, with diversity indexes of 80 percent. Once again, despite the theoretical alignment of interests, owner-operators are running well behind the pack leaders.

There are some bright spots. For example, Marriott sets a high standard among hotel chains for appointing women GMs, with a 20-point advantage. Some third-party managers, such as HEI, Davidson, and Highgate, have also made strides in terms of women GMs but are subpar with 80 percent indexes for women and minorities leading departments such as housekeeping and food and beverage.

Insight #9

Bigger Doesn't Mean More Diverse Below GM

With only 1.6 percent of GMs being black versus their double-digit representation on the front line, the hotel industry has its work cut out to meet its diversity goals. Among the big chains, with respect to black people in hotel management, Marriott, and Kimpton (IHG) have a lead across the board. Hilton, Four Seasons, and Hyatt are a distant second tier some 10 to 15 points below. Bright spots include Kimpton at the GM level and Nomad in food and beverage. Also, a few small management companies, notably Island Hospitality and Marcus Hotels, keep pace with the best chains in diversity in a few categories such as sales and marketing (see Table 4.3).

Table 4.3   Top 10 employers for black people

Rank	Employer	Score
1	Marriott International, Inc.	100
2	InterContinental Hotels Group (IHG)	99.1
3	Hilton	89.8
4	Four Seasons Hotels & Resorts	84.1
5	Hyatt Hotels Corporation	82.8
6	Island Hospitality Management	75.7
7	Marcus Hotels & Resorts	75.7
8	Accor	75
9	Aimbridge Hospitality	74.7
10	Rosewood Hotels & Resorts	68.2

Among management companies, Crescent and Aimbridge have also made more progress than their peers in appointing black GMs but have little representation or bench strength one level below in departments such as food and beverages. Very quickly, diversity gaps become visible as the other operators' indexes sink into the 60s.

Black people constitute 17 to 18 percent of frontline workers in hotels and 13.6 percent of U.S. population. A reasonable long-term goal would be to achieve a representation of black GMs that is equivalent to their population share, which is 13 percent of GM roles. Based on a 35 percent retention rate, promoting qualified black individuals to GM positions can reduce the black GM gap to 250 percent (a total gain of 3109 talents). Therefore, the U.S. hotel industry needs to recruit and develop 5187 black GMs from external sources or international markets to meet its targets in the next decade.

There is little evidence to indicate mergers and acquisitions among third-party management companies and owner-operators will make

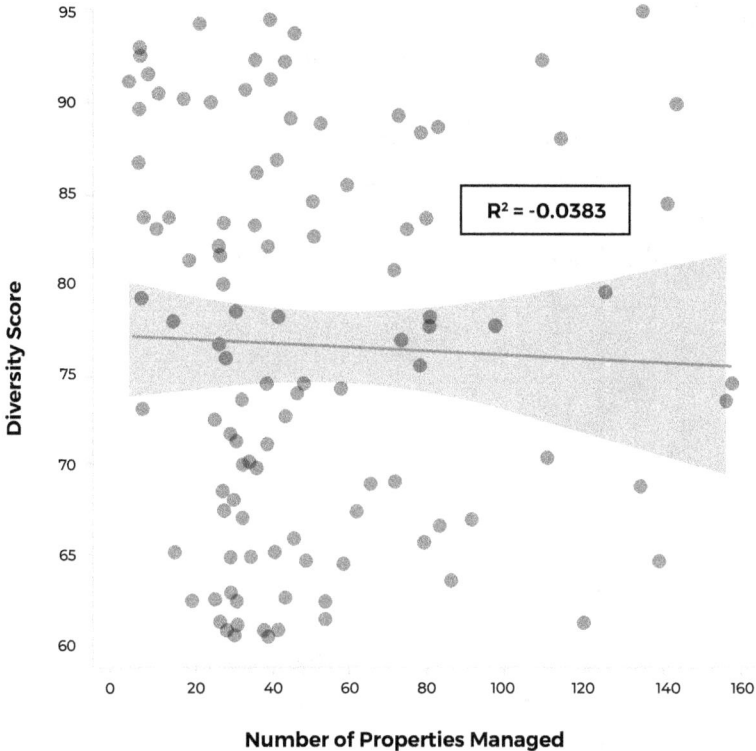

Figure 4.17   Diversity score and portfolio size correlation

a significant difference. Industrywide, there is a negative correlation between the size of the employer and diversity scores (see Figure 4.17). The exception is that there is a slightly positive correlation between diversity scores and size of the employer in properties managed by hotel chains, casinos, and theme parks.

Insight #10

Food and Beverage Is a Bright Spot for Developing Diverse, Elite Talent

High-performing food and beverage departments drive differences in employer talent scores and have the highest diversity representation. It is in these positions where many of the leading employers including Accor, Nomad, Kimpton, Four Seasons, and Park Hyatt outperform their peers. However, smaller operators are the leaders in diverse elite talent in food and beverage including Drury Hotels, SH Hotels & Resorts, MGM Resorts International, Yotel, and Caesars Entertainment (see Figure 4.18). Unfortunately, we have observed that many full-service hotel operators have reduced the number of restaurant outlets, eliminated room service, and postponed rehiring banquet, catering managers, and chefs due to a lack of visibility into group bookings. The net loss of over 100,000 highly skilled food and beverage talents in the United States, and 1 million globally, is perhaps the most significant hit to diverse elite talent in the hotel sector.

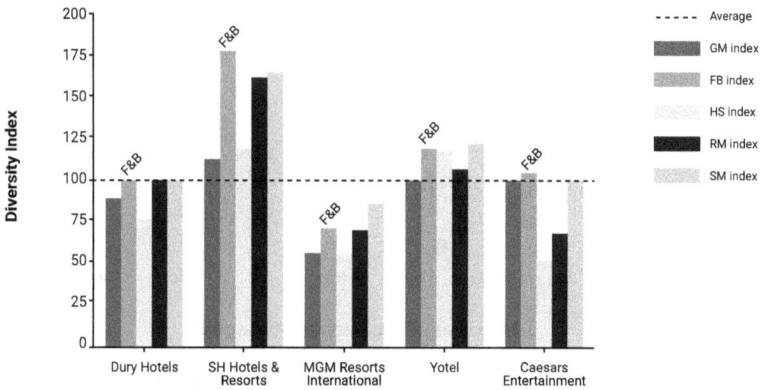

Figure 4.18   Top five companies for diversity in F&B

CHAPTER 5

People First

Establishing a Culture of Ownership

In 2023, inflation remains persistent and real wages remain stagnant for most working people in hospitality, despite significant growth in profits. Demand is surging, and hotels are seeing 90 percent of 2019 revenue in most markets, but EBITDA profit margins are shrinking in most product segments. Despite the projected return of record revenues and $80 billion in profits in the United States by 2025, the hotel industry is struggling due to labor shortages, immigration bottlenecks, and departure of elite talent. According to our analysis, general managers are turning over at 40 percent with average tenures on the job of 16 months, and employee turnover ranges from 75 to 115 percent. Most hotels have 12 job openings despite reducing services such as daily housekeeping and restaurant hours.

The work experience in U.S. hospitality is commoditizing. Hotels risk becoming sweatshops that are losing an entire generation of talent and remain millions of employees short of providing a high-quality customer experience. Fewer people, and equally important, fewer talented individuals, want to work in the once prestigious industry where they could be part of brands that became synonymous with making travel accessible. Furthermore, gender, ethnicity, race, and workplace have become intertwined in inequitable ways with the fortunes of working people and families, exacerbating the socioeconomic divisions in the country.

Economists use Gini coefficient, also known as the Gini index, to measure income inequality, within a population, such as a country or social group. The Gini coefficient measures the inequality among the values of a frequency distribution, such as levels of income. A Gini coefficient of 0 reflects perfect equality, where all income or wealth values are the same, while a Gini coefficient of 1 (or 100 percent) reflects maximal inequality among values, for example, a single individual having all the income while all others have none. In terms of countries, as of 2023, Finland has the lowest Gini coefficient of 0.27, indicating a relatively equal distribution of income among its population, while the United States has a higher Gini coefficient of 0.41, reflecting more income disparities among its citizens, and South Africa with the lowest Gini coefficient among all at 0.63, which indicates a very high degree of income inequality.

One of the drawbacks of the Gini coefficient is that it measures income, not net worth. To the extent that wealth is captured in illiquid assets such as stocks or real estate, it may either overestimate or underestimate income equality. When professional sports are compared to countries, inequality is "off the charts," MLB's Gini coefficient at 0.82 and the NFL and NBA following closely. Next, we analyzed large datasets for the health care, retail, and hospitality industry, respectively, starting with store managers, general managers, and senior hospital managers such as head nurses as our lowest baseline and comparing their income to corporate executives, shareholders, and real-estate owners, taking into account only the income they derived from the business. Since we were seeking to compare business leaders at different levels, working on similar operational and strategic challenges, we did not include frontline or hourly workers in the equation. The data suggest that the U.S. for-profit hospital and health care delivery business has a Gini coefficient of 0.55, which is on the higher end of the spectrum of income inequality among countries, well above the country average of 0.38. Retail scores are lower, with a Gini coefficient of 0.65, worse than South Africa, the country with the largest income inequality and more in line with the global average in 1820 (see Figure 5.1).

In the case of the hotel industry, our large dataset included 130 hotel chains and management companies and 27,300 hotels across the country, including general managers and above including regional operators, corporate-level employees, and the top 150 hotel developers and owners. The U.S. hotel industry's Gini coefficient is an astonishing 0.73, which reflects the disproportionate amount of value being captured by shareholders,

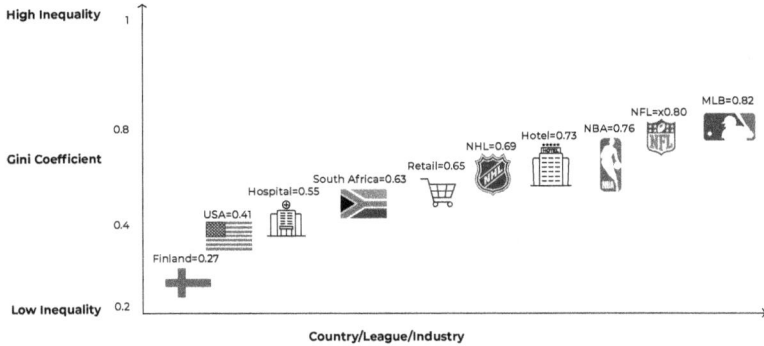

Figure 5.1 Inequality in service industries and professional sports

real-estate and business owners, financiers, and their advisors compared to those who work in the business. This result also calls into question the social impact of unions and government taxes, which seem to have little effect on wealth redistribution, despite the economic rents they extract and their growing influence in the industry.

Meanwhile, hotels are becoming a tax windfall for governments. According to the AHLA, governments have spawned $47 billion in taxes from hotels in 2022. As a generator of taxes, jobs, and tourism revenues, the hotel industry has become incredibly important to government officials at all levels. However, this tax revenue has not been harnessed to solve hospitality's labor shortage and talent crisis. Meanwhile, city governments from New York to Los Angeles are helping unions to become even more powerful and capitalized. For the first time, unions are taking over boutique and independent hotels, starting in markets such as Los Angeles and stating their intentions to take over the entire industry along with other industries such as warehousing and logistics (Amazon) and coffee shops (Starbucks).

So, what can hotel owners and industry stakeholders do to address the growing income inequality in their business, consistent with the values of building a competitive business that is a meritocracy? Besides encouraging brands and management companies to build talent marketplaces to attract diverse elite talent and enable career mobility, how can hotels or any services company change the game to attract and retain talent in this context of labor market turbulence?

One answer is employee ownership. Before discussing how it could work in the franchised hotel sector with hundreds of hotel owners, lenders, and stakeholders, let's take a step back and consider its purpose and relevant case studies of employee ownership.

Employee Ownership

The practice of turning employees into co-owners of joint-stock companies first appeared in the United States in the 1950s in accordance with the Employee Stock Ownership Plan (ESOP) and noticeably intensified in the mid-1970s after the adoption of the law on the guarantees of pensions for workers (Employee Retirement Income Security Act (ERISA)) in 1974, which provided tax incentives to companies implementing ESOP.

The pace of development of this form of private property is quite impressive. While in 1974, there were several hundred ESOP companies with only 100,000 people, in the late 1090s, according to American experts, about 15 million people, or 12 percent of the country's labor force, were covered by various forms of employee ownership in the United States (through savings plans, stock option plans, and, above all, ESOP).

While in the early 1980s, employee ownership was still spread mainly among small closed (private) corporations, by the beginning of the 1990s, it began to spread rapidly, including in its "orbit" large open or public corporations. Among the largest American companies that have established ESOP are Harley-Davidson (see Figure 5.2), Polaroid, Phillips Petroleum, Chevron, Procter & Gamble, McDonnell Douglas, and others (see Figure 5.2).

Most employee-owned companies are still small or medium-sized and have a closed ownership structure. These types of companies make up 85 percent of all employee-owned companies, and there are over 9,000 of them. In about 44 percent of these companies, employees own more than 25 percent of the company, and in about 27 percent of them, employees have a controlling stake. In 700 of these companies, employees own all of the share capital.

Socioeconomic Impact and Bipartisan Support

There is evidence that aligning the financial incentives of workers and the business can triple retention. Today, the bottom 50 percent of the U.S. population

Figure 5.2 Harley-Davidson issues shares to 4500 employees, including hourly factory workers

owns less than 1 percent of equity assets, and white Americans account for 90 percent of stock ownership. A Rutgers study found that women and minorities working at a company with an employee ownership plan had 10 times the median savings of their peers nationally (see Figure 5.3).[1]

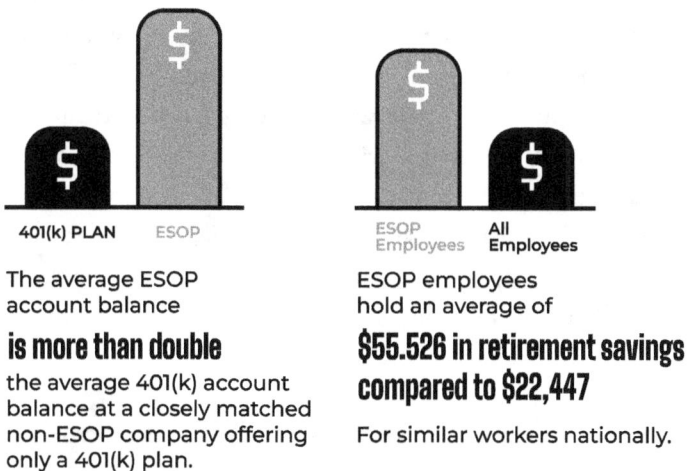

401(k) PLAN   ESOP

ESOP Employees   **All Employees**

The average ESOP account balance

is more than double

the average 401(k) account balance at a closely matched non-ESOP company offering only a 401(k) plan.

ESOP employees hold an average of

$55.526 in retirement savings compared to $22,447

For similar workers nationally.

Figure 5.3 ESOP contribution for salaried workers under $25K

Source: The National Center for Employee Ownership.

Furthermore, there is bipartisan support for employee-owned companies: 72 percent of Republicans, 74 percent of Democrats, and 67 percent of Independents would choose to do business with a company owned by employees instead of those owned by investors or by a government entity. With a host of small- and medium-sized business tax provisions expiring in 2025, it is entirely possible that Congress would pass new legislation encouraging employee ownership, including changes in the tax code that provide pass-throughs above the current 40 percent deduction for ESOP contributions.

Practical Considerations

One continued impediment within the hospitality industry to creating true employee ownership has been the resistance of hospitality owners and operators to undertake the necessary legal and practical considerations required of this change. At its core, employee ownership means that employees both own a significant percentage of the hospitality business (and/or real-estate assets) and can meaningfully contribute to business-level decisions. Ownership without both qualities is ownership only in name, and not in actual substance.

This paradigm creates several issues that hospitality owners and operators must confront. Chief among these concerns are how to structure ownership that will be dispersed among hundreds or thousands of individuals; how to deal with employee-owners who may leave the employment of a given hospitality asset; how to inform employees of the rights and responsibilities that come with ownership and participation in business decisions; how to deal with confidentiality or other issues that may present themselves with the dispersal of financial and operational information of hospitality assets to many people; and how to navigate legal, tax, and regulatory challenges involved in this ownership structure.

Although there are many answers to the problems posed earlier, several possible solutions are described here.

Structuring Employee Ownership and Control

Employees should receive actual ownership or ownership options in the hospitality business and/or asset, and not "phantom" shares, quasi-ownership units, or any other form of constructive ownership. These shares, or units, should be given preferences and rights equal to other shares or units in the business or businesses and, as discussed later, perhaps even additional rights or preferences.

Because any given employee may ultimately own a very small percentage of the business, employee ownership can be structured to vote and act as a "bloc" on matters of business operations. For a simplified example, 10 percent of the total number of shares or units of a given business could be set aside toward employee ownership. This 10 percent ownership could then be held via a holding company, and, in turn, the holding company itself could be owned by employees. On matters in which shareholders can vote, the holding company can hold its own vote, in which the majority of employees or held equity decides the vote of the entire bloc and, in turn, the bloc votes consistent with this decision. In this way, the ultimate voting power of employee ownership is heightened (the bloc would vote the equivalent of 10 percent of all shares or units of the business), and the logistics of managing the voting and preferences of many different employees is lessened.

To heighten the participation of employees in the operations of the company, employees (or, in turn, the employee ownership bloc) should be given information rights, at least consistent with other shareholders or unitholders of the company: for example, the right to see company financial records (monthly, quarterly, or annually). Moreover, employees might be given additional rights above and beyond other shareholders in the businesses. These might include:

- The right to be informed of the salaries and employment contracts of all C-level executives
- The right to participate in, and be informed regarding, employment reviews of C-level executives
- The right to participate in the hiring of C-level executives (and veto the hiring of C-level executives)
- The right to determine broad corporate strategy decisions (e.g., new policies, advertising, large project expenditures)
- The right to assign one director/manager of the company, or have an outsized participation in the election of directors
- The right to collectively negotiate the salaries of certain types of employees

The options for such rights are certainly limitless, but granting additional rights to employees cements the business as an "employee first" organization and furthers the goals discussed in this chapter.

On the financial side, employees can participate in the success of the business in multiple ways. For example, employees can participate in dividends or other forms of distributions, proportionally with their ownership of the business. On a sale, employees can receive liquidation rights or preferences, pegging their ownership to at least some level, regardless of the ultimate success of the venture.

To further the "employee first" nature of the business, employees can be given financial and business training, for example, education on what rights owners of a private company have; financial literacy training on investing and managing money; and specific training on how the operations of a hospitality asset unfold and their abilities to influence business-level decisions.

Further Legal Considerations

Employee ownership creates legal and logistical issues. A nonexhaustive exploration of some of these issues is given later; however, hospitality owners and operators who wish to pursue employee ownership should consult an attorney for insight into how the business' unique structure might influence the issues discussed.

As discussed previously, structuring employee ownership via a special purpose vehicle or holding company that is owned by employees and owns equity in the business and/or real-estate assets is likely preferential. The constituent documents of the entity owning the business or real estate would likely need to be modified to accommodate the existence of this ownership bloc, and, if relevant, dole out special or additional rights to the employee holding company.

To simplify the complexities of employee participation, the holding company can be granted a fixed percentage of ownership in the business or asset-level company, for example, 10 percent. Regardless of the number of employees ultimately involved, the employee holding company would always continue to own the equivalent of 10 percent of the shares or units in the relevant business.

At the employee holding company level, individual employees hold ownership in this entity. For example, ownership might be tied toward longevity of service to the company (those working for longer receive more, or vest a greater amount of equity), type of work (those in certain jobs at the hospitality business may receive more or fewer shares), compensation, or other relevant metrics.

To avoid taxation complications, employees might receive options or profit interests in the employee holding company. This avoids the complexity of an employee being granted equity, worth real money, and being put in a position where they must immediately pay income tax on the grant.

As new employees join the company, additional options/profits interests can be created in the employee holding company. These interests could vest over time, meaning that employees would need to work for the company for a specified duration before their options or units are fully vested, thus partly solving the problem of employee turnover (e.g., an employee may need to work for several years before any equity vests). It may be advantageous to put restrictions on the ability of employees to sell their ownership so that the employee holding company is always owned by employees, not by nonemployee investors (e.g., the shares or units can only be sold to other current employees). Moreover, there may be legal limitations on the class of individuals who can purchase such equity (e.g., accredited investors only).

As cash distributions are made, cash would flow from the asset or business into the employee holding company. At the holding company level, distributions would then be made relative to each employee's equity stake in that business.

Relevant Case Studies of Employee Ownership

Private equity firm KKR adopted broad-based employee ownership as a standard requirement in its deals in industrial and manufacturing businesses, creating billions of dollars of total equity value for over 45,000 nonsenior employees across 25 companies. KKR joined other private equity firms and more than 60 organizations, including pension funds, in becoming a founding partner of Ownership Works, a nonprofit created to support companies transitioning to shared ownership models.[2]

The goal is to build an ownership culture where people think and act like owners. This includes education on the rights and duties of ownership, financial literacy training, and changing organizational processes to provide employees with an increased role in creating an attractive workplace.[3] For example, KKR's acquisition of CHI,[4] a leader in the garage door industry, resulted in 800 employees from factory workers to truck drivers becoming owners of the business. Employees spent $1 million improving working conditions and safety, adding air conditioners, new break rooms, building a new cafeteria with healthier food choices, and creating an on-site health clinic. As a result, work injuries declined by over 50 percent, and retention improved considerably.

Another private equity firm, Apollo Global Management, in collaboration with the REIT Vici Properties, offered 7000 employees at the Venetian and Palazzo operations participation in the "promote" or share of the proceeds after debt and equity investors are paid based on a profitable exit of their $2.5 billion acquisition.[5] For example, if Apollo exits at $4 billion, roughly $1.75 billion will be partially divided up among the nonunion workforce, which could exceed $70 million or $10,000 for frontline employees, in addition to salary, benefits, and annual bonuses. Apollo believes this is the first such offer in the casino and hospitality industry.

According to the National Center for Employee Ownership, 15 percent of ESOP sponsors are in finance, insurance, and real estate, including[6] mortgage companies and brokerages that hire numerous contractors. These companies share financial information with their employees in much the same way that a publicly traded company is required to report.

But ESOPs can be costly to implement, highly regulated, and very technical. They can also complicate the approval of credit lines for mortgages and may not be an efficient model for small hotel owners. They can also be a much more effective tool for acquiring talent at the senior management level.

Instead, synthetic ownership through the careful design of employee bonus structures can achieve the same outcome and build an ownership mentality. For example, under Gary Loveman's tenure as CEO, Caesars Entertainment implemented a quarterly employee bonus program that resulted in quarterly cash bonuses of millions of dollars paid to the front line based on their relative guest satisfaction weighted by customer worth. In other words, those properties and departments that delivered better service to the highest worth customer tiers received the largest bonus. Rather than investing chiefly in product innovation, Loveman's service profit chain model invested in data science and people. These best practices were put into place when the company owned and operated only a handful of Harrah's branded casino hotel properties and resulted in double-digit market share premiums and profit margins that far exceeded its peers by 15 to 20 percent, consistently for more than a decade.

Building an ownership culture that aligns the interests of the workforce, real-estate investors, management companies, and brands can take various forms. Southwest Airlines launched the first profit-sharing plan in the U.S. airline industry back in 1974 and has offered profit sharing to its employees every year since. Within this plan, employees own about 10 percent of the company stock. In 2000, the company offered its employees a "record-setting" $138 million in profit sharing. This tax-deferred compensation represented an additional 14.1 percent of each employee's annual salary. The company shared $230 million with its employees after pulling in a $977 million profit for 2021, bringing back a perk that disappeared in 2020 due to steep losses from the COVID-19 pandemic.

Over the last few years, Delta Airlines has led the travel industry in profit sharing. Airline 2019 profit-sharing totals are presented in Table 5.1.

Table 5.1 *Profit sharing for frontline airline companies*

Airline	Profit sharing pool	Full time employees	Average
American	$213 million	130,000	$1,638
Delta	$1.6 billion	79,636	$20,091
Southwest	$667 million	59,605	$11,190
United	$491 million	79,301	$6,191

On Valentine's Day, Delta "shows the love to its employees when the company's profit-sharing payments hit their bank accounts." This practice, applied in the airline since 2007, also makes a cascading multiplier effect in the communities where Delta people live, work, and serve. In 2022, payout totaled more than $550 million—about 5.5 percent of each employee's 2022 pretax earnings—thus representing one of the most generous profit-sharing programs in the United States.

"The annual payout is part of a substantive one-two punch to boost employees' purchasing power, coming on the heels of the Fed's announcement regarding a five percent pay increase April one for eligible employees." Interestingly, Delta employees can contribute some or all of their profit-sharing payment to their 401(k) or to an emergency savings fund launched this year, which also allows them to earn up to an additional $1000 in savings funds from Delta. The company partners with Operation HOPE and Fidelity Investments to facilitate employees' possibility to earn $1000 in rainy day funds.

The most evident impact is observed in Delta's home state of Georgia, where more than 40,000 employees have received more than $245 million in profit-sharing payments in 2022. But the investment is significant in other states also:

- More than $72 million in New York, home to Delta's hubs at LaGuardia and JFK airports
- More than $48 million in Minnesota, home to Delta's hub in Minneapolis-St. Paul

- More than $43 million in Michigan, home to Delta's Detroit hub
- More than $31 million in California, home to Delta's hub at LAX
- More than $30 million in Utah, home to Delta's Salt Lake City hub
- More than $29 million in Washington, home to Delta's Seattle hub
- Roughly $9 million in Massachusetts, home to Delta's Boston hub

Delta determines its profit-sharing payouts with an equitable and transparent formula: Delta funds the annual profit-sharing pool with 10 percent of its first $2.5 billion of annual profits and 20 percent of annual profits above certain thresholds. Then, the pool amount is divided by the total earnings of all eligible employees. The result is the percentage of earnings Delta will pay out in profit sharing to each eligible employee.

Hotel Owners Must Lead the Way

Hotel owners should use their power over operating capital budgets and legal agreements to provide an alternative to unionization. For the hotel industry to win back talent, hotel real-estate owners must adopt a new model of governance that includes some form of employee ownership and governance, including profit sharing, at the property level.

It should not surprise anyone who knows the hotel industry that conservative hotel chains, brands, and cost-focused third-party management companies will respond reluctantly and follow rather than lead. Hotel owners, starting with private equity, real-estate investment trusts, family offices, and sovereign funds, are driving the bus. These hotel owners can have a direct, immediate, and targeted impact by giving employees, starting with general managers and the executive team of the hotel, ownership stakes in a property, either directly or through their management company.

The implications are transformational. If some type of formal or synthetic employee ownership became more widespread in full-service

hotels, the income of the bottom 50 percent would quadruple. For example, a housekeeping manager's income could quadruple from $24,000
to $106,000. Those on the front line could see similar gains, with their
income increasing from $21,000 to $76,000. The costs would be negligible, as owners would see a decline in their income of 3 to 5 percent.

Finally, as evidenced by the successful employee buy-outs at TPI
Hospitality and Newport Restaurant Group, ESOPs provide another alternative to buying out founders and legacy shareholders, including family
members who have inherited stakes in the business over generations. For
these reasons, employee ownership is an idea whose time has come not
just in hotels but across service industries.

CHAPTER 6

A New Talent Engine

Leveraging AI to Scale Human Capital

America's most important engine of human meritocracy is facing its biggest challenge ever. A generation of talent is leaving the hotel industry as brands are betting on franchising and delegating human capital management to hundreds of third-party managers who lack an employer brand. Reorganization, incremental improvements, and digitalization of the workplace are necessary but insufficient to fill the three million annual openings. Radical innovation supported by technology is required to bring the hotel industry's human capital back to equilibrium. It starts with reimagining the role of human resources from administrator to creator of employee-first platforms such as talent marketplaces that advance meritocracy and accelerate diversity. CEOs and boards of directors can usher in the new paradigm with deal-making focused on establishing talent exchanges within the hospitality industry and with like-minded organizations in adjacent service industries.

Hotel Industry as an Engine of Meritocracy and Growth

Few industries have a track record of generating economic impact and providing upward mobility like hospitality. Overall, immigrants own 29 percent of all restaurants and hotels, more than twice the 14 percent rate for all businesses, according to U.S. census data. Consider the success of people of South Asian origin in the U.S. hotel industry. A majority of these owners are Gujaratis, hailing from India, Pakistan, Uganda, and elsewhere.[1,2] It started in 1942, when a man named Kanjibhai Manchhu Desai left Gujarat,[3] India, in search of new opportunities. He was joined by two Gujarati farmworkers, and they took over a 32-room hotel in Sacramento, California, after the property's Japanese American owner was forced to report to a World War II internment camp. It was far from an overnight success, and white competitors, especially in the rural south, put not-very-subtle "American-owned" signs outside many of their hotels. They gradually expanded by acquiring more properties across the States, focusing on the economy segment. By the 1980s, the second generation of these immigrants started expanding the frontiers of their parents' businesses. By 2007, they owned over 21,000 of the 52,000 hotels in the United States or 42 percent of the market. Furthermore, they have expanded their management companies and launched real estate funds and publicly traded investments in full-service hotel segments in the United States and Canada, led by Hersha Hospitality Management, Noble Investment Group, Vista Hospitality, and others. There were two key factors in their success: flexible "handshake loans" between members of the tribe to acquire hotels and reliance on family as a key source of labor.

Once a family purchased a motel, they would live there, and the family members would do all the tasks needed to run it, from cleaning rooms to checking in guests. There are many other examples of how the hospitality industry has created economic opportunity and upward mobility. Refugees from Vietnam and Cambodia first arrived in Orange County by way of Camp Pendleton in 1975. Among them was a man named Ted Ngoy, who would later be known as the "Donut King." This niche business created an economic pipeline for newly arrived refugees from Cambodia. By the 1990s, there were approximately 1500 Cambodian-owned doughnut shops in California alone. Unfortunately, it is nearly impossible to replicate the success of these immigrants today, even on a regional scale. This is not because informal sources of capital have dried up or because of difficulties with the supply chain or regulations. It's because costs are prohibitive. Today, most hotel and restaurant chains have divested their real estate and are imposing brand standards, resulting in higher capital costs and higher fees. Anti-immigration sentiments are adding to a severe labor shortage; unionization is spreading across the service sector; and most chains have walked away from their role in developing talent and acting as the lead human capital manager for their respective industries. Consequently, profit margins are being squeezed, capital costs are higher, and labor is more expensive and scarce.

Brutal Facts of the Hospitality Labor Market in 2023

At the beginning of 2023, hotel operators are on a losing streak in the talent markets. The same industry that has made significant progress over the past decade in capturing customers with direct bookings has lost 20 percent of its labor market share to other industries. Ironically, these very savvy investors and operators have inadvertently made things worse for themselves by treating HR tech as an afterthought. Most operators continue to invest in advertising and social media on "big tech" third-party job sites and applicant tracking system (ATS) platforms that use their funds to grow their own databases and perpetuate control of the talent markets. The good news is that much of this is within the industry's power to change. The first step is to collect facts, analyze the problem's root causes, and quantify the gap between current strategies and the desired outcome. Consider these five brutal facts regarding the labor crisis confronting hospitality operators in the United States:

Fact one: There are over 10 million job openings in the United States, and hospitality quit rates are more than twice the national average.

Figure 6.1 shows the national job openings and the quit rates across the hospitality, health care, and retail industries. Hospitality and leisure quit rates are at historic highs, at twice the national average for service industries. The retail industry is also experiencing record-high quit rates, followed by health care and social assistance (see Figure 6.1).

Fact two: U.S. hospitality must hire 2.9 million people a year to reach equilibrium, including 1.3 million replacement hires (see Figure 6.2).

Fact three: Even in an optimistic labor market recovery with aggressive recruiting and labor efficiencies, the gap is still 2.4 million.

How can the industry retain and attract sufficient talent to close this shortfall? Consider an optimistic perspective in which college graduates with fewer employment prospects join hotels in larger numbers (organic growth) and the industry successfully adjusts its labor model to become more flexible, pays more competitive wages, and eliminates some

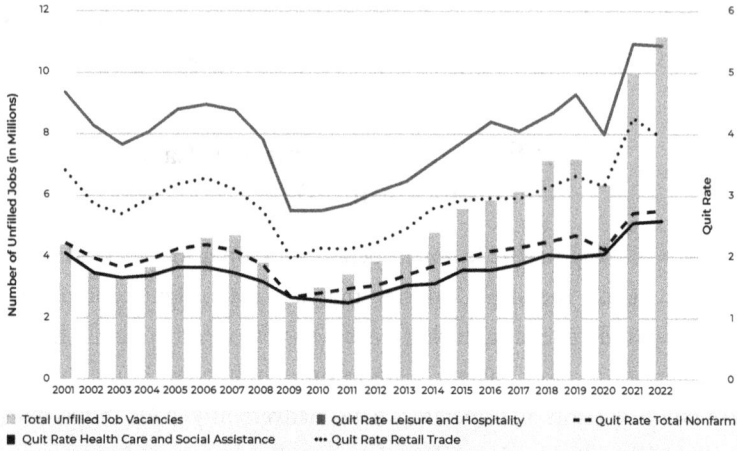

Figure 6.1 Job openings and quit rates in U.S. service industries

Source: The National Center for Employee Ownership.

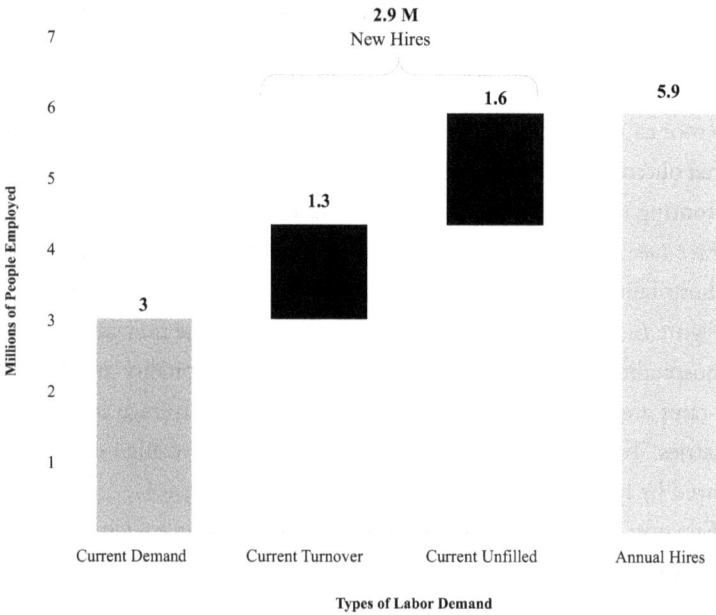

Figure 6.2 U.S. hotel labor market dynamics

positions through efficiencies and service reductions. Let's do the math and see where that takes us.

- *"Bottom up" organic growth*: Hiring new associate and bachelor's degree college graduates, including from hospitality schools. Challenge: even if hotels capture an additional 10 percent of the entire market of two million annual new hires, their turnover is 50 percent. Impact: 100,000 incremental new hires with aggressive assumptions that market share is taken from tech, retail, and other sectors that may suffer from a recession and structural changes that reduce the attractiveness of these sectors.

- *Increasing pay to recapture talent*: Capitalizing on the recession and closing the pay gap versus other industries to convince those who have left hospitality to return, including those who work in the gig economy. Challenge: research says people left to seek a better working culture and more flexibility, not just higher compensation. There is no evidence that changing compensation alone will work. That said, let's assume hotels increase pay by 20 percent and owners agree to offer supervisors and above more cash incentives such as profit sharing. Impact: 200,000 incremental new hires with aggressive assumptions that market share is taken from tech, health care, gig jobs, and so on.

- *Efficiencies through digitalization*: Eliminating frontline positions using technology like mobile apps for check-in and consolidating departments such as front desk, housekeeping, and restaurants. Challenge: most jobs and pricing power are in full-service, group, and luxury hotels that require service. Impact: reduces hiring needs by 100,000.

- *Attracting talent from other industries hit hard by the recession:* An example is retail, which shed 25,000 jobs in August 2022 alone and continues to shed jobs heading into 2023. Challenge: other than the economy sector, hotels have a mixed record of hiring retail, even in functions such as finance. Training costs are higher than anticipated, and turnover risks are extremely high. Furthermore, delivery and logistics businesses, including Uber, are growing with average hourly pay, adjusted for taxes, of two to three times hourly wages in hotels. Impact: 100,000 incremental new hires.

In conclusion, these optimistic scenarios generate an incremental 500,000 employees. Where does that leave us? Even with the optimistic scenario, the current strategy leaves a gap of 2.4 million for the U.S. hotel sector.

Fact four: The top 16 hotel operators are in a class of their own. Almost half of the top 80 largest hotel operators, representing 70 percent of branded properties, have abysmal talent and diversity scores. We analyzed the quality of talent at the top 80 hotel operators, addressing 12,000 hotels, and developed an algorithm to rank talent, from frontline employees to general managers.

Talent ranking algorithm

$$f(x) = (\text{Service Score} \times w) + (\text{Brand Score} \times w) + (\text{Market Score} \times w) + (\text{Experience Score} \times w) + (\text{Stability Score} \times w)$$

$$\text{Service Score by Department} = \text{Service} - \left[\frac{\text{Rooms} + \text{Location}}{2} \right]$$

Brand Score = Brand Prestige by Product Segement [1 (low) and 5 (high)]

$$\text{Market Score} = (\text{REVPAR } \Delta \, \%) \times \text{Number of Rooms Available}$$

Experience Score = Industry Experience

Stability Score = Job Hopping Frequency

We summarized our findings in the talent share matrix chart, which shows a company's share of elite talent on the X-axis and the number of properties managed on the Y-axis. We classified high-performing hotel operators from a talent perspective into two buckets: "high potentials" (talent scores above the median, high growth, and below-average portfolio size and growth) and "stars" (talent scores above the median, high growth, and above-average portfolio size and growth). A few hotel operators are "stars" with quality talents that stand above the rest, alongside a few notable small brands and management companies. However, over 50 percent of the branded hotels are managed by underperforming management companies with below-average talent scores and less than one star performer per property, whose average tenure is under 24 months. What about progress in diversity, equity, and inclusion? We also ranked the top 80 hotel management companies for diversity—the proportion of elite talent who are women and minorities in their property-level supervisor and above ranks over four years (2018 to 2022). We then performed regression analysis to ascertain the correlation between the quality of talent and diverse elite talent for the same employers. There is a 92 percent correlation between a change in the company's quality of talent score and its diversity talent score (see Figure 6.3). We analyzed these results by brand segment (i.e., economy versus luxury) and product type (i.e., resort versus airport hotel), and the results were within a 10 percent confidence interval.

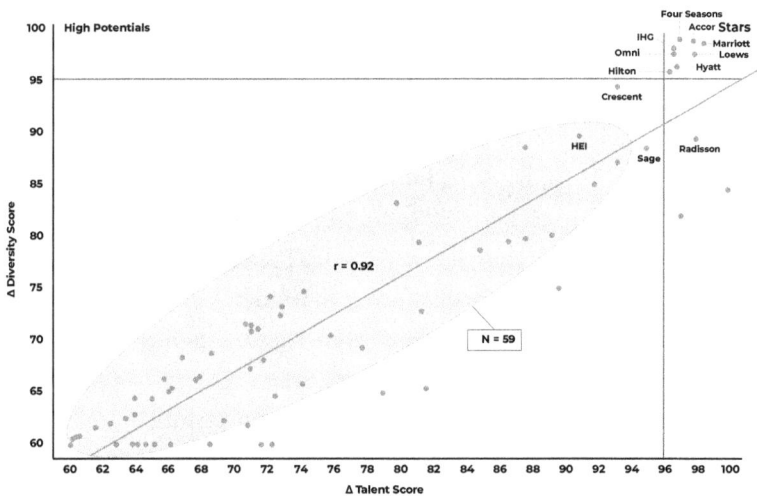

Figure 6.3 Relationship between employer talent and diversity score

If managerial diversity were a performance key performance indicator (KPI) with equivalent importance to revenue indexes, many of these operators would be out of business. Furthermore, owner-operators—who in theory have the most stakeholder alignment—rank among the worst in diversity, equity, and inclusion (DEI). This demonstrates that aside from brands, most of which are publicly traded or owned by institutional investors, the industry has not made significant strides in diversity at the property management level.

Fact five: Radical innovations—the broader adoption of the hybrid work model, wholesale changes in job qualifications, and a paradigm shift in hospitality recruiting—could generate an additional one million talents, closing the labor shortage to 1.4 million.

- *Semi qualified "hidden workers"*: People with service industry experience who are either unemployed, employed part time, or have left the workforce and are screened out by legacy HR tech due to the flawed recruiting process and ATS filters that require a college degree. Based on a recent Harvard Business School and Accenture study, we estimate the potential gain to be 500,000 people. The challenges include significantly increased recruiting, training, learning, and development costs of 5 to 10 times per employee to $5000 per year for the front line.

- *Legal immigration*: Qualified hospitality workers such as those trained by hotel chains in countries such as Mexico, the Caribbean, Ukraine, India, and China, where large numbers are seeking to exit. We estimate the potential gain to be 100,000 supervisors and above. The additional costs, including visa sponsorship, relocation and housing, assistance with language barriers, cultural adjustment, and other assistance, will be $35,000 per employee.

- *Hybrid work models*: People with service industry experience who need to work from home to take care of family or who have intentionally left the hospitality industry to pursue the hybrid work model that is now the norm in other sectors such as technology and professional services. What if the industry changed its labor model to permit finance, accounting, human resources, revenue management, purchasing, and even general managers to be hybrid? This would also enable department heads and supervisors on the property to demonstrate their leadership potential. We estimate the potential gain, including attracting new talent into the industry, to be 400,000. Additional costs include accelerated training and development, but there are also potential savings in labor, benefits, and other costs. While they would be expensive and risky, these radical innovations could generate an additional one million talents, closing the gap to 1.4 million. There is only one option to close this gap to 500,000 or less: increasing retention to 75 percent.

The Solution: Building a Talent Engine of the Future

Clearly, addressing the labor/talent crisis in hospitality requires more than stewardship: significant innovation, including new processes and technologies, is needed to increase retention and attract new talent into the industry in parallel. Hotel operators continue to bet on legacy HR technologies, including job sites, ATS platforms, and static internal job boards. These passive platforms filter out 80 percent of "hidden workers" and use generic artificial intelligence (AI) that delivers inaccurate matches. Research also confirms that across industries, internal job boards have failed to advance meritocracy because they are not widely used by over half of women, minorities, and individuals outside a company's privileged social networks.

One of the potential solutions to address the labor/talent crisis in hospitality is to leverage AI in talent management. AI aims to create machines and systems that can perform tasks that normally require human intelligence, such as reasoning, learning, decision-making, and perception. AI can be a powerful tool that can achieve remarkable results when used effectively and ethically. This is especially relevant in the human capital management domain, where bias is a big challenge and the business environment and workforce needs are constantly changing.

The talent engine of the future is a network of interconnected and interdependent actors and entities that collaborate to create value and achieve shared goals. This network uses data and AI to create new processes for talent acquisition, learning, internal mobility, compensation, and rewards.

What Does the Future Look Like?

Imagine a talent engine that acts as a vibrant community, attracting hidden workers, legal immigrants, and freelancers, including a hybrid and remote workforce. It uses data from independent third-party sources and algorithms to help organizations identify rising and elite talents both within and outside their organization (see Figure 6.4).

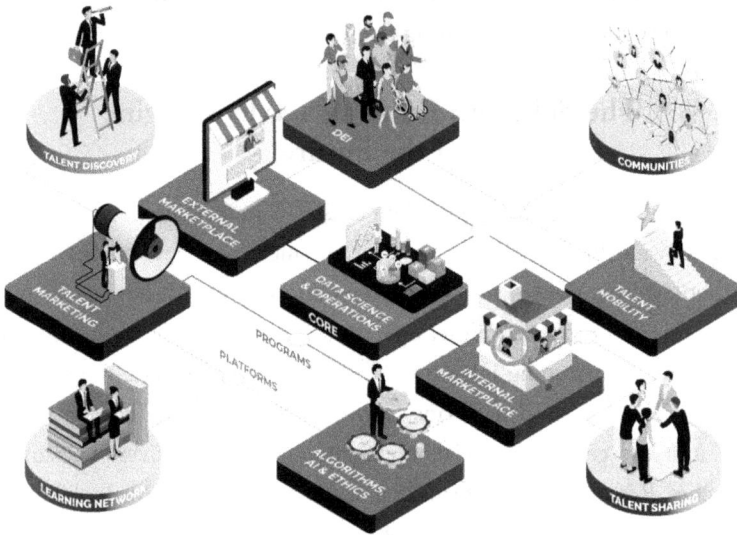

Figure 6.4 Components of a talent engine for service industries

The talent engine is powered by AI-powered analytics and includes the following modular components:

- *Data science and operations*: Building scalable solutions to source, rank, and appraise elite talents with leading employers; writing and testing algorithms that use data science and AI to predict matches between diverse talents and employers in service industries.
- *External marketplace*: Matching diverse supervisors and above talents from service industries with career opportunities at leading hospitality employers; includes full-time, contract, part-time, and gig opportunities.
- *Internal marketplace*: Matching diverse supervisors and above talents from inside multiunit organizations with career advancement opportunities, including laterals and promotions, across departments, functions, business units, and geographies.
- *DEI*: Closing the diversity gap by sourcing diverse elite and rising talents—50 percent women, 33 percent minorities,

and LGBT supervisors—from within and outside hospitality; providing diverse candidates with career opportunities both internally and externally.

- *Talent mobility*: Providing tools to accelerate career paths, including assessments for elite and rising talents to access both lateral and promotion opportunities inside organizations.
- *Talent marketing*: Inspirational content, including GM interviews, talent tier awards, and marketing campaigns that share human stories and promote careers in hospitality. Employers can also create communities based on sponsored content or organic content.
- *Algorithms, AI, and ethics*: Developing and testing algorithms that generate predictions of talent rankings, tiers, and matches—using data science to generate employer rankings for the overall quality of talents and DEI by company type, region, and brand segments.
- *Communities/mentors*: Enabling talents to share their stories, chart career paths, form peers and connections, and engage in hospitality-specific communities both internally and externally, including mentorship, references, and reviews.
- *Talent discovery*: Innovative applications that source hidden workers and talents from outside hospitality, including those outside the traditional workforce, engaging these hidden workers in the external marketplace, learning zone, and communities.
- *Learning network/zone*: Providing a hub for experiential learning, including courses and certificates from leading industry providers and employers, and providing an empowering platform for user-generated content from industry professionals sharing best practices and innovations.
- *Talent sharing*: Brokering talent exchanges between complementary organizations from different geographies or adjacent industries, including both short-term exchanges and long-term talent-sharing deals, enabling the fluid movement of people between business partners.

Talent Experience

Individuals are drawn into the talent engine that leverages AI to provide personalized recommendations based on interests, preferences, goals, and skill levels. These learning communities provide a sense of belonging, trust, and accountability among the talents in an organization. Talents can also take advantage of professional communities that use AI to identify potential mentors, mentees, peers, or experts who can provide support, advice, or feedback.

An experiential learning zone uses natural language processing (NLP) to analyze an employee's queries and feedback and generate relevant responses or suggestions (see Figure 6.5).

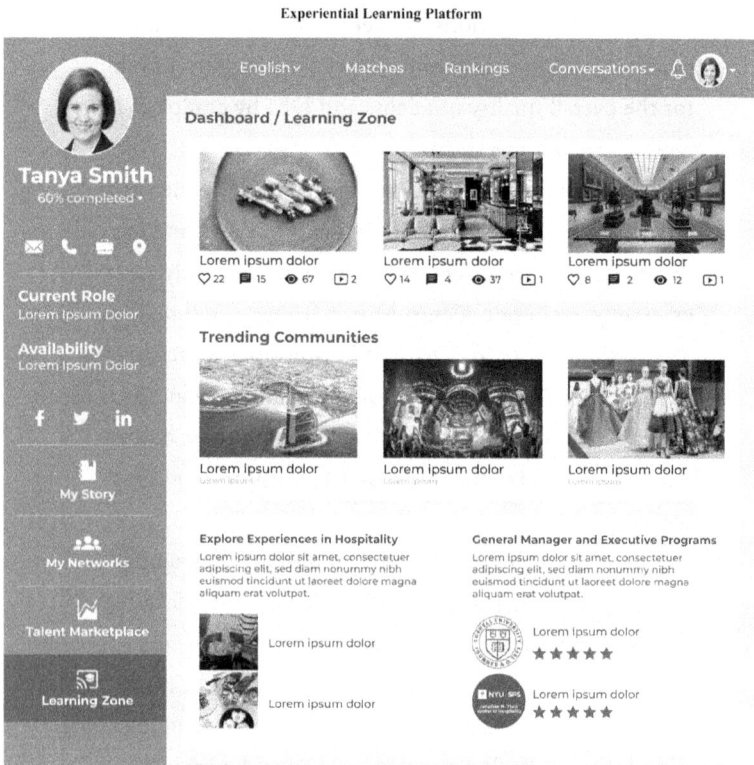

Figure 6.5 Experiential learning platform

Talents can utilize augmented and virtual reality (AR/VR) training, which is an immersive and interactive learning experience that simulates real-world scenarios. For example, the training includes moments of truth in customer service and develops conflict resolution skills, adapting the difficulty of the training according to the employee's performance. AR/VR training can also use computer vision and speech recognition to capture the employee's gestures and voice and provide real-time feedback on whether his or her tone reflects the brand's tone and voice.

Experiential learning can use AI to create personalized learning paths for employees based on their skills, career pathways, and preferences. AI can also help match employees with suitable projects, assignments, or gig jobs that can provide them with hands-on experience and exposure to different roles or functions.

What Data Do Hospitality Talents Deserve?

Given that most hotel general managers last an average of 22 months in their respective roles, using AI to gather up-to-date information on a large scale is essential to collecting a statistically valid sample size. Talent deserves to see employer rankings at the property level to gauge the quality of the executive team, the elite talents who are running departments at the property, and the diversity, including women and minorities, among supervisor-level and above team members.

From 2018 to 2022, MogulRecruiter's Data Science team analyzed over 50,000 hotel executives in the United States and 10,200 hotels across 50 metropolitan statistical areas (MSAs). We mined data from LinkedIn and others to draw significant takeaways about the hospitality industry's diversity gap and distribution of elite talent. We ranked talent by evaluating service performance, market difficulty, and brand quality. We then adjusted for market difficulty and credited those who are improving none-category leading brands.

By using machine learning and AI, we were able to gauge how each employer's managerial talent is performing at the property level. After identifying the number of employees that rank within the top 10 percent, we determined each employer's proportion of elite talent relative to the properties operated and indexed them against their competitive set. Diversity also comes into play among the employer's elite talent, starting at director positions and above, by splitting employees into groups by position, evaluating the diversity of each group, and crediting employers for having diverse candidates where diversity is low. An employer's final rank depends on how diverse their managerial talent pool is compared to other employers.

A hotel employer property review should be AI-enabled, gather data across websites, social media, and other channels, and include the following:

- Quality of the hotel general manager and the executive team of the hotel as reviewed by existing and former employees
- Quality of the parent brand or management company, and whether they invest in training, advancement, and local communities across their network of properties
- The owners' overall reputation, including a track record of investing in capital projects to improve hotels and their investment in employees at the specific property in question

The first two principles are reflected in the prototype design screens of MogulRecruiter's Talent Marketplace solution, which provides users with this experience (see Figure 6.6). Adding the owner's track record will be possible as our AI capabilities grow over time and provide further insights at the property level, where most talents are employed (see Figure 6.7).

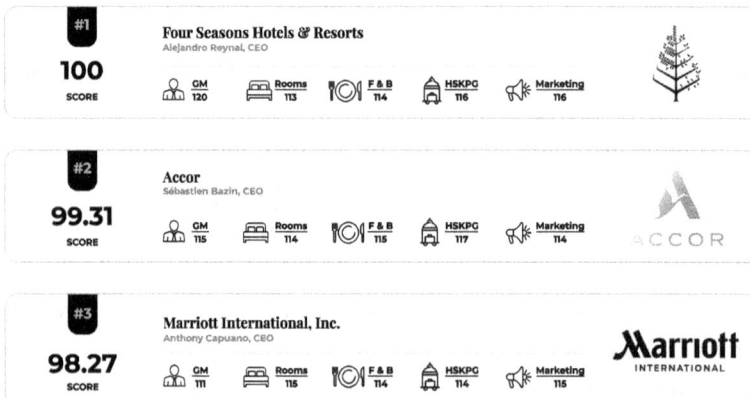

#1	Four Seasons Hotels & Resorts				
100 SCORE	Alejandro Reynal, CEO				
	GM 120	Rooms 113	F & B 114	HSKPG 116	Marketing 116

#2	Accor				
99.31 SCORE	Sébastien Bazin, CEO				
	GM 115	Rooms 114	F & B 115	HSKPG 117	Marketing 114

#3	Marriott International, Inc.				
98.27 SCORE	Anthony Capuano, CEO				
	GM 111	Rooms 115	F & B 114	HSKPG 114	Marketing 115

Figure 6.6 Hotel employer rankings: alternative perspective

Mogul Rankings

Markus Lambert	MEGA MOGUL	+12 •	1
Tanya Smith	MEGA MOGUL	+3 •	1,487
Jason Padilla	MEGA MOGUL	-14 •	1,488
Derek Ortega	RISING MOGUL	+1 •	1,489
Austin Sandoval	RISING MOGUL	+2 •	1,490

See all leading Moguls

Property Rankings

The Pierre Taj Hotels	+3 •	589
Gild Hall Thompson Hotels	+4 •	590
The Peninsula Hon... The Peninsula	-2 •	591
The Carlyle Rosewood Hotels	-1 •	592
Park Hyatt New York Hyatt	+1 •	593

See all leaders

Company Rankings

Thompson Hotels	+7 •	12
The Peninsula	-5 •	13
Taj Hotels	+2 •	14
Rosewood Hotels	-2 •	15
Hyatt	-2 •	15

See all leaders

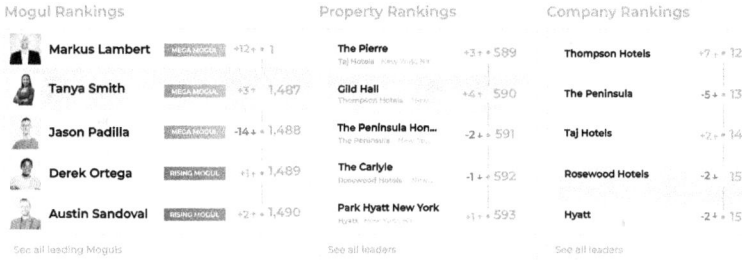

Figure 6.7 Employer rankings: talent perspective

Employer Experience

Finding and matching talents with relevant opportunities is a challenging task for employers. This is where industry-specific algorithms add value: proactively identifying the talents who have the potential and suitability to perform higher level roles based not just on their skills and experience but their daily performance. The talent engine can learn to match rising talents with projects and roles that best suit their preferences.

For example, one use case of industry-specific algorithms is finding and matching talents to a general manager position at a property level. The AI matching system can identify talents who demonstrate their capability to perform the job, such as assistant general managers, hotel managers, and primary directors, and expand the pool of talents by looking into other industries that have similar or transferable skills and experience (see Figure 6.8).

The matching system can also be utilized in autopilot mode, which can process job descriptions and use industry-specific variables to search through a database and crawl the Internet. It can also contact the most suitable talents with personalized messages that match the employer's brand and tone. The system can also help employers by providing a simple and intuitive chat interface that is powered by the GPT model to create and manage their job postings.

A dashboard provides insights into talent pipelines by position and geography, including talent tier, worth, experience level, and readiness for promotion. Employers can "drill down" into each position to understand the distribution of talent by multiple dimensions, including brand, product type, geography, and union experience (see Figure 6.9).

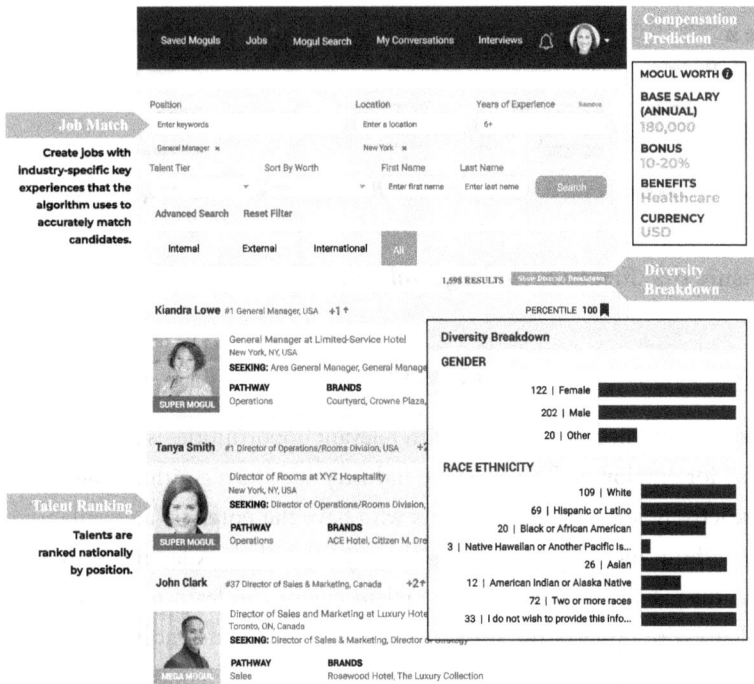

Figure 6.8 Industry-specific AI search engine

Yield Management for Talent Acquisition

A talent engine can also create cost efficiencies so human resources can be more productive and aspiring talents can receive relevant and timely inquiries for opportunities that make economic sense. For example, AI can be used to establish dynamic pricing models that reflect the supply and demand of talents for each role based on various factors such as market conditions, seasonality, trends, and events. Yield management can provide valuable data and insights for budgeting, reduce recruiting and marketing costs, and significantly improve the productivity of HR teams.

The Science of Employee Relationship Management

Building a proprietary talent engine would enable the hospitality industry to establish an AI-powered database and target talents through behavioral segmentation into new workforces and alternative compensation models.

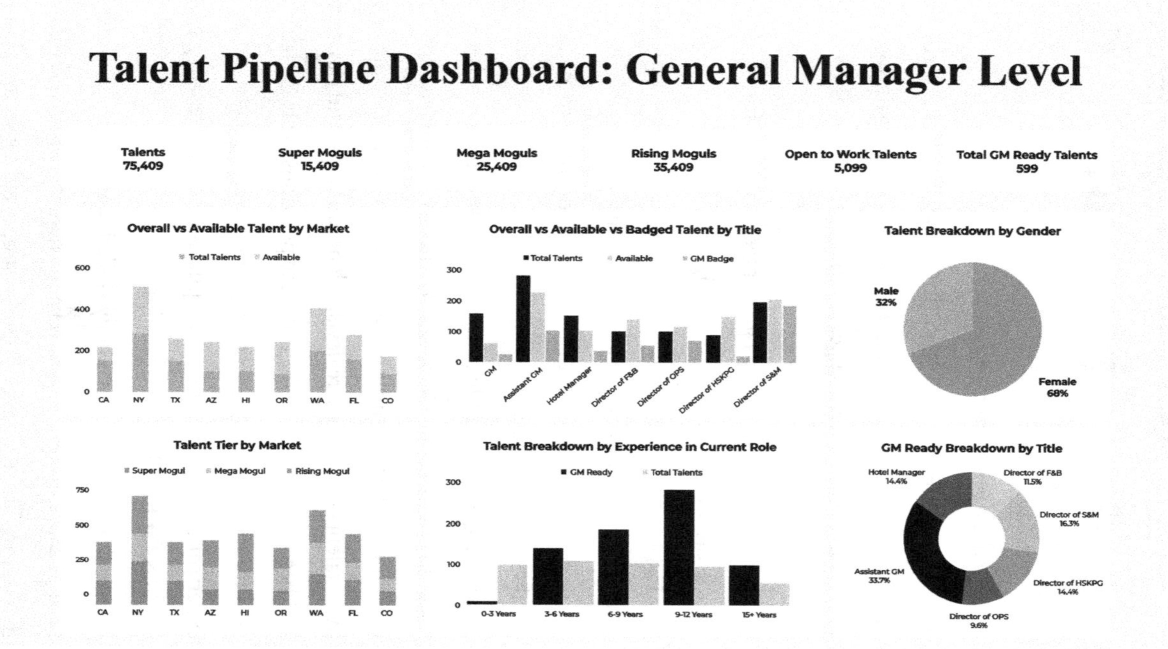

Figure 6.9 Talent pipeline dashboard: general manager level

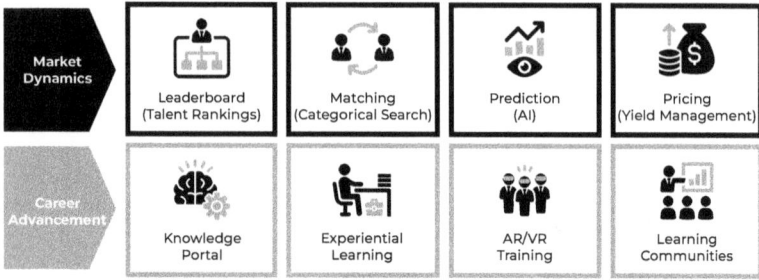

Figure 6.10 AI-driven talent engine

Employee relationship management (ERM) tools of the future could address the following three workforce models that are gaining traction, with over 50 million Americans expected to be working on them by 2030:

- A hybrid work model with a guaranteed base pay for hourly wage positions, starting with the gig model and extending into full-time hourly positions. Depending on the supply and demand of talent for a particular position, wages could be set by the market for a period of time as an incentive to attract highly skilled workers.

- A flexible gig work model, starting with restaurants, where it has already gained traction, taps into six million workers. It can be used as a scouting system, and, over time, some of these talents can garner reviews, talent rankings, and pay tiers and become candidates for full-time positions. This is viable on a meaningful scale if vetting, payment, insurance, and experiential training systems are put in place to prepare gig workers for frontline service roles.

- A virtual work model for highly skilled, analytical positions such as accounting, finance, revenue management, and digital marketing. These experts could be supported by secure cloud-based platforms on a project, seasonal, or semipermanent basis.

The Path Forward: From Steward to Market Maker

It is widely acknowledged that the hotel industry is not known for R&D or being an early adopter of new technologies. Building a platform where hospitality employees, who represent 300 million workers worldwide and generate 10 percent of global gross domestic product (GDP), can garner recognition and fair compensation for their contribution to the business seems like a daunting task. But the industry is prolific at deal-making and has an impressive track record of integrating new technologies, including reservation systems, channel managers, and loyalty program partners. On the customer side of the service profit chain equation, hoteliers have proven that experimentation is a critical enabler of management processes that build culture. Successful implementation of a talent engine similarly requires licensing, integrating, and partnering with many innovative technologies, including start-ups.

The innovation process must be supported by a transformation in the composition and role of the HR function from a "top-down" planner to a facilitator of a "bottom-up" transparent marketplace that includes internal and external talents.

CEOs and boards should incentivize internal mobility into HR, which must be seen as part of a larger systems approach to executive talent management. Within HR, there should be roles for brand marketers, strategists, dealmakers, and technology integrators. It starts with the realization that one of the most effective ways to promote retention, career ambition, and internal mobility is to champion a free market approach by managers, starting at the highest levels of the corporate organization, and incorporate it into the operating units of the organization, regardless of whether they are managed or franchised. But to do this, it is necessary to change the corporate organizational structure and key management processes of the HR function. The current composition and structure of HR are not set up to innovate.

Rather than a tenure-based appointment like in academia, HR executives should have "term limits" like those imposed on certain government offices. HR should become a rite of passage for every senior executive to become a C-suite leader. Departments such as talent acquisition, training and development, compensation and benefits, and organizational learning should require two- to 3 year rotations that include the highest performing directors and VPs from technology, operations, marketing, and other functions, across business units and geographies.

Once corporate HR is reset, the entire corporate office, including strategy, corporate development, finance, and legal, needs to move boldly toward cutting "talent-sharing" deals within the industry and with complementary organizations in other service sectors. For example, a hotel brand or operator in part of the industry value chain, such as Extended Stay America (ESA), could develop career paths and exchange talent with a complimentary hotel brand that manages full-service properties, such as Four Seasons. Talent-sharing exchanges would attract and retain new team members better suited to start their careers in the budget or limited-service segment and, conversely, those ready to move to full-service or luxury operations. Talent exchanges could also extend into other complementary industries. For example, a hotel operator could develop a talent exchange platform with a restaurant chain where its best-in-class regional managers could become food and beverage operators at full-service and luxury hotels. As talent exchanges are implemented in the retail, education, and health care industries, they could help manage labor supply and demand changes by developing a multidisciplinary workforce. By partnering with software companies to build a talent engine, hospitality leaders can create a virtuous talent cycle: an employer brand that attracts people and strengthens the industry by providing career opportunities, both inside the organization and externally.

By adopting this new perspective, the industry can begin to attract people who are looking for growth and value culture as much, if not more, than compensation. Continuously linking culture, leadership, and mobility can increase the talent pool and retention. The result of these efforts can be an organization that can confidently invest in its people who reach their human potential, becoming industry leaders themselves.

Implementation Challenges in Operationalizing an Internal Talent Marketplace

Economic history is replete with examples where nation states established new comparative advantages by creating competition and rivalry among their internal companies and suppliers, preparing them to compete internationally. There are also numerous business school case studies that demonstrate how multiunit service companies, from banks such as JP Morgan to casinos such as Caesars Entertainment, allocate performance-related bonus payouts based on the results of internal competition and require category leaders to support their underperforming peers, resulting in improvements to a company's long-term performance. Others have put aside funds for internal competitions to create new products, services, and lines of business supported by third-party-facilitated internal innovation processes whereby employees can form teams and launch experiments, such as Shell Gamechanger, which has become institutionalized across the company's global divisions and inspired breakthroughs in sustainability that have generated billions of dollars of value for shareholders. Similarly, a talent marketplace can elevate employee engagement, incentivize and reward performance, and facilitate innovation.

Key Factors in an Open Marketplace

For talent marketplaces to work inside companies—with or without an enabling technology platform—senior management must address governance, transparency, and awards.

Regarding governance, there is a growing discrepancy between the views of human resources executives and those of rising and elite talents in service businesses. Most human resources executives surveyed want controls such as who should be internally mobile, at what price, and when. In contrast, high-performing talents want the freedom to choose their career paths and the right to experiment in ways that often make human resources and most service operators uncomfortable.

Our research into the engagement needs of the talent pool across the service industries we surveyed—hotels, restaurants, retail, and logistics—suggests that other than a few basic rules, the market should be self-regulated. To be sure, while all talents should be made visible to enable mentorship and build a culture of meritocracy, there should also be access tiers for different levels of the organization. For example, the front line could see the career paths and rankings of supervisors all the way to the property GM, but their access to talent ranking and worth data could be more limited. HR executives could also have access tiers relevant to the scope of their duties, progressing all the way to the CHRO whose data access should be companywide.

Ultimately, every organization will have to create new processes, including dispute resolution mechanisms, that reflect their values and culture. AI-enabled algorithms can address some of these concerns, such as rewarding undersupplied rising talent with higher compensation and greater internal mobility, but may lag in addressing other issues. An example of an issue facing many companies is the organizational cost of the talent exchange process. This is primarily an issue of internal talent transfer pricing. For example, the National Football League (NFL) established a process where teams that develop diverse managers that are poached by another team get compensated by the NFL with draft picks and other forms of compensation. If hospitality and service companies were to take this approach by giving credit in performance reviews, paying larger bonuses, and attributing widespread recognition to the business leaders who hired and developed these highly sought after talents, it could assuage their concerns about "taking another one for the team." Governance is critical, but creating another bureaucracy to consolidate the power of the corporate office will slow down the process and could defeat the larger purpose.

Next Steps: Achieving Stakeholder Alignment

In conclusion, even disruptors such as Airbnb have made minimal impact on the hospitality industry's consumer or employer branding strategies, let alone its labor model. With interest rates rising, inflation, and banking risks, the capital markets are not likely to change their perspective on the primacy of franchising. Given these realities, what will it take to overturn hospitality's "big tech-driven" orthodoxy and escape the trap that has enveloped brand managers, operators, human resources, information technology, and an entire ecosystem?

- Boards and CEOs must reinvent the HR discipline in hospitality. For reform to be successful, HR directors at the property, regional, and corporate levels should be individuals who have worked in operational roles, including in other industries, and are tech-savvy. Aside from certain administrative disciplines, HR should be compensated in line with other operating roles and become a mandatory rotating position for anyone who seeks to ascend to the role of hotel general manager. This cross-functional approach will facilitate collaboration across departments and between properties and regions, as well as the often too-distant corporate office. The goal should be to escape the recruitment management system (RMS)/ATS trap by either sourcing or developing an alternative talent search marketplace, including a search engine and matching system based on a hierarchy of essential skills, relevant categorical search parameters, and talent ranking that is based on independent third-party data sources. For example, a task force could be created to write algorithms that use third-party customer service and hotel product data to rank both internal and external talent and chart their predicted career paths. For example, identify star front desk agents who could be promoted to front desk supervisors, then rooms directors, and subsequently to assistant GM to hotel GM.
- Chief marketing officers must balance their short-term objectives with the long-term health of the brands they manage. This requires measuring human capital as a component of brand equity. Category leading brand managers in a position of strength relative to real estate investors can adjust the way marketing, program, and loyalty program fees are allocated, reallocating budgets to supporting hotels in the acquisition, training, and development of frontline and

supervisory-level talent. They can also begin developing brand standards for employee workspaces and lead by example by implementing these designs and work environments in their managed hotels. Brand managers can organize coalitions of owners who are willing to test new approaches and use their marketing funds to build talent databases, provide applications for customers to review and tip employees 1:1 to adopt transparent scorecards for their brands, benchmark owners and third-party operators on the quality of their talent, and quantify the investments in human capital that properties should make and in what areas of operation. Employee loyalty programs and big data partnerships with travel and service companies, rather than the next customer rewards scheme, should become their focus for the next decade.

- HR executives can reduce spending on algorithmically driven advertising and instead invest in databases and technologies that source hidden workers from other service industries such as retail, education, construction, and military veterans. HR can stop collecting resumes and instead require candidates to share experiences that can be mapped to competencies and categorical search groups specific to hospitality, such as brand segments, turnarounds, and new openings, and other service industries such as restaurants, retail, airlines, and health care. To attract hidden workers, human resources can rely less on computer-based assessments to screen candidates in anything except for highly technical roles where strong quantitative and analytical skills are required, as financial controllers or revenue managers.

- Chief information and technology leaders must view talent management as an R&D problem worthy of greater investment than property management systems, hotel websites, and customer loyalty programs. The hotel industry spends an average of 2.5 percent of room revenue on technology, or $22.5 billion annually, but only 5 percent of this is allocated to HR technologies. Technology leaders can run quarterly experiments and create task forces with cross-functional teams of HR, operations, finance, and technology partners whose goal is to run talent pool experiments for difficult-to-fill roles at the most complex hotel properties. Budgets can be set aside for low-cost experiments outside legacy HR tech, including ATS and job sites, that use resume parsing applications and instead independently test algorithms that score a pool of candidates and compare results.

- The private sector cannot rebuild hospitality brands and infrastructure on its own. State, county, and city governments should allocate 25 percent of their budgets to attract local talent. They should partner with hospitality leaders and nonprofit organizations to help attract talent, subsidize training and development at local colleges, and fund workplace support systems, such as childcare for local hotel workers. Only recently have some jurisdictions, such as Estes Park, Colorado, used bed taxes to subsidize housing and childcare costs for local hospitality and tourism workers. In November 2022, the city raised its hotel bed tax to 5.5 percent, up from 2 percent, and earmarked funds from the increase—an estimated $5.3 million in 2023—for housing and childcare initiatives. These taxes, along with city, county, and state sales taxes, add a cumulative 14.2 percent to the cost of a nightly stay in the city, funding new workforce-related initiatives. According to Colorado tourism officials, at least 17 municipalities have imposed a new bed tax or modified an existing one over the past year, seeking to replicate this model.[4]

CHAPTER 7

Cross-Cultural Advantage

Rescuing Globalization

Globalization, as we've known it, is quickly unraveling. A discontinuity—from globalization to the "clash of civilizations"—is disrupting the free movement of people and information with massive implications for the hospitality and travel industry. The war in Ukraine is likely to be just the first of what historian Augustus Norton called "irredentist campaigns" as democracy continues to backslide in the face of rising religio-political and ethnic conflicts. This discontinuity renders defunct the multinational approach to developing human capital while upsetting the apple cart built under the U.S. leadership since World War II. For hospitality companies, it disrupts the prospects of building a single company culture that is predicated on a shared set of values, beliefs, and norms that facilitate localizing western products and services. Instead, the assertion of local values, practices, and legal systems supported by a larger role for protectionist governments leads to the rise of national champions. Hospitality leaders must begin to prepare for a multipolar world with power centers organized around religious, cultural, and even tribal identities, starting with the Sinic, Islamic, and Hindu regions along the fault lines outlined by the late professor Samuel Huntington in the "clash of civilizations" (see Figure 7.1).

If the controversy over the potential ban or forced sale of TikTok is any indication, it's conceivable in the multipolar world that national security-driven data controls and regulations will mandate new data firewalls for the travel industry. National committees may subject marketing initiatives such as travel databases, airline, and payment partnerships with banks to government approvals. If relationships between Washington

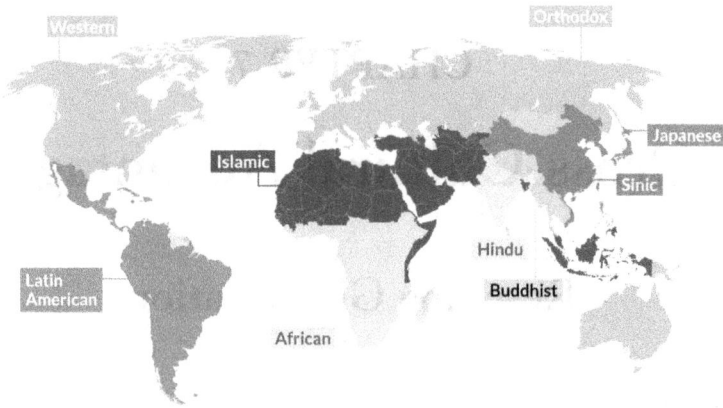

Figure 7.1 The clash of civilization and the remaking of world order

Source: The clash of civilizations and the remaking of world order by Samuel P. Huntington.

DC, Beijing, and the Gulf Cooperation Council (GCC) further deteri-orate, national governments may force the restructuring or sale of hotel and airline loyalty programs, their databases, technology applications, and their algorithms to domestic parties. In this context, hotel chains may have to break up into separate companies, not just for China but other regions too. Brands may be forced to enter into master franchise agreements with approved national entities who co-own their intellec-tual property and rights to inspect and effectively control their databases, starting with their deals with national airlines. These government enti-ties could demand exclusive territorial licenses and treat certain fees paid by hotel owners as a revenue stream for their country's travel marketing fund. Such developments could drastically change the western franchis-ing model and accelerate the rise of regional competitors.

New regional alliances and organizations, for example, the Indo-Pacific region or between China, Russia, and the GCC, will be formed, creating new regimes overseeing a fragmented set of rules addressing intellectual property, talent, and information flows. In this turbulent con-text, new corporate structures and organizational models are required for developing and managing talent across borders in an unstable multipolar world. The purpose of this chapter is to discuss how innovative technolo-gies can enable hospitality companies to build cross-border talent engines that may result in the only remaining source of sustainable competitive advantage. The discussion of a global strategy or strategic pivot starts with understanding the economic factors underlying deglobalization and unpacking the layers of the structure that are unraveling in the 2020s.

The Beneficiaries of Economic Globalization

In the post-World War II era of American hegemony, cross-border capital flows and global supply chains were established between the United States, Europe, and northeast Asia. Cross-border mergers and acquisitions accelerated the globalization of industries represented by integrated cross-border supply chains not seen since the early 1900s under the British Empire. The expansion of the European Union, NAFTA, the rise of the Asian tiger economies, and the emergence of free enterprise zones in China further accelerated globalization. The largest beneficiary was the shareholders of global corporations who benefited from access to consumers in developing markets, a stable cost of capital with low inflation, and citizens in the west who accessed relatively cheap goods, services, and low energy costs. But globalization also greatly benefited people living in many developing countries who received higher wages along with knowledge from skills, training, and career opportunities from western and Japanese corporations in markets such as China, India, and Brazil. Despite its damage to the environment and toll on human rights, the globalization of production facilitated the rise of China, South Korea, and the ASEAN region, eliminating poverty for over 400 million people through a state-led model of capitalism in less than 30 years.

While western and northeast Asian business leaders and shareholders gained access to highly skilled talent in developing countries, many retained a Eurocentric worldview about capital markets, worker rights, and the protection of intellectual property. A universalistic worldview informed how boards of directors and CEOs built, organized, and managed their global businesses. In this context, category-leading firms such as P&G, LVMH, Toyota, and Samsung achieved global economies of scale through their global supply chains; for example, the components of a stereo system in the 2000s were sourced, assembled, and produced in over 90 countries. These companies adopted a "top-down" global strategy, supported by corporate functions and global brand teams measured by worldwide profit and loss statements, based on the logic that "a firm's competitive position in one national market is significantly affected by its competitive position in other national markets."

Today, the DNA of leadership in the hotel industry reflects this top-down model of headquarters-driven globalization. According to our research, of the 140 largest American-, Canadian-, British-, Australian-, and European-based hotel brands and operators, only four CEOs have been either educated or worked in an executive role outside the United States and Europe, and only 8 percent of their senior management teams and 5 percent of their board of directors are foreign nationals from nonwestern countries. The story is similar in Asian and Middle Eastern-based multinationals in hospitality and travel. Ironically, despite globalization, international experience, a critical dimension of diversity, is largely absent from the discussions and metrics in Environmental, Social and Governance (ESG) reports and DEI disclosures of most hospitality and travel companies.

Defining and Measuring Globalization and Its Reversal

Broadly speaking, extrapolating from the late Susan Strange, a founding scholar of international political economy, there are four legs of the chair or pillars of globalization:

1. *Production flows*, the integration of supply chain of both goods and services measured by the sum of imports and exports as a percentage of gross domestic product (GDP)
2. *Information flows*, including the creation and dissemination of knowledge, intellectual property, research and development measured in part by the growth of shared search engines and applications on the Internet
3. *Financial flows*, or the cross-border movement and integration of capital flows, including private, public, and informal debt and equity markets
4. *People flows*, namely the growth of people and highly skilled talent across borders enabled by agreements such as those underpinning USMCA or the European Union (see Figure 7.2)

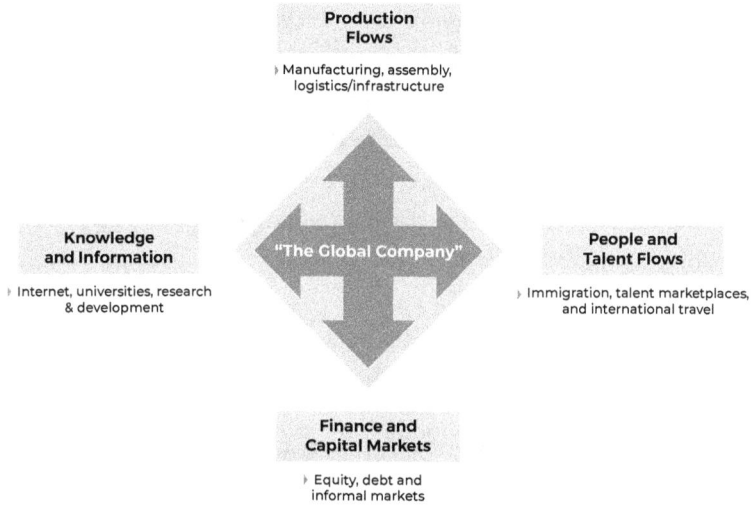

Production Flows

⟩ Manufacturing, assembly, logistics/infrastructure

Knowledge and Information

⟩ Internet, universities, research & development

"The Global Company"

People and Talent Flows

⟩ Immigration, talent marketplaces, and international travel

Finance and Capital Markets

⟩ Equity, debt and informal markets

Figure 7.2 The four pillars of economic globalization

Challenges to the Existing World Order

With respect to production flows, the degree of integration of global value chains (GVC)—a measure of the value of intermediate goods that are either imported or re-exported for other countries to export—has been in decline since 2008, even within the European Community prior to Brexit (see Figure 7.3). Trade tensions are compounding a shift that has been underway since the financial crisis in 2008–2009 and the United States has adopted the highest tariffs in its recorded history.

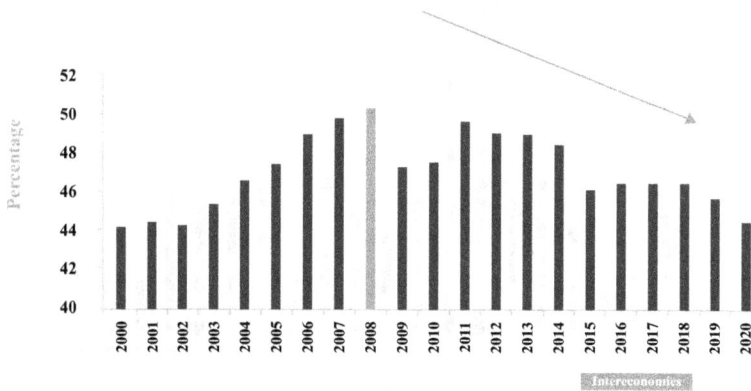

Figure 7.3 Participation in global value chains

Source: UNCTAD-Eora database, Natixis.

Today, political economists discuss "slowbalization," measured by decelerating trade, investment, and smaller GVCs. Put differently, slowbalization is the process by which countries and regions deglobalize and adopt protectionist practices to achieve greater perceived self-sufficiency. Cross-border investment, trade, bank loans, and supply chains have all been retreating or deteriorating relative to world GDP—both inward and outward foreign direct investment (FDI) flows have declined as a share of nominal GDP (see Figure 7.4).

The sharp decline in bilateral portfolio flows between the United States and China is reflected in both China's reduced ownership of U.S.

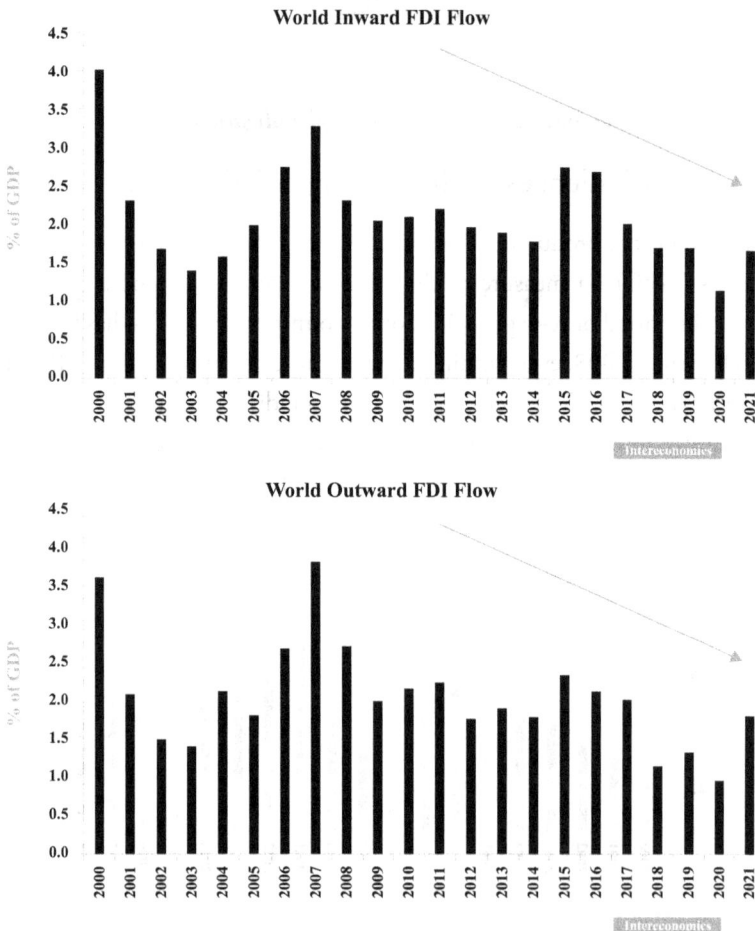

Figure 7.4 World inward and outward FDI flow

Source: UNCTAD.

treasuries and the reduced foreign ownership in Chinese long-term securities due to regulatory changes. With the reduction in cross-border lending, all forms of cross-border financing have become more difficult. This is also evident in the fragmentation of the global capital markets and the introduction of new alternatives to the U.S. dollar as the world's reserve currency. For example, there is compelling evidence of a decoupling of the U.S. and Chinese equity markets—leading China-based companies such as *Alibaba* have opted for secondary listings in Hong Kong, and the IPO of Aramco, which valued the company at $1.7 trillion dollars, is listed on the Saudi Stock Exchange. China, Russia, India, and several Latin American and GCC countries have bilateral and multilateral programs to lessen the U.S. dollar's dominance over international trade seeking to use new financial technologies to settle transactions in their own currencies.

A Decline in Global Talent and Information Flows Has Huge Implications for the Hospitality Industry

Information flows are also suffering with the raising of digital firewalls, followed by a wave of "technology decoupling," most seriously in the semiconductor industry but also in software including Internet infrastructure, social media, and cloud and data storage. Rules on privacy, data, and espionage are rupturing. New government regulations addressing data management have been disrupting cross-border data flows by imposing localization requirements for privacy or national security reasons. For example, China's Internet security law has required foreign operators like Apple to store user data with local companies since 2017. More recently, U.S.-based companies such as Airbnb and LinkedIn have exited China after being subject to greater censorship and data controls addressing their users not just in China but around the world.

Talent is also constrained from moving to the greatest opportunities due to changes in corporate strategy or market access in other parts of the world. In the Middle East, countries such as Saudi Arabia have legislated plans to nationalize the workforce, including hospitality, requiring that most managers be local citizens rather than expatriates. Rising anti-immigration sentiments and outdated systems in the west, reflected in a waiting period for a U.S. visa still reaching over 500 days for prospective Indian travelers, and the backlog of H1B visa applications are accelerating investments in offices set up closer to remote talent. According to the UN, new regulations and policies hostile to foreign investment are at record highs of 40 to 50 legislations passed a year.

People flows, measured by legal immigration of skilled talents, are lower and facing severe bottlenecks in the United States and Europe. According to Skift, international travel is also under indexed relative to the postpandemic economic recovery and is poised for recovery but set back by higher prices and reductions in corporate travel due in part to the economic recession and the timing of China's reopening[1] (see Figure 7.5).

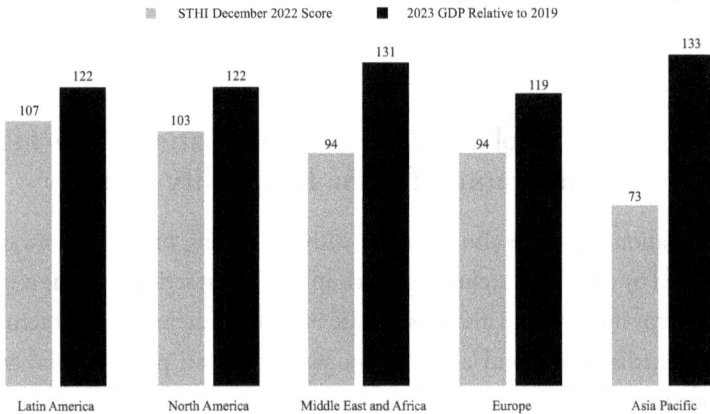

Figure 7.5 Travel recovery by region

The Talent Problem Facing the Multinational Hospitality Industry

From the customer's perspective, the travel industry is inherently global as hotels, airlines, and online travel agencies compete for their leisure, business, and government dollars and deploy global loyalty programs, sales organizations, and advertising campaigns to capture and gain their loyalty. However, from an operational standpoint, the hospitality industry has never been truly global: hotel and food and beverage operations are managed as decentralized regional or country-specific business units. Operators are global in name only: from a talent management standpoint, hotel operators are a classic case of what the late University of Michigan professor C.K. Prahalad called "traditional multinationals" that view their business as a portfolio of national opportunities led by expatriates who oversee "local server factories" of talent.[2] The benefits of such a structure and its associated management processes include responsiveness to local customers and stakeholders. Particularly in the case of regions with language and cultural barriers, costs, including redundancies and difficulties of technology transfer and internal turf wars, usually far outweigh the benefits (see Figure 7.6).

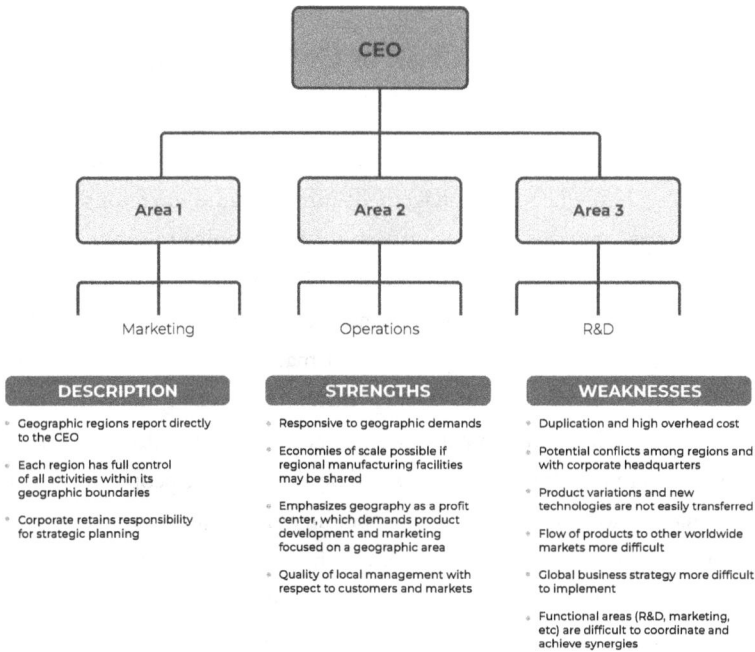

DESCRIPTION	STRENGTHS	WEAKNESSES
• Geographic regions report directly to the CEO	• Responsive to geographic demands	• Duplication and high overhead cost
• Each region has full control of all activities within its geographic boundaries	• Economies of scale possible if regional manufacturing facilities may be shared	• Potential conflicts among regions and with corporate headquarters
• Corporate retains responsibility for strategic planning	• Emphasizes geography as a profit center, which demands product development and marketing focused on a geographic area	• Product variations and new technologies are not easily transferred
	• Quality of local management with respect to customers and markets	• Flow of products to other worldwide markets more difficult
		• Global business strategy more difficult to implement
		• Functional areas (R&D, marketing, etc) are difficult to coordinate and achieve synergies

Figure 7.6 Multinational organizational structure

Under the multinational structure, the role of the corporate office in hospitality is focused on mergers and acquisitions, development, loyalty marketing, and support services such as finance and procurement. Hospitality companies utilizing matrix patterns combine the characteristics of brand/product and operations-centric geographic designs in a hybrid that uses "the administrative structure of the company to balance and integrate the roles/responsibilities of its business, geographic, and functional unit." Under this structure, talent management is relegated to locals as the corporate office spends much of its time on business development and cleaning up a legacy of inconsistent, tired, and incoherent brands (i.e., Sheraton, Hilton, Holiday Inn), scaling their growth in countries such as China and the UAE. Regardless of the matrix variant, other than the CEO, there are few executives with global profit and loss responsibility and the lead factory remains in the corporate headquarters where the global brand manager's role in operations and talent management is symbolic and tactical in nature.

What's New: The Clash of Civilizations Disrupts Global Talent Flows

As talent disruption unfolds in the coming years, hotel operators who have placed heavy bets on management infrastructure in regions such as Asia, Europe, and the Middle East have a hard choice to make—either retreat to being highly decentralized, franchised organizations or continue evolving toward becoming global human capital companies that develop and manage talent flows, such as general managers and culinary talent, across borders. Those who can leverage their scale by using emerging technologies including AI and talent marketplaces to build multilingual, elite talent pools in multiple geographies will be able to move people around to meet market needs required for new openings and acquisitions. In theory, global hospitality companies can achieve higher retention and employee engagement and outperform their peers by a wide margin.

As a case in point, the U.S. hotel industry is facing a severe labor shortage of over two million job vacancies while there are at least 100,000 job vacancies in the United Kingdom. An additional 90,000 job vacancies are forecast for the GCC region by 2026. Historically, key source markets for recruiting staff in the GCC, including the Philippines, Egypt, the South Asian subcontinent (India, Pakistan, Nepal, Sri Lanka), and Africa, are insufficient to meet the demand of large integrated resorts and new destination markets. On the other hand, markets such as China, India, Thailand, and Ukraine are seeing a surplus of over 400,000 highly skilled talents, trained by leading brands in functions such as food and beverage management and rooms management, seeking employment and experience outside their home markets.

To accelerate the movement of talent flows, some national governments are beginning to focus on immigration reform, raising the prospect that cross-border hospitality talent mobility becomes more fluid. As a case in point, German Chancellor Olaf Scholz's Cabinet approved issuing "opportunity cards" for people with more than 2 years of professional experience in their home country, targeting industries such as hospitality and information technology. Other noteworthy examples where innovative immigration policies are being adopted to grow long-term talent flows in hospitality and tourism include Canada and Australia, where indigenous travel has become a strategic objective of national governments, and Thailand, whose luxury resorts depend on multilingual GMs capable of hosting leisure travelers from China, India, Europe, the Middle East, and other regions.

As Freedom House reports the 17th consecutive year for the decline in global freedom,[3] hospitality companies are also joining 220 businesses in other industries committed to hiring 22,725 refugees from countries such as Afghanistan, Venezuela, and Ukraine. There will be a growing need for such initiatives in the coming decade. The UNHCR estimates the total number of people worldwide who were forced to flee their homes due to conflicts, violence, fear of persecution, and human rights violations (the so-called "displaced people") surpassed 100 million in 2022, of which 22 million were classified as refugees, a 200 percent increase from a decade earlier. A typology of displaced people, including those associated with human rights violations such as religious persecution and self-determination movements, is shared in Appendix IV.

The complication is a parallel and contradictory trend—the concurrent nationalization of talent flows in many of the largest talent-sourcing markets. The root cause is democratic backsliding with autocracies on the rise including, paradoxically, significant deterioration of rights and freedoms in western countries including minority rights in the largest democracies such as India. According to the Economist Intelligence Unit's 2022 Democracy Index, there are only a handful of full democracies remaining such as Canada, France, the United Kingdom, and Australia (see Figure 7.7).

⊡ **Authoritarian regimes**   ☰ **Hybrid regimes**   ▦ **Flawed democracies**   ■ **Full democracies**

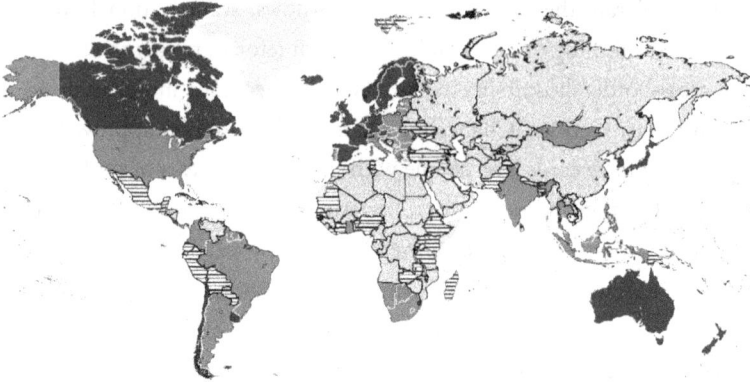

Figure 7.7 Global map by regime type 2023

Source: www.eiu.com.

Cultural relativists increasingly question whether value judgments should be made across cultures. President Xi's unveiling of the "Global Civilization Initiative," which contends that countries "should refrain from imposing their own values or models on others and from stoking ideological confrontation," is a case in point.[4] A by-product of this initiative is that China, intentionally or not, is leading the process of reversing the core values underpinning the process of globalization that underpins their economic success. Another example is "Saudization." In 2019, the Minister of Labor and Social Development Ahmed Al-Rajhi issued a decision to "Saudize" hotel management in properties classified as three-star and above, resorts, hotel suites, and villas.[5] The ministry's decision stipulates 100 percent Saudization of jobs in the tourism hospitality sector in a number of roles and an initial rule of 70 percent in sales, events, and conferences. The decision has banned employers from recruiting expatriate workers, transferring their services, assigning work to them, or using them in the jobs mentioned in the decision, whether directly or indirectly.

In June 2023, Sequoia Capital, a 51-year-old leader in the venture capital industry, announced it will split into separate American, Chinese, and Indian entities that will drop the company name, sever all investor connections, and operate as independent local entities.[6] The significant shift in strategy from a globalized connected world with cross-border investments in Chinese start-ups such as the category leading ride delivery company Didi to "local first" capital sources. According to Bain Capital, this echoes trends in worldwide private equity capital raised for investments in China, which is down 77 percent in the last 6 years to $25 billion as China's share of committed capital has fallen to 25 percent of Asia's share, excluding real estate.

Glocalization: A Model for the 2020s and Beyond

Glocalization, a combination of the words "globalization" and "localization," is not meant to simply convey customization of products and services to local needs. Glocal is derived from the Japanese word "dochakuka" and refers to the interface of the global and the local. For global service companies, the goal is no longer building a single culture and advancing homogenization, centralization, and scale. In contrast, glocal companies manage talent, information, and knowledge flows in all directions. For example, Whirlpool created new washing machines to assist Indian women in washing sarees that had broad applications and became a global product. They specifically considered the unmet needs of their Indian consumers. Indian consumers of Whirlpool had a recurring issue with five-foot or longer sarees getting tangled in washing machines. Whirlpool then collaborated with a local business partner who created a new washing machine that catered to regional customs and tastes. This was part of a wave of new product and service development across the Asia-Pacific region. Whirlpool learned that placing a refrigerator in the living room is a common practice among Asian consumers. These insights led to significant design changes and refrigerators were built in vibrant hues like red and blue to make them suitable for living room furnishings. By adopting glocal strategy, Whirlpool has been more successful in gaining market share from competition from both local and international brands because it meets local needs and preferences, at lower costs, due to the global sourcing and technology advantages of the company.

The Human Resource Function of the Glocal Company

Many hotel CEOs still believe that their company valuation and future corporate success depend on tapping the international marketplace, especially in Asia and the GCC region in the Middle East. To build a more local talent pool and reduce costs for owners, hotel CEOs have recently set goals to hire 25 to 50 percent local general managers that are developed or sourced from within a country market. However, according to our research and interviews of over 200 hotel general managers and regional leaders, in the wake of rebuilding after the pandemic, the traditional multinational HR function is lagging and needs radical innovation to realize its glocal dream.

The GMs we interviewed contend that international experience is not often equated with career progression; many managers who are presented with such opportunities view it instead as a veiled demotion. Moreover, managers posted abroad feel "out of the loop," isolated from, and ignorant of, the activities of corporate headquarters. Staffing of cross-border assignments is often rushed, little cross-cultural or language training is provided to the expatriate, and foreign assignments are often too short to acquire local expertise. Relocation is still extremely stressful on family life. Spouses in dual-career families are reluctant to interrupt their own jobs to move abroad. Finally, the division of authority between brand, country, and regional managers is often mixed, and solutions that change reporting structures into matrix reporting usually augment rather than relieve such confusion. Many GMs point out that few if any of their peers who ascended to regional roles ever became a hotel CEO.

The glocal company adopts innovative solutions to these problems by focusing on the strategic and personal levels. Given the scale of hiring required to reopen after the global pandemic, the need to develop truly global managers—both expatriates and indigenous personnel—has never been more important.

The U.S.-based industry leaders in other global sectors such as consumer products, technology, and oil and gas ensure that the global HR function remains at the core—rather than the periphery—of their strategic decisions. They view international experience as a prerequisite for an executive appointment, appoint executives and board members that reflect these priorities, and communicate this viewpoint throughout the company. They encourage local autonomy in decision-making, but also create processes to instill the company's vision, values, and strategic goals throughout their subsidiaries. Such companies also focus on developing both local and expatriate managers. They know that true competitive advantage is gained by combining the expatriate's knowledge of corporate practices with the specialized expertise of the local manager. Training for international assignments is extensive; spousal and family concerns are recognized and met. The global company works diligently to create a pool of experienced international managers, who will form the basis for future success.

Key Strategic Issues Facing Service Industry CEOs in a Clash of Civilizations

For service operators based in far-flung regions, in the context of deglobalization and instability in a multipolar world, decentralization seems justified because the corporate center can provide little guidance in serving the tactical needs of foreign employees, customers, owners, and other stakeholders including governments. However, the corporate overhead and technology costs of further decentralization alone far exceed the benefits. Consequently, most service companies seeking to salvage their footprint, fee income, and international growth will grapple with three fundamental challenges:

1. The first is to exit geographic markets with the most management-intensive model, preferably by franchising, joint ventures, or other business models, that perpetuates brand standards; it involves crafting exit strategies that balance potential long-term fee income streams that perpetuate brands against the capital requirements and management time required to build and integrate operational infrastructure and the inherent political, economic, and financial risks of brand dilution in geographic markets. The hotel industry's disappointments with the potential opening of Cuba, its ongoing growth challenges in India where domestic luxury incumbents maintain the

luxury segment, and its hastened retreat from Russia after decades of investment are examples where the actual cost of equity capital was far greater than financial models suggested, resulting in huge losses. The success of Yum China Holdings, Inc. (spun-off from Yum!) and the casino industry's structuring of separately listed companies in China for the purposes of establishing a presence in Macau and the pros and cons of Conrad Hilton's spin-out of Hilton International are relevant case studies for how service companies could adapt and restructure to protect their brands while meeting the requirements of regulators. However, while this is a topic that merits more research and case studies, it is not the focus of this book.

2. The second challenge is for hospitality executives to learn from their strategic failure in the global pandemic and the Russia war and act multilaterally by pooling resources in advance of a crisis. The long-term goal should be to create and finance a multilateral regime to protect their employees and those working under their flag in the properties and, if necessary, to work with NGOs to manage the logistics of their movement across borders. Hotel CEOs can start by writing a global humanitarian charter for hotel employees so that properties can serve as a haven, to protect the rights of women, minorities, and displaced people. The largest hotel chains should be the permanent members of this standalone organization that should not be affiliated with any specific national organizations or governments. Hotel CEOs should assign an executive from their social responsibility or ESG teams to champion ad-hoc policy initiatives and establish funding mechanisms for a new international organization for hospitality workers, whose members are participating hotels and restaurant operators and owners, hospitality schools, and nonprofits.

3. The third challenge is to reset and establish a sustainable competitive advantage within the largest foreign hotel operations, where a separate entity could be publicly listed or exited with valuations comparable or even better than those in western markets. This challenge is made difficult by the growing presence and influence of well-capitalized national and regional competitors with deeper government relationships and local expertise in areas such as

construction and design, food and beverage, and digital marketing. To gain a potential advantage, international operators must attract and empower local talent and adapt their cultural advantages such as meritocracy, diversity, and inclusion to their advantage. This requires building a global talent engine that acquires and develops talent in each region of the world and converts these talents into international managers faster and cheaper than their regional competitors. Let's focus our attention on this topic by analyzing the first and most important case study of where hotel chains can focus to reset their brands: the People's Republic of China (PRC).

Seeking Extraordinary Talent: China Case Study

One way to consider the merits of building a global talent engine is to consider China as a case study. In glocalization, category-leading western brands appear committed to the China market for a sizable portion of their revenues, growth, and innovation. According to our analysis, 20 to 30 percent of the valuation of the top five western-based hotel stocks is tied to either profits or future growth value expectations in China. Consumer interests are continuing to converge as tech-savvy Chinese millennials are seeking the latest brand innovations. Pfizer, Apple, Nike, the

NBA, Procter & Gamble, Starbucks, KFC, Wyndham, Disney, General Motors, Intel, and Microsoft are the agents of social integration and have spent decades investing in China. For these reasons, we turn our attention to the challenge of talent management in China.

Historically, the key advantages for China have been its relative ease of doing business and its cutting-edge infrastructure. But now the long-term reason for being in the market is access to China's talent, which, despite rising labor costs, remains unrivaled in most measures of productivity. As large markets go, other than India, there are few geographic alternatives to attracting a talent pool on a scale anywhere near China, with over 100 million service employees trained in managing western brands, eager to learn English, and adopting new mobile applications and artificial intelligence at a breathtaking pace.

Market leaders in China have built leadership teams over decades, starting with expatriates, and evolving to promote local hires based in the PRC into the most senior positions. For example, Hilton grew its share of China-born hotel general managers from just 10 percent in 2005 to over 50 percent by 2022, a remarkable achievement that provides human capital assets that can eventually be deployed around the globe. Hilton aims to have 1000 hotels in operation in the market with 100,000 team members, including 85 percent local general managers and 30 percent female general managers. This is a realistic goal given the findings of our research, which includes surveying 12,000 hotel general managers and property executives in China who are based on our platform, Mougulan ("seeking extraordinary talent"). We discovered that China's elite hospitality talent, the top 10 percent of hotel general managers according to our algorithm, is 58 percent women (compared to 35 percent in the United States) and a decade younger than their U.S. counterparts. These elite talents have also risen to general manager positions in an average of just 7 years, or 36 percent faster than their U.S. counterparts. Reflecting the country's low salaries for the hotel industry, the average estimated worth of the top 10 percent of general managers is 742,000 Chinese Yuan or U.S. $107,000, compared to an average of $164,000 for those based in the United States. Outside of the tier-three cities, the vast majority of China's elite hospitality talent is multilingual and at least semifluent in English and seeks work experiences outside the PRC.

Therefore, in the coming years, China will provide the industry with an undervalued, high-performing, and diverse global talent pool of hospitality executives.

Furthermore, while the media bemoans the Chinese exits of Airbnb, LinkedIn, and western social media, consider the success of these American-based biotech, entertainment, retail, and hospitality companies in building "glocal organizations" in China:

Retail: Walmart China has over 400 stores across 169 Chinese markets and employs 100,000 people. They committed $1.2 billion to build distribution and logistics across China in the next 5 years to open at least four new Sam's Club stores, 15 additional shopping malls, and more community stores in the capital of China's Hubei province.

Hospitality: Starbucks, which has over 6,000 stores across 230 cities in China and generated an estimated $3 billion in revenues, employs over 60,000 people, headquartered in Shanghai where they have built China-specific store concepts since 2010. Starbucks also remains committed to investing $130 million to launch a global roasting facility in its coffee innovation park.

Biopharma: Pfizer is China's market leader in cardiovascular and antibiotics, has invested $1.5 billion within China, and is the country's leading foreign biopharmaceutical company with four state-of-the-art manufacturing plants and 11,000 employees in over 300 cities.

Sports: NBA China, the separate company the league set up in 2008 to manage its retail deals with Alibaba and a 5 year $1.5 billion content deal with Tencent, is now valued by the league at $10 billion to $15 billion. The league has offices in Beijing, Shanghai, Taipei, and Hong Kong, and 500 million fans watched NBA programming on Tencent during the 2018 and 2019 seasons and 21 million fans watched game six of the 2019 Finals, according to NBA data. The league also has more than 200 million followers on social media in China. In March, the league opened the second-largest NBA store outside of North America in Beijing. Despite their current challenges, the NBA's success in building the game in China is remarkable and inspired their creation of a separate entity in Africa.

The massive government stimulus after the pandemic also represents a once-in-a-generation opportunity for the most innovative U.S. brands to ramp up investing in China and target its domestic market. As part of its post-COVID-19 stimulus plan, China will be investing trillions of RMB into service sectors. The ramped-up spending will aim to spur infrastructure investment, backed by as much as 2.8 trillion yuan ($394 billion) of local government special bonds. So, what should a western hospitality executive do to build extraordinary talent in China, in 2023 and beyond?

Over time, industry leaders have built a unique collective ability to understand patterns of thought and behavior or "Wenhua," reflected in Chinese culture. For example, westerners believe in 360° feedback and are used to a "thick-skinned" work environment where employees, business contacts, and government officials can be openly criticized. In contrast, the Chinese believe in Confucian-based harmony and that "chou" or smelly criticism on an individual level can be dangerous, and when necessary, should be done privately and diplomatically. Criticism of government or public officials is often considered treason.

The Chinese concept of "face" or Mianzi means respecting and complimenting others so that they give you face in return. Incumbents who view the Chinese market as a source of talent innovations that can be exported to their home markets will retain employees and scale organizations. It is also likely that as Beijing's priorities have permanently shifted with higher importance placed on social purpose, environmental sustainability, and the growth of domestic market consumption, a new generation of category leaders can seize the day and build profitable domestic businesses in China. For example, hospitality brands could focus more on local community initiatives supporting the 30 million migrant workers, mostly mothers who comprise nearly one-third of China's hotel labor market and live apart from their families, with an annual trip home.

Building and retaining a leadership team in China today requires establishing and widely communicating a clear plan and message for how it will improve the country. Consider the case study of Tesla. Tesla invested $5 billion into its Chinese factory to sell cars in the country and Tencent is one of its biggest shareholders. No foreign company has invested in a bigger Chinese factory than Tesla, which aims to have 100 percent of parts locally sourced by 2023. Tesla is developing a Chinese design and engineering center to develop new cars specifically for the China market. Their approach to the China market has resulted in various concessions including tax credits, subsidies, faster approvals, and preferential loans. Prices for Tesla's Model three sedans are like those of local manufacturers such as NIO Inc. and Xpeng Motors while undercutting global players such as BMW and Daimler AG.

Many American legacy brands have found a second life in China due to deep local partnerships, including General Motors (Buick is the #1 selling car) and Howard Johnson (which, almost extinct in the United States, has over 100 five-star hotels in China). This has happened in large part because the local partners have made a positive social impact with local and provincial governments and are effective for their equity investors

and lenders. In all cases, business leaders must maintain strong relationships with government officials who are measured on job growth, wealth creation, and social capital. Having transformed their country, most Chinese business leaders are now motivated by "Wang Ming" or a higher level of "total dedication." Offering a brand or business that becomes a new global standard and improves the environment or has positive social impact scores the highest.

CHAPTER 8

Winning Moves

How Hospitality Can Score Big with AI

Source: ai.io

Having once again demonstrated its resilience in the face of long-term labor shortages, inflationary pressures and geopolitical uncertainty, the U.S. economy remains the envy of the world. However, two parallel and contradictory trends—the spread of the union contagion pushing into new sectors and the growing pull of the freelancer gig economy (which represents 56 million Americans or 36% of the workforce)—reflect elevated levels of distrust in the corporate world and all levels of government. These trends have spilled into a now turbulent technology sector which is shedding thousands of jobs being replaced by artificial intelligence, accelerating the discontinuity called "a talent disruption," the title of my book. In many traditional industries, even business leaders in touch with the times are scratching their heads and asking, "Where did all the workers go?" However, there is an industry that continues to defy the odds and thrive in the labor market, with an abundant supply of talent and unit labor economics that remain favorable: professional sports.

Like hospitality and travel, the sports industry is thriving due to pent-up demand post-pandemic. But that's where the similarities end. Unlike travel and hospitality, which have reduced their services and amenities resulting in lower customer satisfaction, or the entertainment industry, which was embroiled in long strikes paralyzing their ecosystem, the sports industry has grown its offerings and generated new revenues by leveraging its robust talent pipeline. While other industries remain stuck in defensive labor wars, the sports industry is making people the brands, generating new digital and consumer product related revenue streams. Hence, it's worth asking, what is the sports industry doing differently with respect to human capital management? What's their secret algorithm?

As part of our research into developing talent marketplaces, our team of data scientists analyzed data from over 3000 players in five major sports leagues based in the U.S.: Football (NFL), Basketball (NBA), Baseball (MLB) and Hockey (NHL). We went through a discovery process mapping salaries, income distribution, upwards mobility, and talent lifecycles within each league against other industries. Our team also analyzed the organizational structures, budgets and strategies adopted by the highest performing teams. The iterative process of testing uncovered a number of surprising insights. We have summarized our findings in three lessons in human capital management that corporate executives can learn from professional sports.

Lesson #1: Data Science Is King. Take Your Touchy-Feely Style Somewhere Else

The sports industry has come a long way in the 20 years after Michael Lewis' bestselling book, *Moneyball: The Art of Winning an Unfair Game,* highlighted how independent analysts from outside baseball uncovered the mispricing of talent and capitalized on informal market inefficiencies. Today professional sports teams have an average of 28 full time employees focused on data science assessing human capital. The old-school touchy-feely scouting system is gone. The differences in identifying and pricing talent before and after the data science models in sports were implemented were so significant they enabled small market teams to compete effectively against their larger rivals who have 40–100x their operating budgets. Unsupervised machine learning models that incorporated new data and algorithms enabled leagues and teams to engineer meritocracy in recruiting, promoting and compensating players with math prepared by analysts who have few presuppositions and biases.

In the years since data science was implemented, unionization, team salary caps and calls for improving DEI have not negatively impacted the meritocratic systems used by professional sports teams. Over the past few decades, the sports industry has developed predictive models and advanced algorithms using the latest biomechanical data assisted by camera footage, wearable devices, and motion capture. These breakthroughs have enabled the industry to grow from 10,000 to over 10 billion data points. At their corporate offices, human capital teams build sophisticated models that track and analyze a wide range of performance data—from pitch velocity and bat speed in baseball to sprint speed and agility in soccer—providing inputs that generate a detailed assessment of an athlete's impact on team success. Additionally, with the emergence of generative artificial intelligence, teams have been able to expand their talent scouting and performance analysis to new markets on a global scale. A prime example is the partnership between Major League Soccer (MLS) and aiScout, a sports talent discovery platform. This platform analyzes high-quality videos from individual talent profiles and drone-captured footage during games using advanced video analysis algorithms that are scaled through supervised machine learning.

The resulting insights into players' skills and performances, including metrics like speed, acceleration, and accuracy, are shared with sports teams. These advancements are breaking down traditional barriers and opening unprecedented opportunities for athletes at all levels to pursue their dreams. In this context, artificial intelligence has evolved from being a tool to being a peer and partner in human capital innovation. Unsupervised machine learning is widening the global sports talent pipeline, allowing teams to discover more undervalued athletes and make informed decisions about investment and compensation, ensuring it is directly tied to proven on-field contributions. While industries such as hospitality continue to rely on job sites, applicant tracking systems, outdated personality tests and the biases of old school recruiters, the sports industry is using artificial intelligence to grow its talent pool and generate new revenue models in every corner of the earth.

Lesson#2: Use Artificial Intelligence to Determine a Talent's Worth

With respect to pay for performance, professional sports teams such as the NBA use analytics to assess key drivers of revenue production such as attendance, sponsorship, content and advertising and playoff optionality to generate the net present value (npv) or lifetime worth of a player. Each player's value is situational and determined based on the context of a specific team, considering a player's marketability and leadership role in developing talent. A player's worth can be compared to his or her replacement value and adjusted for injury risk.

In recent years, fantasy sports websites have empowered fans to compute a player's value above replacement, transforming this analysis into tangible metrics, such as betting dollars. For instance, one such metric gaining prominence in fantasy baseball circles is Standings Gain Points (SGPs). SGPs offer a standardized measure to evaluate a player's impact on a team's standings in the league, particularly for statistics measured by ratios or averages like batting average or earned run average.

To illustrate, let's consider the formula for calculating SGPs for batting average in fantasy baseball:

$$SGP_{BA} = (Player_{BA} - League\ AVG_{BA}) \times Conversion\ Factor_{BA}$$

Where:

- $Player_{BA}$ represents the player's projected or actual batting average.
- League AVG_{BA} denotes the league average batting average.

- Conversion Factor$_{BA}$ is the factor used to convert the difference in batting average into a standardized unit (e.g., points).

By utilizing SGPs, fantasy baseball enthusiasts can effectively gauge a player's value above replacement and make informed decisions when managing their teams. This data-driven approach underscores the importance of employing data science methodologies over traditional consulting reports when assessing talent worth in sports. In contrast, legacy service industries such as hospitality use backwards looking consulting studies and job sites to benchmark compensation, often purchasing data from the same sources that treat human capital purely as a cost. They fail to adjust these generic datasets for context such as degree of difficulty, product quality and competitive factors that could help determine if an employee is a clutch performer or an overvalued asset who has benefited from easier assignments and other economic factors.

Lesson#4: Use AI to Develop Talent From Farm to Table

Next, we turn our attention to talent acquisition, learning and development. Sports teams draft players from high school and college into their vertically integrated minor league "farm teams." These minor league teams cultivate rising talents and remodel professionals with new skills and renewed confidence. The most successful sports organizations build 20 percent of their stars through this owned and operated "farm system."

Unfortunately, the business model in hospitality is going the other way: franchising is fragmenting the workforce as 5 out of 6 people work for third party managers contracted by real estate owners. Given skyrocketing costs, the ROI on a bachelor's degree in hospitality is over a decade, leading to declining enrolments and higher attrition, while most community colleges are limited to teaching hospitality trades like culinary arts.

Generative artificial intelligence has the potential to change this predicament and give rise to a new talent ecosystem. Hospitality companies could build bench strength and compete more effectively with the gig economy by building AI powered talent scout apps and establishing talent sharing deals to create an ecosystem of employers. AI could be used to identify skills gaps in the workforce and employers could be compensated for training and developing rising talents for each other. For example, Hyatt could partner with Chef Daniel Boulud to develop its culinary talent in French cuisine, and they could train his future managers in accounting and finance of restaurants and catering.

A more radical innovation is Talent Sharing. Rather than working for a company, talents join a network of employers where they can choose to be trained and work. For example, Hilton could work with Starbucks and Mayo Clinic—to enable culinary and restaurant management talent to be ranked, put into tiers, priced, and moved between relevant brands and properties. After they have completed their training and demonstrated their worth, elite talents could have the option or right to become free-agents and receive bids from multiple employers in the network.

Owners and franchisees can also lead the way in human capital R&D by pushing profit sharing down to the front-line. They can leverage AI to inexpensively source talent off the beaten path and experiment with floating wages that reflect supply and demand like gig apps in hospitals that use yield management to determine wages for nurses. Franchisees who are owner-operators can also build shared talent networks with each other to offer career paths.

Some argue that if hospitality invests in AI similar to sports, it will exacerbate inequality and put millions of people out of work. But with millions of unfilled positions rendering businesses incapable of meeting demand, hospitality leaders should leverage artificial intelligence to build a new factory operated by fewer and more productive employees who are well-compensated. It starts with adopting the best practices of the sports industry and leveraging AI to scale human capital and score big.

CHAPTER 9

Anthropomorphizing Robots

Autonomous Hotels of the Future

Photo by DALL-E

Prompt: Create an image showing a hotel arrival manager, a hotel intern, and the humanoid robot Natasha in a luxury resort lobby awaiting welcoming their guests.

Imagine that you are eagerly organizing a weekend getaway for your daughter's 16th birthday. You're on the hunt for a boutique luxury resort, ideally located within a 2 hour drive from your home, to accommodate her and her 100 closest friends for an unforgettable celebration. Given her immense love for Bollywood, you're seeking a venue that can truly make her feel like a celebrity on her special day. Your checklist includes booking 50 double-bed rooms, 5000 square feet event space capable of hosting a dinner for 100 guests with live entertainment, and a facility that can sustain a vibrant dance party well into the night.

AI Travel Planning

Opting for the efficiency of technology, you turn to the AI assistant on your preferred Internet search engine. Your initial input includes the date, geographical location, desired resort class and amenities, specific room types and floors, catering needs for food and beverages, and spa treatments. The AI system efficiently processes your criteria, returning a curated list of boutique lifestyle and luxury resort options that meet your specifications. Among these, you focus on the one boasting the highest accolades for hosting social events.

Carefully reviewing the presented choices, you compare amenities, ratings, and pricing for each element of the potential experience. Your attention is drawn to a particular luxury resort located on Ocean Drive in Santa Monica. This venue stands out with its celebrity chef-led restaurant renowned for catering upscale events, a rooftop nightclub offering panoramic views of the Santa Monica Pier and the Pacific Ocean, capable of accommodating a 100-person group. It's highly praised for social events and includes a star meeting planner, aligning impressively with 92 percent of your search preferences, including valet parking.

You land on the property's website, and its AI-enabled booking engine asks you questions about your daughter's personality and interests, such as her preferred genres of music, food and favorite treatments and services in the spa and salon. It turns out your daughter is a big fan of Bollywood Bhangra dance and movies, she loves Southern Indian vegetarian cuisine, and she is passionate about curated fashion such as jewel embroidered Sarees and Lengha dress. Based on your answers, the hotel site generates an itinerary which includes a package with preference-matching percentages, pictures and videos of each activity, customer reviews and a la carte pricing options.

The booking engine lets you delve into an Augmented Reality (AR) experience to explore and personalize every aspect of your event. Picture yourself virtually walking through the finest suites and rooms, getting a feel for the event space, and browsing the dining options. You also get to customize your event down to the last detail – from selecting the theme-matching decor, lighting, and music, to arranging how the food is presented and where guests will sit. You even have the freedom to tweak things like the color scheme, the layout of the tables, lighting of the event, and the seating arrangements. And for an extra touch of excitement, you add a special Bollywood Bhangra dance performance and a live chef food presentation.

Once you're happy with the preview, you reach out to the event planning team to finalize everything. This includes confirming the hotel room allocation, pinpointing the exact room locations, and setting times for the dinner and party. The event planner promptly sends over a quote. You then secure your booking with a deposit and complete the payment. Excitedly, you share the party preview with your daughter and the guests, stirring up anticipation for the celebration. Remarkably, the entire process of searching, planning, booking, and communicating is streamlined and efficient, taking just 30 minutes.

Arrival Experience

Arriving at the hotel a day before the party, your family of three looks forward to a relaxing day and a chance to check out the event space for any last tweaks. In the lobby, the arrival manager, and a hotel intern, accompanied by a humanoid robot named Natasha clad in traditional Indian attire, warmly welcome you, celebrating your daughter's 16th birthday. The intern hands you the hotel's signature welcome drink. After some friendly exchanges, Natasha scans your retina, enabling a unique check-in process via a text message code. Once scanned, she efficiently checks you in and instructs her robotic colleague, Henry, donned in a virtual hotel uniform, to take care of your luggage and guide you to your room.

As Henry escorts you to your room, Natasha briefs your wife on the latest preparations for your daughter's birthday celebration. She connects you to the VIP event host, who greets you via a tablet. The host enthusiastically shares that her team, along with the chef, are dedicated to crafting an unforgettable experience for your daughter and the guests. Natasha also reminds you to utilize the hotel's mobile app for event planning. Through the app, you can stay updated with live progress on the event's organization and make any necessary changes on the go.

Luxury Suite Experience

Upon being verified by the robot via biometric check-in, you use the barcode sent to your phone to access your two-bedroom suite. You're immediately welcomed by a digital display of Bollywood art, a favorite of your daughter's, adorning the walls and her preferred Indian pop tunes playing softly. In the living room, a high-tech mirror catches your eye, showcasing a range of clothing options through augmented reality, from contemporary designs to traditional Indian wear, all available for rent from an online retailer with the promise of delivery to your suite within 3 hours (see Figure 9.1).

Figure 9.1   Fashion mirror—image by DALL-E

In the master bedroom, you're comforted to find a bed equipped with pillows designed to support your pregnant wife's needs. Nearby, the "NASA Analyzer" stands out - a cutting-edge, non-invasive medical diagnostic tool, compact enough for deep-space missions, capable of analyzing various sample types and measuring a wide array of analytes. Intrigued, you scan its QR code to learn more about this advanced technology.

Your exploration leads you to the second bedroom, where birthday decorations, balloons, and a personalized note from the General Manager await, all celebrating your daughter's special day. Feeling a bit peckish, you peruse the kitchen, finding it stocked with your family's favorite drinks and a digital menu that offers room service from the hotel's casual eatery, alongside recommendations from local venues and the hotel's own restaurants, all tailored to fit your family's unique dietary preferences based on your "live to 120" AI genomic profile.

You switch on the TV, greeted by a personalized welcome message. Eager to catch up on your favorite Netflix series right where you left off at home, you navigate to your customized entertainment channel. This unique feature seamlessly integrates with your personal Netflix, Hulu, Paramount, and other streaming accounts, allowing you to continue your viewing experience without missing a beat, enveloped in the comfort of your suite.

AI Enhanced Event Experience

The following day, with excitement building for the birthday celebration, you quickly open the mobile app to confirm that the party preparations are on track, and everything is set for the event. After ensuring all is in order, you head down to the lobby. Greeted by a robot, you receive warm birthday wishes for your daughter. The robot then guides you to the rooftop, where an eagerly awaited party is set to unfold (see Figure 9.2).

As you ascend to the rooftop, the VIP event manager welcomes you with a delightful glass of Mango Lassi. Holding the refreshing drink, you stroll around to survey the setup. The rooftop has been transformed with a vibrant Bollywood theme, complete with event organizers dressed in Punjabi attire, and the energizing rhythms of Bollywood music inviting you to dance.

Figure 9.2   Birthday Party—image by DALL-E

While mingling with other parents on the rooftop, another alert captures your attention. A guest messages to say they'll be bringing an additional five people. This news briefly unsettles you, as the party was meticulously planned for 100 attendees. Without hesitation, you access the hotel app to communicate with your VIP event host. You request extra seating to accommodate the unforeseen guests. They respond promptly, assuring you of a swift resolution. Comforted by their quick action, you let go of your concerns and once again immerse yourself in the joy of the party.

Food and Beverage Experience

At the party, you and your guests relish the array of foods and drinks thoughtfully customized by the hotel to align with the theme and preferences of your gathering. The menu, prepared with attention to dietary needs, offers vegetarian, dairy-free, and gluten-free options. Organically sourced from local farms, the food is presented in a visually appealing manner, segregated into vegan, vegetarian, and meat selections. The spread includes vibrant and tasty dishes like Samosas, Panipuri, and a variety of Biryani, catering to the refined tastes of culinary enthusiasts. The beverage options, including Mango Lassi, Masala Chai, Nimbu Pani, and Thandai, are equally refreshing and delightful.

The chef and sous-chef add an entertaining twist to the evening by personally presenting the entrees. They engage the guests with stories about the origins and cultural significance of each dish and drink, interspersed with humor and interactive food chemistry tips for the kids, such as balancing spices with yogurt. The culinary team's appearance culminates in a well-deserved standing ovation, photo sessions with the teens and their parents, and heartfelt thanks from the attendees.

The party is full of excitement, with you thoroughly enjoying the chef's presentation and the delectable food. You express your gratitude and admiration for her team's efforts. The arrival of a group of Bollywood dancers, performing your daughter's favorite Bhangra dance, elevates the celebration. The party peaks as the chef presents a triple-layered birthday cake while everyone sings 'Happy Birthday' to your daughter, accompanied by the legendary voice of Lata Mangeshkar in the background. The event concludes on a high note, leaving everyone content and delighted.

Post Event Experience

The next day, you receive the captured videos and photos through the event planner app, allowing you to instantly download and share these cherished moments on social media. Shortly thereafter, you're invited to review and tip the hotel team, including the event planner, chef, and even the robots, for their exceptional service and contribution to a memorable celebration.

How AI Powers the Semi-Autonomous Hotels

Thanks to advances in artificial intelligence and robotics, such customer innovation scenarios are not farfetched. Academic research from the University of Kong and Sejong University in Seoul has validated that the fit between robots and brand personality influences consumer reactions.

High-contact robots, which handle tasks like check-in and dining services, are best suited for brands that are exciting, trendy, youthful, and imaginative.

AI at the Operational Core

The semi-autonomous hotels will be a place where human and machine intelligence work together to create a seamless and personalized experience for guests, supported by an AI-adjacent workforce. In this context, AI can enable hotels to run more efficiently by using an AI-enabled operating system that integrates disparate systems and external data sources. The operating system will act as a unifier that connects various components, such as property management systems (PMS), revenue management systems (RMS), customer relationship management (CRM), point of sale systems (POS), and human resources information systems (HRIS). It employs sophisticated algorithms to refine operations, inform decisions on daily pricing, staffing, marketing, and inventory control, and effectively bridges the gap between "soft" data including digital bookings and guest preferences and "hard" data that captures the nuanced expertise of hospitality personnel.

To achieve the vision of a semi-autonomous hospitality, three key technologies are leveraged: Intelligent Process Automation (IPA), Robotics Process Automation (RPA), and Natural Language Processing (NLP) to redefine the customer experience pre-stay, during the stay, and post-stay (see Figures 9.3 and 9.4).

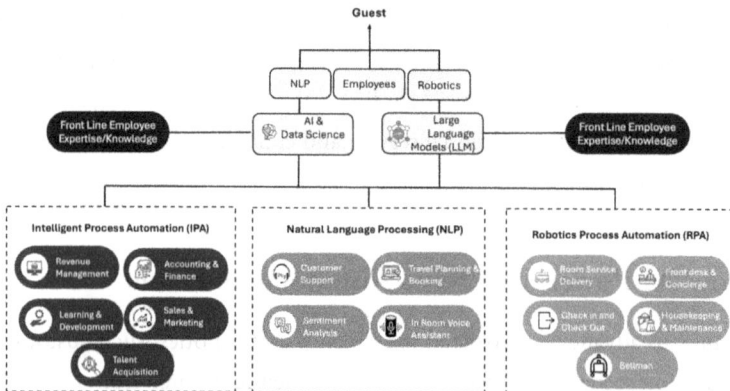

Figure 9.3   Framework for achieving semi-autonomous operation

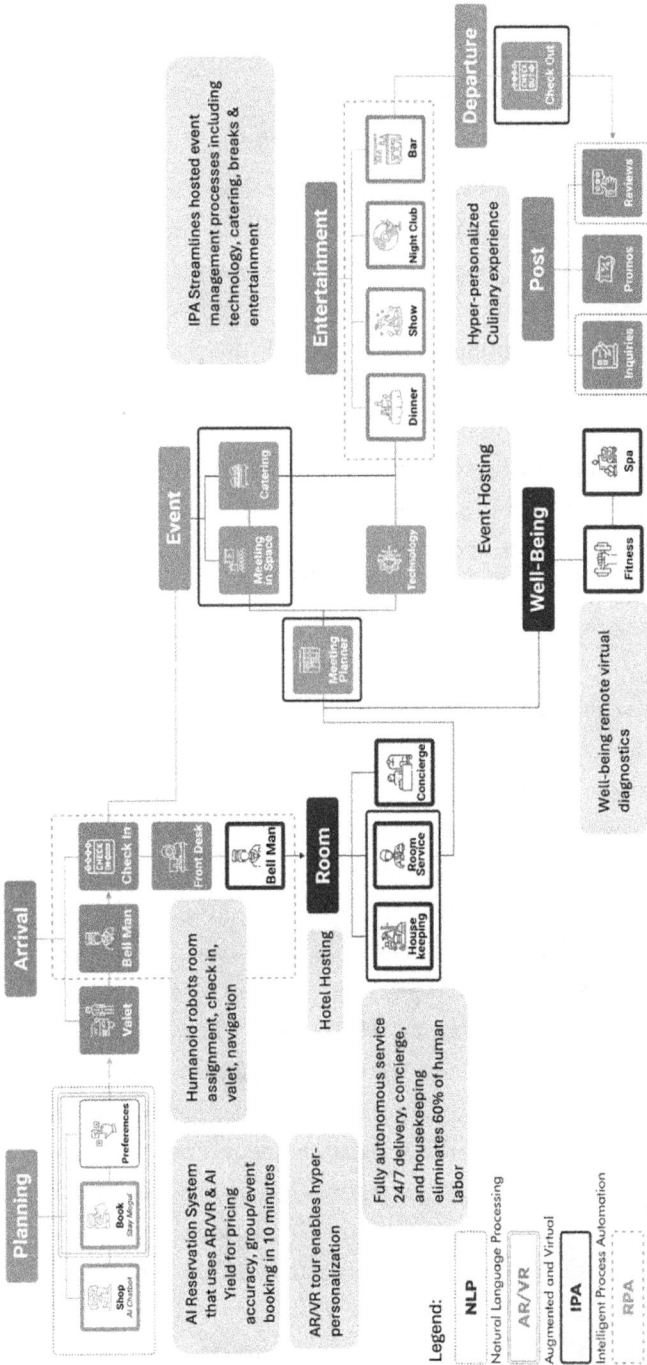

Figure 9.4   Semi-Autonomous hotel guest experience

Here's how these technologies are going to be incorporated to achieve semi-autonomous hospitality:

Natural Language Processing (NLP):

Implementing Natural Language Processing (NLP) significantly elevates customer service and operational efficiency. NLP models can be integrated into various systems, including the reservation system, in-room service voice assistants (part of the Property Management System), and the Customer Relationship Management (CRM) system. Key areas where NLP makes a difference include:

- **Pre-Stay:** Intelligent chatbots, powered by text-generation NLP models, will be integrated into the booking engine, mobile app, and social media platforms. These bots will handle natural language queries from potential guests about room availability, booking conditions, amenities, and special requests. By providing instant responses, chatbots can enhance customer satisfaction by making essential information readily accessible, thereby reducing the need for human intervention. Each interaction with these chatbots will be logged and analyzed to gain insights into guest preferences and market trends, allowing hotels to tailor their offerings and enhance their communication channels, including FAQs.

- **During the Stay:** Rooms will feature voice-activated devices integrated with the Property Management System (PMS), enabling guests to interact with services using simple voice commands. These interactions, managed by speech recognition models, will cover services such as room service and housekeeping. This integration not only personalizes the guest experience but also improves operational efficiency by automating routine requests, thereby allowing staff to focus on other critical tasks. The data gathered from these devices will be analyzed to optimize service delivery, identify peak request times, and enhance guest satisfaction.

- **Post-Stay:** After their stay, guests will interact with the Customer Relationship Management (CRM) system where NLP will automate responses to common inquiries about bills and refunds. Additionally, sentiment analysis will be applied to reviews and feedback across various platforms. This automation will expedite responses and improve the efficiency of administrative processes. By analyzing guest feedback, hotels can derive actionable insights, tailor marketing campaigns, and refine services to better meet the expectations of future guests.

Robotics Process Automation (RPA)

RPA will concentrate on automating labor-intensive, customer-facing tasks to enhance service delivery. Some of the areas that will be automated are:

- **Room Service Delivery:** Service robots will manage order intake, inventory, and delivery directly to guest rooms, ensuring timely and accurate service.
- **Front Desk and Concierge:** Automating check-in/check-out processes and providing 24/7 concierge services to enhance guest convenience and satisfaction.
- **Housekeeping, Engineering and Maintenance:** Robots will handle cleaning tasks such as vacuuming, sweeping, and wiping surfaces, as well as routine maintenance checks, ensuring a consistently high standard of cleanliness and upkeep. Remote and smart engineering systems, equipped with IoT sensors, will monitor, and manage building infrastructure, optimize energy use and automating maintenance through predictive analytics to quickly address any issues.
- **Valet Services:** Automating luggage handling and delivery to guest rooms to streamline the arrival and departure experience.

Intelligent Process Automation (IPA):

Automating essential back-office functions is vital for achieving semi-autonomous hospitality. This may require partnering with third-party technology providers to streamline operations. Key functions to automate include:

- **Accounting and Finance:** Automating financial transactions, reporting, and auditing processes to ensure accuracy and reduce manual effort.
- **Revenue Management:** Implementing automated pricing and inventory management systems to optimize revenue and enhance profitability.
- **Sales and Marketing:** Utilizing IPA to manage customer data, execute marketing campaigns, and analyze performance metrics for more effective strategies.
- **Learning and Development:** Automating training modules, instigating and tracking employee progress to foster continuous improvement and skill development.
- **Talent Acquisition:** Streamlining recruitment processes, from sourcing candidates to onboarding, to attract and retain top talent efficiently.

Talent Engine

Semi-autonomous hotels are powered by a Talent Engine at their core, acting as a vibrant community that attracts hidden workers, legal immigrants, and freelancers, including a hybrid and remote workforce. It uses data from independent third-party sources and algorithms to help organizations identify rising and elite talents within and outside their organization.

Data Science and Operations are the core of the Talent Engine, where data is used to find, evaluate, and rank the best talents based on their merits. The Talent Engine also features a two-sided talent marketplace that connects the top talents with projects, including opportunities outside the organization. Moreover, the Talent Engine offers learning and development opportunities for talents, using AR/VR and experiential learning, to advance their career goals.

The Talent Engine also acts as a central data repository for training the language models. Each humanoid robot has a profile where employees can contribute to its knowledge base. These profiles detail the contributions of each talent, showcasing the data and knowledge imparted to the robot, along with the dates and times of the training sessions. Employees who participate in training the robots earn lifetime royalties, enabling them to create lasting wealth as front-line workers.

Leveraging AI and Data Analytics, the Talent Engine plays a crucial role in performance management by effectively managing and enhancing performance across all levels of operations. These technologies allow operators to analyze vast amounts of data, providing deep insights from regional operations down to individual properties. This comprehensive approach helps identify areas for improvement across the entire portfolio.

AI models delve deep into customer feedback and reviews, as well as individual employee performance metrics. By meticulously analyzing this data through the Internal Human Capital Management (HCM) System, the AI identifies skill gaps and recommends specific training, educational resources, and experiential learning opportunities tailored to enhance employee capabilities. This fosters an environment of continuous improvement, ensuring that service standards are not only bolstered but consistently maintained across all operations.

This strategic use of AI in performance management allows operators to optimize every aspect of the service profit chain, from employee development to customer satisfaction. As a result, they can deliver exceptional service consistently, solidifying their position as a leader in the hospitality industry.

Reservation System

The progression toward a data-driven, algorithmic approach in yield management not only maximizes revenue and reduces the need for intermediaries such as channel managers, online travel agencies, and meta search engines. But an AI-driven booking engine doesn't just sell and book a room. It constructs an experience that matches customers with accommodations and experiences which starts with their stay preferences, such as bedding type, music genre, soap and shampoo brands, towel types, shower temperature, and other preferences. The reservation system also matches customers to branded robots, otherwise known as hosts, that can adopt the service style and tone of voice, methods, and frequency of communication the guest seeks on the specific travel occasion.

Personalizing the Future of Travel Marketing

Semi-autonomous hotels transform the landscape of hospitality by learning and predicting guest preferences, creating a marketing approach that feels almost telepathic. When a potential guest interacts online, the AI begins crafting a unique experience. A couple planning their anniversary weekend at a luxury resort could virtually stroll through a romantic sunset beach walk, construct their meal, design their dinner food presentation, and select an eco-tourism tour before booking their stay.

Moreover, AI integration extends to real-time, on-site customization during the stay. Here are some ways semi-autonomous hotels can create bespoke customer experiences, typically reserved for luxury customers:

- **Hyper-segmentation**: Semi-autonomous hotels can use advanced analytics and machine learning to hyper-segment their customers into psychographic dimensions that speak to their service style, such as bohemian luxe, which describes rising technology and entertainment entrepreneurs who prefer to cherish curated local discoveries and informal and relaxed service style typically seen in independent and boutique hotels.
- **Lifestyle Programming**: Each individual hotel could have an open-source content channel that features appraised local musicians, entertainers, and other creatives. Using data from various sources, such as social media and purchasing trends on applications such as Spotify and Netflix, hoteliers could introduce content from up-and-coming local artists that match a customer's interests.

Advancing Sustainability

The semi-autonomous hotel is driven by the vision of providing guests with the information and tools they need to advance sustainability in all aspects of their experience. Using sensors, Internet of Thing (IoT), and advanced analytics, the customers can accomplish the following objectives:

- **Minimizing Food Waste**: AI analyzes the guests' preferences and dietary needs and predicts the optimal amount and variety of food to prepare, thus avoiding food waste. AI is fully integrated into the chef's procurement system and suggests locally sourced ingredients that have lower environmental impact and support local farmers, proposes catering menus that are more plant-based, seasonal, and organic, and tracks the environmental impact of each ingredient, such as the CO_2 emissions, water usage, land use, and biodiversity loss. Excess food is automatically routed to local food banks and charities in an integrated supply chain.

- **Reducing Carbon Footprint**: The semi-autonomous hotel model motivates guests to reduce their carbon footprint during their stay by tracking and analyzing data such as transportation modes, travel distances, energy and water consumption and creating a carbon footprint report at the end of the stay. Guests will be incentivized with discounts for lowering their carbon footprint during their stay and consuming less energy.

- **Decreasing Energy Consumption**: The semi-autonomous hotel model saves energy by using intelligent devices and sensors that control the lighting, heating, cooling, and ventilation of the rooms and facilities according to the occupancy, weather, and time of the day. The semi-autonomous hotel model also relies on renewable energy sources, such as solar panels, wind turbines, and geothermal systems, to run the hotel and lower its reliance on fossil fuels.

Enabling Health and Wellbeing

Frequent long-haul travel negatively impacts health and reduces life spans due to changes in time zones, nutrition, sleeping pattern, air quality, and other factors. The semi-autonomous hotels could integrate into well-being data apps connected to the room's remote diagnostics and share information to selected health care providers. The science of sleep is also fertile ground for innovation: smart beds with sleep tracking sensors, temperature control, and an adjustable base can enhance sleep quality for guests. Smart bathrooms could provide urine and nutrition analysis to detect any health issues or deficiencies and recommendations to a customer and their health care provider. Smart mirrors can project the overall health statistics of the guests, such as blood pressure, heart rate, body mass index, and stress level, offering suggestions for better decision-making and well-being. Smart food menus can generate curated food options based on the guests' nutrition needs, preferences, and allergies. In a world where healthcare is becoming more remote and personalized, these technologies will enable customers to improve their well-being through actionable data that leads to better decision-making, saves time and money, and prevents disease.

Semi-Autonomous Hotels: Incubators for Strategic Innovation

Employees are still the most critical component of the semi-autonomous hotels. Without the expertise and creativity of the hotel employees who are part-owners of the property and compensated for their creation of intellectual property, building the semi-autonomous hotels will be impossible. Anthropomorphizing robots, which has captured the world's attention, is the next frontier in lifestyle hospitality. As hotel managers evolve from static programming of their properties to content creators in a world of AI-powered entertainment, new revenue models are created including streaming events and partnering with studios to produce pulse-racing, spine-tingling material to communities that relish drama. In the process, the stars of the show such as celebrity chefs, event planners, and their teams can receive a share of the royalties.

The semi-autonomous hotels must foster a culture of innovation among its employees. The hotel will not require a dedicated R&D department, but artificial intelligence will facilitate collaboration between hospitality experts, data scientists and engineers by prompting them to explore new ways of enhancing hospitality and improving service innovation. AI will automate experimentation with innovative ideas, learn from failures, and share best practices across a network of properties.

Responsible AI

These innovations undoubtedly enhance the overall guest experience; however, they also bring forth significant ethical and security considerations. The OECD[1] defines AI as "a machine-based system that can, for a given set of human defined-objectives, make predictions, recommendations or decisions influencing real or virtual environments." It classifies AI cases into one of the following seven types: hyper-personalization, recognition, conversation and human interaction, predictive decision and analytics, goal-driven systems, autonomous systems, and patterns and anomalies. Responsible AI requires establishing global auditing standards and requirements, starting with authenticating AI-generated content, user testing and content traceability in areas that protect consumers and employees. It's imperative that the semi-autonomous hotels address the following dimensions of Responsible AI effectively:

- **Privacy and Security:** The gathering and storage of guest data for personalization and automation can give rise to substantial privacy concerns. Guests may fret about the utilization of their data, who possesses access to it, and whether it receives adequate protection against potential breaches. The advent of generative AI has made social engineering increasingly accessible, rendering humans more susceptible to breaches than AI-powered systems. Semi-autonomous hotels have embedded comprehensive security features. Guests can activate a fully encrypted stay feature, ensuring that their data and information are thoroughly concealed and stored separately, thereby guaranteeing protection against privacy and personal data breaches even in the event of a security breach.

- **Bias and discrimination:** AI algorithms can inadvertently reflect the inherent biases of the data they are trained on. To mitigate bias and discrimination in AI-driven hotels, a comprehensive approach involves diverse and representative training data, regular bias audits, and transparency in AI decision-making. Implementing ethical AI guidelines, offering human oversight, and continuously monitoring algorithms for emerging biases are crucial. Providing mechanisms for guest feedback, considering third-party audits, and collaborating with legal and ethical experts further ensure compliance with laws and regulations. These measures collectively aim to reduce legal and reputational risks while promoting fairness and equity in the guest experience.

- **Job displacement:** The automation of tasks through AI has raised concerns about potential job displacement among hotel staff. The scope of Responsible AI should include auditing all recruitment-related software starting with applicant tracking systems and job sites for systematic bias. The truth is that the process was deeply flawed prior to the advent of AI, filtering out semi qualified workers, most notably women, minorities and military veterans and exacerbating historic labor shortages. However, semi-autonomous hotels aim to empower employees by enabling them to acquire new skills, including AI-related knowledge. The goal is to build an AI-adjacent workforce, certified by the Responsible AI Institute (RAII). Employees focus on enhancing AI systems, collaborating with data scientists and robotic engineers, and elevating the overall guest experience through valuable feedback. This shift toward a future where laborious tasks are handled by robots presents an opportunity for a more fulfilling and innovative work environment.

- **Accessibility:** Ensuring that AI-driven technologies are accessible to all guests, including those with disabilities, can be challenging. To achieve this, AI systems are meticulously crafted with inclusivity as a fundamental principle which includes features like voice commands and user-friendly interfaces, AI-powered apps with real-time voice instructions for navigating the property for visually impaired guests. By placing inclusivity at the forefront of their design philosophy, semi-autonomous hotels aim to provide an equitable and enjoyable experience for all guests, irrespective of their physical or cognitive capabilities.

- **Data Ownership and Control:** Travelers need to know when AI is used and how it's employed, as well as how and where to provide timely feedback and complaints. To ensure transparency and prevent potential disputes, semi-autonomous hotels establish explicit guidelines regarding data ownership, leaving no room for ambiguity. Furthermore, semi-autonomous hotels prioritize granting guests significant control over their data, allowing individuals to manage and dictate how their information is used. This commitment to guest empowerment underscores the hotel's dedication to responsible data management and privacy, fostering trust and confidence among all patrons.
- **Advancement of Secure AI:** Prioritizing the development of AI models that pose no harm, which includes the publication of a Model Card for every new iteration of an AI model upon deployment. This Model Card comprehensively outlines the model's usage and provides insights into the safety assessments conducted to evaluate its reliability and security.

The semi-autonomous hotels ensures compliance with national and international responsible AI guidelines which includes actions such as, sharing safety test results and other critical information with the government to ensure it passes the standard test scenarios, developing standard tools and tests to ensure that every innovation is tested for safety and trustworthiness prior to making it public, and develop principle and best practices to mitigate the harms and maximize the benefits of AI for workers.

Conclusion: Back to the Future

In *Back to the Future*, Marty (Michael J. Fox) says "This is heavy" a bunch of times throughout the trilogy. Whenever he's bewildered or confused in time travel gone awry, he uses his catchphrase. At one point, Doc (Christopher Lloyd) asks him about the turn of phrase: "There's that word again, 'heavy.' Why are things so heavy in the future? Is there a problem with the Earth's gravitational pull?"

As quantum computing progresses, industries are converging. Like most disruptive technologies, semi-autonomous hotels will benefit from learning and collaboration with industries at the forefront of robotics and automation such as the hospitals of the future. As a case in point, advanced computer vision, including the processing abilities of its visual and voice sensors—the robots' nerves and sensory organs—are rapidly advancing with machine learning. More power-dense batteries have made it possible for a humanoid robot to move its legs quickly enough to balance dynamically and navigate stairs, ramps, and unsteady ground. These trends don't necessarily mean there will be fewer people employed in hospitality. On the contrary, thousands of talents can train Large Language Models and develop humanoids with different service styles and personalities. As artificial intelligence continues to progress at a breathtaking pace, the line between science fiction and reality becomes increasingly blurred. The dawn of AI-driven hospitality is going to reshape travel in ways we could not imagine a few years ago.

CHAPTER 10

A Call to Action
Responsible AI

Introduction

In November 2023, the long-simmering fault-lines in the debate over AI safety reached a new crescendo with the non-profit board of OpenAI, the creator of ChatGPT and DALL-E services, voting to fire its founder & CEO Sam Altman. Within the U.S. technology community, two opposing factions have emerged: the "doomers" or self-described "safety-first technocrats" led by venture firms such as General Catalyst (in partnership with the Biden Administration) who are forming cross-disciplinary committees and non-profits that create protocols and playbooks; and the "humanists," also known as the "techno-optimists" led by libertarian firms like Andreesen Horowitz who believe entrepreneurs rather than policymakers (who are seeking to relitigate regulation more broadly) or non-profits who have never built things are most capable of ensuring technology is a force for good. The debate risks tearing Silicon Valley apart and given the heightened risks for investors, negatively impacting U.S. leadership, with unintended consequences such as AI offshoring that may benefit regions such as the E.U, that have established regulatory frameworks, countries such as China where businesses are engaged in multi-year state-sponsored AI initiatives.

Over the past few years, the "doomers" or safety-first technocrats have been gathering momentum. There have been considerable multilateral efforts to establish an agreed upon terminology, development guardrails, auditing standards and compliance systems for the responsible development and release of generative artificial intelligence. Policymakers around the world, including the EU, U.S., UK, Canada, Japan, and Australia were frantically enacting new AI regulations. The EU's proposed AI Act seeks to heavily regulate a group of systems that threaten human rights and safety including automated hiring and real time biometric surveillance. These precipitous developments raise an important strategic question for executives in hospitality and travel: should they regulate AI and if so - when, how, and where?

Defining the Problem

Artificial intelligence (AI) can be defined simply as "the capability of a machine to imitate intelligent human behavior." The OECD defines AI as "a machine-based system that can, for a given set of human defined-objectives, make predictions, recommendations or decisions influencing real or virtual environments." It classifies AI cases into one of the following six types: hyper-personalization, recognition, conversation and human interaction, predictive decision and analytics, goal-driven systems, autonomous systems and patterns and anomalies (see Figure 10.1).

Moderna used AI and robotic automation to produce 1,000 mRNAs a month, a molecule that was essential to the vaccine's development and production scale. The health care industry is investing billions of dollars in AI to advance precision health and responsible health care intelligence. Examples of use cases in precision health include apps that analyze dietary habits and provide reports on the nutritional intake of each menu on personal mobile devices starting with senior care facilities and children with chronic diseases. With respect to health care intelligence, AI algorithms are analyzing medical imaging data to identify early signs of disease, with far greater accuracy than human doctors and at a lower cost. By combining these innovations with the power of genomics, machine learning and AI will transform the healthcare[1] industry and eliminate its labor shortages in the coming years.

The travel industry has been experimenting with AI, automation, and robotics for at least a decade including automated lighting, automated vehicles, and biometric identification. In China, Alibaba has been working with international hotel chains on full-service robot hotels that check customers using biometrics, deliver room supplies and meals in restaurants and even act as bartenders. In the U.S., an M.I.T. backed restaurant[2] chain called Spyce created the first robotic restaurant that delivers meals in less than 3 minutes priced 40 percent less than comparable quick service brands; its technologies have been adopted by Sweetgreen, a fast-growing[3] brand that claims to be "all in on automation." Online travel agencies such as booking.com are introducing AI trip planners that predict travel

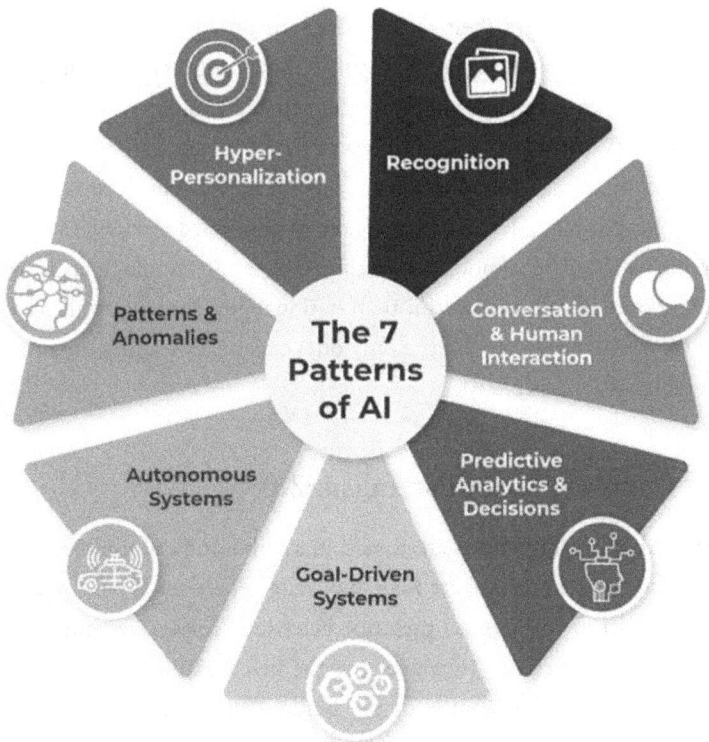

Figure 10.1 The Seven Patterns of AI.

Source: Artificial Intelligence & Responsible Business Conduct report, OECD

intent and create visual lists of destinations and properties. The goal of these companies and a wave of new travel AI start-ups is to establish automated systems that don't just imitate human intelligence, but far surpass it in terms of the scale of data, learning and predictions required to personalize the customer experience.

A Renewed Sense of Urgency

After decades of investments, trillion-dollar big tech companies such as Microsoft (Open AI/Chat GPT) and Google (Bard) gave premature birth to AI in the public domain. They claimed their primary motivation was to carefully test generative AI on a large scale with real users to garner feedback akin to what start-ups do when they launch an imperfect minimum viable product (MVP) ripe with flaws and defects. However, skeptics contend they accelerated its launch to defend their turf in businesses such as search engines and to raise large amounts of capital at high valuations to pre-empt their rivals. Observers noted their timing was no coincidence: it capitalized on rising anti-China sentiments among polarized Western governments who were not capable of bipartisan legislation.

Few in Washington D.C., Ottawa or Brussels were surprised that the CEOs of these big technology firms advocated AI regulations, such as open innovation and levels of transparency they failed themselves to provide the public. The paradox is that these Western technology firms, who have become far more powerful than national governments with respect to their wealth and scale, are the only ones capable of leading the process to establish Responsible AI.

The Promise of Multilateralism 2.0

Global AI regulatory efforts are rooted in a philosophy of multilateralism that Princeton scholar Robert Keohane characterized as "a persistent and connected set of rules, [that] prescribe behavioral roles, constrain activity and shape expectations," thus affecting the behavior of all actors. In the early 1990s, after the collapse of the Berlin War, Keohane defined "the new multilateralism" as "the practice of coordinating national policies in groups of three or more states, through ad-hoc arrangements or by means of institutions." When multilateralism works, nations and civilizations recognize their fates are indivisibly linked, and their interactions are based on generalized principles of conduct and expectations of diffuse reciprocity. Since 2021, ad-hoc multilateral efforts at advancing Responsible AI—multilateralism 2.0[4] - have been quite inclusive, involving big tech, start-ups, government representatives, academics, non-governmental organizations, and members of civil society. The objective is to establish adaptive and interoperable AI regulatory frameworks and harmonized standards such as those being developed by the U.S. National Institute of Standards and Technology (NIST), requiring "red teaming" as a testing system.

Perhaps most notably, international organizations such as the World Economic Forum's AI Governance Alliance (which published recommendations on precise and shared terminology, model and system traceability and knowledge sharing that prioritizes social progress) and the OECD (whose comprehensive framework addresses data relevance and representativeness, data quality, understanding systems decisions, transparency to the user and data subject, bias testing and robust systems testing) organized summits featuring a diverse cross-section of experts that appeared aligned with new standards and protocols for AI engineering. In 2022, the Responsible AI Institute (RAII) created a global certification program that has been adopted by certain industries such as financial services who have implemented its programs in automated lending. G7 leaders have also agreed on International Guiding Principles on AI

In the U.S., President Biden released his Executive Order[5] on Safe, Secure and Trustworthy AI which followed the U.S. Commerce departments AI Risk Management Framework which took a sectoral approach in negotiation with major AI companies. Critics have remarked that these efforts are little more than vaporware. Unlike the E.U's AI Act, which calls for testing and documentation, these initiatives lack teeth and will require legislation and are subject to judicial review and can be revoked by a future administration.

The Limits of AI Sovereignty

Given the stakes for national security in an unstable multi-polar world, governments are not betting on multilateralism 2.0. Hence, the race is on and AI sovereignty reigns supreme. As a case in point, Germany's research minister Bettina Stark-Watzinger framed the new EU AI Action Plan[6] as a way to achieve "technological sovereignty" and avoid dependence on outside powers. This came weeks after Germany announced its own multi-billion-dollar AI fund citing "AI sovereignty" in a global competition against the U.S. and China as Berlins' top priority.

At recent AI summit in London[7] that included Chinese representatives, UK Prime Minister Rishi Sunak, a Stanford MBA who has financed many technology start-ups in his career, argued that "only governments can properly assess the risks to national security" and that "only nation states have the power and legitimacy to keep their people safe." The problem is that people have historically low levels of confidence in their government leaders, irrespective of whether they are democracies or not. It's also difficult for citizens to place their faith in many of the same politicians who failed to enact meaningful regulations on Internet search or social media. They failed to ban data brokerages that sell users data to organizations based anywhere in the world. Furthermore, some of the proposed regulations – like requiring AI to know why the system does what it does in each case - are not just utopian, they demonstrate that most legislators fail to grasp even the basic concepts of AI.

Geopolitics is throwing more fuel on the fire. While some Western politicians believe it's best to leave Beijing out of the process altogether, the irony is that China is the only major G20 country that has enacted regulations addressing hate speech on social media, curtailing children's[8] time playing video games and regulating surveillance technologies and facial recognition. As Elon Musk points out, how could a global governance model possibly exclude China?

The paradox of Responsible AI is that the superpowers today are not governments – they are big technology firms. Multilateralism 2.0 is appropriately described by Ian Bremmer as a new "techno-polar world order." The more viable resolution is self-regulation with Elon Musk, Satya Nadella, or Jensen Huang playing the role of Captain Kirk in the U.S. Enterprise, chairing AI governance, resolving disputes and dispatching multinational inspection teams that put out fires and advise governments how to manage risks.

Recommendations for the Hospitality and Travel Industry

Chaos is not an option for travel and hospitality, an industry that thrives on stability. The unprecedented "techno-polar" context should not dissuade CEOs in the travel and hospitality industry from establishing a process for collective AI security. Regrettably, the hospitality industry is widely regarded as a sleeper with respect to cybersecurity as evidenced by the recent attacks that paralyzed MGM resorts and resulted in Caesars Entertainment paying multi-million-dollar ransoms to hackers. Over the past decade, most of the world's largest hotel chains, including Hyatt and Marriott, have been hacked several times, resulting in the travel records and credit card information of over 40 million people being exposed and huge fines from governments such as the UK. Compounding the situation is the fact that hospitality and travel firms generally outsource their software development, security, and technology infrastructure to consulting firms who rely on a network of offshore vendors. Most travel and hospitality firms and their franchisees lack the expertise to audit AI engineering in house and are not trained in writing large language models.

Given these realities, the industry should move quickly to establish a process to regulate AI, prioritizing the following three initiatives: (1) Creating a single multilateral organization for responsible AI in travel and hospitality including an auditing and certification process managed by an independent third party; (2) Adopting new corporate governance standards that mandate AI literacy for all employees and board directors that sit on an AI committee of the board; and (3) Prioritize multilateral projects that establish new standards and protocols for the use of artificial intelligence in human capital management.

Responsible AI requires establishing global auditing standards and requirements, starting with authenticating AI-generated content, user testing and content traceability in areas that protect consumers including privacy. For example, as travel planning, hotel bookings and check-in get automated, there are serious risks not just to privacy but security. If terrorists hack into a hotel reservation system and direct a target into a specific hotel room or vacation rental home and subsequently take over the cameras and launch an attack, it would have devastating consequences for the entire travel industry. Encrypting personal information, including names and contact information, could be a first step toward privacy and security.

Travelers need to know when AI is used and how it's employed as well as how and where to provide timely feedback and complaints. Other issues to explore include synthetic data and media which can speed up developments such as customer value scoring for the purpose of determining a reward program tier but are likely to exacerbate bias or even create new biases. Hotel and airline websites should publish a Model Card for each new version of an A.I. model that is deployed including how the model is used, as well as information on safety evaluations conducted to test the model.

To diversify the supply base, hotels and airlines must work together to establish an open-source innovation platform that shares best practices and is overseen by independent experts. To foster trust with consumers, travel and hospitality companies should require their teams and vendors develop "secure by design software" rather than endless patches to fix software vulnerabilities that are commonplace today. It's imperative that new travel AI standards and protocols don't perpetuate the dominance or control of AI development by either big technology firms or the handful of incumbent technology players who presently dominate the supply base of vendors in platforms such as online distribution, reservations, revenue, and channel management, as well as human resources technologies.

Regulations are long overdue to address AI's growing role in human capital. At present, few AI-powered tools for recruitment and selection are fully explainable and interpretable or can prove they do not disadvantage a minority group. The scope should include auditing all recruitment-related software starting with applicant tracking systems and job sites for systematic bias. The truth is that the process was deeply flawed prior to the advent of AI, filtering out semi qualified workers, most notably women, minorities and military veterans and exacerbating historic labor shortages. Upgrading human resource departments in travel and hospitality to become sufficiently technology literate should be the highest training priority. New regulations should force HR software firms to be transparent about their data practices and provide operators the ability to use artificial intelligence to engineer their own talent marketplaces and reduce their dependence on third party human capital software intermediaries. It's time for executives in the travel and hospitality industry—which accounts for 300 million global employees that represent 10 percent of the global workforce—to demonstrate to its consumers that it can self-regulate itself. By creating global standards and a transparent process for Responsible AI, executives in travel and hospitality can limit existential business risks and ensure new technologies make a positive impact on the future of humanity.

CHAPTER 11

Final Thoughts

Hospitality's Great Reset

On July 4, 2023, 15,000 employees from the most iconic hotels in Los Angeles, including brands such as Ritz Carlton, Fairmont, Hyatt, Inter-Continental, and Hilton, as well as recently unionized independent and boutique hotels were on strike. While the immediate dispute revolves around wages and work rules, the glaring issue is widening income inequality plaguing the industry. Unless a new mindset is adopted, this strike may just be the beginning, threatening the entire service sector, derailing the travel boom, and leading to job losses and a recession. During the pandemic, hotels received $15 billion in federal bailouts and returned to profitability quickly by cutting jobs and guest services such as daily housekeeping.

Fast forwarding to 2023, hotel profits in Los Angeles County have surpassed prepandemic levels, despite a growing dependence on contracted labor. Frontline workers, mostly women and minorities, struggle to afford a place to live in cities where they work and are forced to move further away due to lower hourly wages than Uber drivers. In a UNITE HERE Local 11 survey, 53 percent of workers said that they either have moved in the past 5 years or will move because of soaring housing costs.

Case Study: LA Hotel Workers Strike 2023

These 65 full-service hotels, worth more than $5 billion and generating an estimated $500 million in operating profits combined, are at the heart of this conflict. The workers, including room attendants, cooks, and dishwashers, are demanding an immediate five dollars an hour raise with an additional three dollars an hour in 2024 and 2025 plus 28 percent more benefits. This amounts to a 40 percent raise. The hotel coalition (which represents 42 of the hotels) offered $2.50 now and $6.25 over the next 4 years, for a raise of $8.75. Assuming they settle at $10 an hour raise, this equates to $1 million or 8 to 10 percent of net operating profits on average for these full-service hotels, representing a significant increase in fixed costs that underscores the magnitude of the conflict. The dispute underscores why market-based approaches such as profit sharing, ownership, and other variable pay including tips and bonuses should be part of the solution.

Inequality and the Root Causes of Talent Disruption

The underlying issue goes beyond the current hotel strike in Los Angeles. It is a symptom of the growing income inequality within one of our country's most profitable hospitality industries that has a Gini coefficient of 0.73, worse than South Africa (the worst ranking country for inequality according to the World Bank) or Major League Baseball (the worst ranking professional sport for income inequality). The hospitality sector is grappling with a shrinking talent pool, losing 20 percent of its labor market share to the gig economy and other sectors. Workers cite concerns such as affordable housing, long commute times, and 30 percent increased workloads. From a customer standpoint, service levels are deteriorating price increases that have outpaced inflation by two to three times since 2021.

The End of Hospitality as We Know It

Prior to the pandemic, the U.S. hotel industry was doing well, generating annual record profits of $80 billion to $100 billion for 12 consecutive years. However, by 2018, the hotel factory was overstressed, with 10 million unfilled positions and 60 percent employee turnover preparing for a record hotel development pipeline. Despite labor shortages and rising costs, these symptoms went unheeded. Consequently, hotel brands have lost their luster, reflected in declining customer loyalty and product and service inconsistencies.

Due to structural changes in the labor markets, accelerated by global pandemic and innovative technologies, hospitality, health care, and other service sectors are now facing long-term labor shortages with aging professionals and shrinking talent pipelines. Compounding the issue are the impacts of structural changes in the industry itself. Long gone are the days when hotel chains like Marriott operated most of its hotels and was the largest employer, grooming the industry's elite talent and generating the majority of its cash flows from owned and operated properties. Today, over 250 camouflaged third-party management companies employ 80 percent of the hospitality industry, including restaurants, and operate over 80 percent of branded and independent properties in the United States, on behalf of institutional investors, private equity, and family offices. As hotel chains focus on distribution, real-estate owners have emerged as the new power brokers: the financial strategies of REITS, PE firms, and family offices directly impact operations.

In this context, the U.S. hotel industry, whose revenues are expected to recover to prepandemic levels by the end of 2023, is beset with three major operational problems that negatively impact its growth and profitability. The first is the quantity of labor and quality of talent. The second is declining customer loyalty despite the context of pent-up demand. The third is an absence of corporate strategy and brand differentiation.

Labor Shortage Turns Into a Talent Disruption

First, as the fastest growing sector postpandemic, the hospitality industry is in dire need of qualified talent. Labor costs are skyrocketing, customer service is deteriorating, and double-digit wage pressure is negatively impacting profitability. Labor accounts for over 50 percent of a full-service hotels' cost structure and increased productivity, via highly qualified candidates, is the key to reining in runaway costs. Millions of talented experts and future general managers in key roles such as sales and marketing, revenue management, and finance have left the industry. Despite increasing wages by 15 percent, the average hotel has 11 full-time openings (versus 12 after the pandemic) and operators are experiencing 9 to 10 percent quit rates, the highest of any sector.

To suggest existing methods are inadequate is a gross understatement. Legacy systems including generic applicant tracking systems (ATS) and one-size-fits-all job sites generate inaccurate matches and filter out semi-qualified and "hidden workers." Current and prospective employees are fed up with the hiring and promotion process. Talents complain about lack of transparency in compensation, job duties, and working conditions as well as health and safety risks.

For hotel and restaurant owners, the direct and indirect costs are staggering. Search firms charge an average of $40,000 or 25 to 40 percent of first-year salary for a supervisor and above. When management time is factored in, talent acquisition and onboarding costs range from 50 to 75 percent of a first-year salary of $100,000 for supervisors and above.

Customer Experience Further Deteriorates

The second roadblock to recovery is historically low customer satisfaction and loyalty scores. This is the result of 2 years of record price increases that outpace inflation and understaffed hotel properties, with employees performing the jobs of two or three people. Leisure and business travelers and those who combine both experiences in a trip ("bleisure") and are accustomed to hotel service, such as valet, housekeeping, and restaurant service, are losing confidence in hotel brands, scoring them poorly for responsiveness and "value for money." Despite pent-up demand for leisure travel and corporate events, consumers have attached declining value to loyalty programs: Research from Deloitte found that hotel companies and airlines have seen their loyal business traveler client base shrink rapidly. That has challenged brands to extend premier status to members and adjust their benefit programs. Meanwhile, luxury customers are beginning to migrate to virtually hosted self-serve alternatives such as homestays, vacation rentals, timeshares, and other alternatives.

Customer satisfaction and employee engagement data reveal that most third-party hotel management companies perform far below acceptable levels required to regenerate customer loyalty. This is not surprising given that many third-party management companies maintain a sweatshop mentality akin to steel factories at the turn of the century, delivering short-term cost savings reinforced by short-term real-estate owners who routinely subject their contracts to 30 day terminations and accounting policies and budgeting processes that encourage contract labor disincentivize investment in employees.

Opportunity for Corporate Strategy and Leadership

The third issue facing the industry is an absence of corporate strategy and brand innovation. Hotel chains have adopted remarkably unimaginative and uninspiring strategic intents that lack differentiation or deep purpose required to differentiate their brands or attract new talent into the business. Put differently, hotel owners, brands, and operators have chosen to compete on the same dimensions of competition such as design differentiation and iconic architecture. Deeply held beliefs or toxic orthodoxies are maintained by a homogenous community of senior management, hotel owners, Wall Street analysts and the media, unions, industry events, and hospitality schools. As a case in point, "asset light" franchising is widely considered the most superior business model despite being devoid of a formula for building human capital and perpetuating blind spots that render the industry vulnerable to further unionization and government intervention.

The LA hotel strike of 2023 is a case study in the absence of foresight and corporate strategy in the C-suite. For the last 40 years, with a few exceptions, hotel industry CEOs and boards have been dominated by real-estate and finance DNA, mirroring a mostly white male elite social class of real-estate owners, financiers, lenders, and developers. Research and development, a nonexistent line item in the financial statements of hotel chains, is a fraction of that seen in health care, retail, or other service businesses and has been focused on solving real-estate problems with corporate design centers that feature new beds and coffee machines rather than service innovations such as new beds and televisions. Rather than rationalize, retire, or upgrade existing brands, hotel chains have spent more management time adding over 200 undifferentiated brands in the last decade. Meanwhile, full-service hotel brands issue an average of 500 standards focused on room amenities, reservations, and cookie-cutter loyalty programs with few requirements for recruiting, training, and developing talent in their hotels.

From an owner's perspective, a key lesson from the pandemic is that existing hotel products are relatively inflexible, labor intensive, and travel dependent. Moreover, the traditional hotel service model, enhanced with texting and kiosks, doesn't resonate with customers accustomed to apps that provide transparency into hosts, one-to-one reviews, and tipping such as Uber, Airbnb, and DoorDash. Hence, hotel owners are facing compressing margins, increasing capital intensity with more product standards, and larger fixed costs, rendering them highly vulnerable in an economic downturn.

Furthermore, for a new generation of talent, hotel brands lack a reason for being, let alone a social purpose, that attracts talent. Other than through minor operational changes, such as the elimination of plastic straws and placing customers in charge of requesting new towels, the industry has failed to address ESG in a meaningful way. In fact, hotels and resorts are one of the worst contributors to climate change. Hotels create 1.9 billion pounds of waste each year (enough to fill 37 million suitcases), use 219 billion gallons of water a year (equal to one person taking a shower nonstop for 277 years), and use 84.7 billion kwh/year (enough energy to power 64.5 million TVs).

Jumping on the bandwagon of publishing ESG reports, hotel chains have announced goals to reduce emissions, but those pledges have remained, if not entirely, focused on operational carbon via reductions in fossil fuel use, waste, and water usage and not on construction. With no real definition of net zero, hotels can easily obtain meaningless certifications, such as those from LEED, that falsely inform travelers of their sustainability practices. Embodied carbon, the term that encapsulates all the harmful greenhouse gases emitted during renovation and construction of a building, remains an outsized part of any hotel project's footprint. Embodied carbon in hotel-related construction contributes to at least 21 percent of global emissions compared to only 1 percent for hotel operations. According to Bloomberg, the hotel industry's definition of net-zero carbon emissions is subject to obfuscation and is therefore "a big lie." Very few hotel projects in the United States have advanced sustainability through reduced embodied carbon such as the Citizen M in Los Angeles, which was built using prefabricated construction in China.

Rounding out a mixed record in ESG, the hotel industry has made little progress in DEI at the property level over the past few decades. Women and minorities, respectively, comprise 60 and 40 percent of the hotel frontline in the United States. However, only 17 percent of U.S. hotel general managers are women and 8 percent minorities. In the United States, black people represent 13 to 17 percent of the front line and less than 0.5 percent of hotel general managers. Among the top 150 hotel CEOs, only two are minorities, both of whom own family-controlled businesses and there has never been a minority female CEO in any of the U.S.-based hotel companies.

As the SEC makes information more transparent to shareholders with nonbinding "say on pay votes," pay equity and executive compensation have become contentious issues in many industries including hotels, casinos, and online travel. Hospitality continues to reflect wealth disparities, as corporate executives make 400 × that of hourly workers in their properties, and real-estate investors generate record yields and billions of dollars in returns on invested assets while compensation for property-level hotel executives barely matches inflation. Paradoxically, achieving meritocracy, including promoting and rewarding talented employees, is made more difficult by the growing power of unions that impose tenure-based criteria for promotions and work rules that constrain innovation.

The Need for Effective Industry Governance

Despite a labor shortage of 1.6 million workers and a need for 2.4 million net hires a year in the hotels sector, one of the main hurdles is the lack of leadership. Various parties extract billions of dollars in fees from hotels for branding, asset and hotel management, taxes, union dues, and discretionary fees, yet accountability and oversight are murky. The industry's governance structure is becoming a disaster, with brands, owners, third-party operators, cities, and municipalities pointing fingers at each other. Hotel chains focused on franchising use legal arguments to avoid accountability while enjoying the benefits of revenues from the topline and owner-funded marketing budgets. Meanwhile, cities and municipalities extract $46 billion in taxes from the industry but prioritize advertising over addressing labor-related problems such as housing for workers.

Empowering Workers and Addressing Recruitment Challenges

Unions are spreading to independent and boutique hotels and workers have few alternatives but to join them to have a voice. However, hotel owners, driven by short-term profit goals, perpetuate the talent death cycle by hiring third-party managers to cut costs and buying and selling properties an average of every 5.5 years. Unlike airlines, frontline employees in hotels have no ownership stake or role in management decisions. Hotel operators have been inefficient in recruiting talent, relying on legacy technologies that filter out millions of semiqualified hidden workers. The industry needs to adopt AI-driven HR technologies and build transparent talent marketplaces that reward high performers and facilitate meritocracy.

There are three nonexclusive strategies that the hotel industry, as well as other service industries including health care providers and retailers, can pursue to create value and attract elite talent into their businesses:

Strategy #1: Investing in AI to Accelerate Self-Service Through Automation

Hotels could reduce labor costs through automation and robotics, eliminating many frontline, event management, and back-office departments. These concepts have been initiated in East Asia, where technology companies such as Alibaba are experimenting with semi-automated, full-service hotels including check-in and delivery robots using facial recognition and biometrics. This can also help rationalize brand portfolios and adjust standards such as housekeeping, restaurant hours, and amenities. However, this approach risks a clash with organized labor, increased government intervention at the state and local levels, cannibalizing existing brands and prolonging the recovery of business travel. Therefore, it's a classic low-cost disruption that is more likely to be generated from an industry outsider or a new platform than incumbents.

Strategy #2: Empowering Employees with Ownership and Deep Purpose

Hotel owners, led by private equity, should extend their best practices into hospitality and make frontline employees partial owners of real estate, giving them financial literacy and a voice in governance. As employee ownership scales, the workforce rather than the corporate office could be leveraged to develop a purpose for the company and its brands. This model gives rise to a new generation of future hotel owners, including economically disadvantaged groups currently being targeted in DEI-related initiatives. Implementing AI and new marketplace technologies could help identify, develop, and advance diverse, elite talents across an internal network of properties, including franchisees and like-minded external organizations, to cycle talent into new career opportunities. This would require a departure from current practices of hoarding talent in fiefdoms with brands and franchisees competing against each other and therefore create new legal and technology-related costs. However, it's likely to attract new talent into the industry at lower acquisition costs and generate more labor productivity.

Financial investments in the human resources technology sector are projected to reach $76 billion by 2030. Advances in information technology, predictive analytics, and artificial intelligence in HR processes will enable professionals to perform their usual duties more efficiently, but risk trapping them in a big tech ecosystem. New technologies, including artificial intelligence, provide opportunities to rethink approaches to retaining highly skilled and "promising" employees, as well as organizing the company's activities, to create brand-centric platforms, processes, and tools to take leadership positions through the implementation of the most innovative human capital practices, such as augmented and virtual reality-based learning and simulations, in the entire history of the service industry.

Within the talent engine, people analytics have become indispensable. Predictive analytics and working with big data are imperative to scale a multiunit service business: the analytical tools predict many important factors affecting the effective work of the company (e.g., employee behavior), calculating compensation models, the likelihood of turnover, motivating employees depending on their personal characteristics, and so on. A built-in and cognitive system analyzes the career experience and personality of the applicant and then offers career opportunities. With the consent of the user, the platform can use one's data from social networks and send it to the employer. In other countries, governments have been using machine learning and other technologies to determine and share a "social score" for every citizen.

As new AI-enabled marketplaces have emerged, the talent disruption has extended, from software developers and data scientists on platforms such as toptal.com and turing.com to creative industries such as writers, publicists, artists, and designers on upwork.com to highly specialized and regulated professions such as intellectual property and immigration attorneys on platforms such as legalzoom.com.

The topmost case in point is the health care industry, the largest source of jobs in the U.S. economy. Facing severe labor shortages and cost pressures, hospitals quickly evolved beyond hiring "traveling nurses" for several weeks at a time and are tackling the shortage of registered nurses with marketplace applications such as ShiftKey and CareRev that offer shorter gig work shifts and use algorithms to determine hourly compensation. Providence began using gig workers a year ago and has so far filled 13,000 shifts for nurses and other medical professions at its hospitals and nursing homes. The scope of the health care talent marketplace is likely to continue growing due to inflation, cost pressures, and a once-in-a-generation change in priorities among talents seen in the first ever unionization of "burned out and exhausted" resident physicians at teaching hospitals in markets such as New York City.

Strategy #3: Reinventing the Franchise Business Model

The cyclical hotel business, like the entire tourism ecosystem, is still in a vulnerable state, due to potentially permanent cutbacks in corporate travel, inflation, rising interest rates, geopolitical instability, long-term labor shortages in the airlines including pilots, and new environmental and other government regulations. An entire generation of travelers is also becoming accustomed to Airbnb, which is seeing a more affluent customer mix and is introducing new initiatives targeting business travelers. Of course, there are family offices and entrepreneurs in economy and limited-service hotels who have managed to adapt and even capitalize on the new challenges through mergers and acquisitions, but the business is now, in the literal sense of the word, turbulent. A permanent shrinkage of the business and its employment base and tax revenue is conceivable in many markets and across the country.

In this context, hotels could reset the franchising fee model and partner with cities to redirect funds, such as program fees and tax revenues, to support workforce-related initiatives. Asset managers could reallocate capital reserves to performance-based employee bonuses and housing allowances. Although this shift in priorities may not be what unions are seeking, it represents a step toward addressing the industry's talent disruption.

Conclusion

Today, service industry's stakeholders around the globe are rethinking their human capital strategies and deeply held beliefs or orthodoxies, starting with those pertaining to the definition of employees and what constitutes a workforce. Long-term changes in talent markets are calling into question traditional practices and legacy technologies regarding recruiting, training, and compensation. Conventional thinking is that the gig economy is focused on low-skilled hourly workers such as drivers, dog walkers, housekeepers, and plumbers. While the gig economy is certainly transforming frontline labor, its disruption is rooted in redefining the nature of work, compensation, and the market value of highly skilled talent, across service industries.

Based on empirical research, surveys, and interviews with the industry's frontline employees, the following themes emerge as opportunities to reset hospitality and mitigate the talent disruption:

- *Data-centric human capital solutions*: Rather than focus on marketing and advertising, service companies need to establish new platforms that differentiate their employer brands. Some of the solutions include:

- o Building an internal talent engine that can nurture and develop high-potential talents within the organization;
- o Using data-centric algorithms to rank and pay talents without bias based on their performance, skills, and potential; and
- o Incorporating gig as a work type into their core operation, allowing them to tap into a diverse and flexible pool of talents who can work on demand and on specific projects.

- To expedite innovation and the process of experimentation, service companies should *create an R&D center to experiment with AI and other innovative technologies such as GPT models and their applications.* This will require a change in the priorities of brand management, corporate development, procurement, and other corporate functions to focus more on deal-making and investments in emerging HR technologies and start-ups that can help build talent databases, rather than legacy platforms.

- *Employee ownership at the unit and operating company levels*: Aligning the interests of the general manager and executive team with the success of the business owners; making headlines when a general manager makes $1 million or more from profit sharing and exits; pre-empting unionization, but also working with labor unions as necessary to implement employee ownership and provide the workforce with financial literacy and experience to become business owners themselves 1 day. Success will be achieved by those organizations that can quickly scale ownership and profit-sharing concepts across their portfolio.

- *Measuring and reporting human capital*: Translating quality and depth of management, skills, and expertise into intangible assets that are amortized; establishing metrics and key performance indicators, using the income approach, starting with the worth of elite talent and the lifetime value of the earnings of the property leadership team, benchmarked internally and externally similar to customer and financial metrics; assigning cross-functional task forces led by elite talent whose aim is to develop rising talent and quantifying the value created from such initiatives; an integrated approach to reducing turnover and building human capital reflected in the cash flows of the property.

- *New leadership competencies*: Breaking down silos and redefining HR by rotating leadership of its core functions among corporate executives, including marketing, operations, technology, finance, and development. For a new generation of CHROs to be a fundamentally different type of leader—a tech savvy "digital leader" who can use big data and AI to develop a culture of innovation—expand risk appetite with more external hires and create conditions for accelerating the time from front line to general manager and general manager to CEO.

- *Establishing social purpose from the bottom up, not top down*: Allowing each property to determine how to best make social impact and advance ESG or the aspects of ESG it finds most relevant, rather than dictate goals set by the corporate office; a truly "glocal" company that is less Euro-centric that develops local brands, products, and services to create new wealth in every geographic region in response to consumer and market needs.

Structural changes in the labor markets, big data technologies, immigration bottlenecks, human capital disclosures, and a growing sense of urgency to improve diversity are long-term trends contributing to a discontinuity or "talent disruption." For service industries such as hospitality, the talent disruption marks the end of labor as we know it. In this context, the capital markets are quickly distinguishing between companies that are implementing gradual changes from those that are building or acquiring new competencies that build human capital in response to a truly turbulent socioeconomic and geopolitical environment.

In conclusion, incremental measures including wage increases, daily pay, or gig shifts will have minimal impact on the deep-rooted issues facing the service sector including the hospitality, health care providers, and the retail industry. It is crucial to fundamentally reconsider the labor model to defeat the ongoing talent disruption. Failure to act strategically will only accelerate the crisis and permanently shrink employment in an industry that has a rich history of entrepreneurship. It is time for collective action and innovative solutions that prioritize worker well-being, address income inequality, and revive the travel boom. By investing in human capital, the hotel industry can create a more equitable and prosperous future for all stakeholders involved.

APPENDIX I

Table AI.1 Value migration to new intermediaries

Label	1 Jan 18 2018 Market Cap ($MM)	1 Jan 18 % Share	1 Jan 19 2019 Market Cap ($MM)	1 Jan 19 % Share	31 Mar 23 2023 Market Cap ($MM)	31 Mar 23 % Share
Marriott	49,750	20.1%	36,780	18.6%	51,290	9.4%
InterContinental	12,040	4.9%	10,430	5.3%	11,670	2.1%
Other Chains	26,048	10.5%	4,578	2.3%	20,399	3.8%
Hilton	25,660	10.4%	4,038	2.0%	37,530	6.9%
Hyatt	8,888	3.6%	20,620	10.4%	11,970	2.2%
Expedia	18,990	7.7%	11,470	5.8%	14,880	2.7%
Booking.com	88,420	35.7%	7,163	3.6%	99,860	18.4%
TripAdvisor	4,859	2.0%	16,640	8.4%	2,800	0.5%
Airbnb	–	0.0%	78,370	39.7%	78,540	14.5%
Google Travel	–	0.0%	7,436	3.8%	199,200	36.7%
VC Backed	–	0.0%	–	0.0%	1,973	0.4%
Timeshare	13,135	5.3%	–	0.0%	13,056	2.4%
Total	247,790	100%	197,525	100%	543,168.42	100%

Table AI.2 Valuation of health care companies, March 2023

Hospitals and Delivery							
Company	Ticker Symbol	ROIC	Value Creation ($M)	TEV/ EBITDA	Market Cap. ($M)	Weight	Price/ Book (Current)
HCA Healthcare	HCA	16.0%	$3,607	8.8×	$73,107	34%	NM
Tenet Healthcare	THC	7.3%	$302	6.3×	$6,077	3%	5.5×
Universal Health Services	UHS	7.3%	$92	8.0×	$8,982	4%	1.7×
Community Health Systems, Inc.	CYH	2.7%	($256)	9.0×	$643	0%	NM

(Continued)

(*Continued*)

Company	Ticker Symbol	ROIC	Value Creation ($M)	TEV/ EBITDA	Market Cap. ($M)	Weight	Price/ Book (Current)
Select Medical Holdings	SEM	6.5%	$25	8.9×	$3,288	2%	3.2×
Acadia Healthcare Company, Inc.	ACHC	7.2%	($25)	13.3×	$6,598	3%	2.4×
Encompass Health Corporation	EHC	9.9%	$132	9.6×	$5,395	3%	4.6×
Modiv-Care Inc.	MODV	2.6%	($48)	14.4×	$1,190	1%	3.1×
Teladoc Health, Inc.	TDOC	–2.2%	($380)	NM	$4,212	2%	1.5×
DaVita Inc.	DVA	7.2%	$126	7.4×	$7,333	3%	11.4×
CVS Health Corporation	CVS	6.7%	($682)	6.6×	$95,422	45%	1.4×
Total/ Weighted Average		9.8%	$2,893	7.7×	$212,246	100%	1.5×

Table AI.3 Valuation of traditional retail companies, March 2023

Traditional Retail							
Company	Ticker Symbol	ROIC	Value Creation ($M)	TEV/ EBITDA	Market Cap. ($M)	Weight	Price/ Book (Current)
Walmart	WMT	9.7%	$3,075	11.8×	$397,475	30%	5.3×
Home Depot	HD	31.5%	$12,551	12.1×	$299,534	22%	212.1×
Costco	COST	17.6%	$3,032	20.9×	$220,354	16%	9.8×
Kroger	KR	8.2%	$381	6.5×	$35,421	3%	3.3×
Walgreen Boots Alliance	WBA	2.7%	($2,786)	10.0×	$29,836	2%	1.4×

Traditional Retail							
Company	Ticker Symbol	ROIC	Value Creation ($M)	TEV/ EBITDA	Market Cap. ($M)	Weight	Price/ Book (Current)
Target	TGT	12.2%	$1,610	13.1×	$76,250	6%	6.4×
Lowe's	LOW	25.3%	$4,401	10.2×	$119,253	9%	NM
Dollar Tree	DLTR	8.6%	$198	8.0×	$31,757	2%	3.7×
Dollar General	DG	10.8%	$882	10.6×	$46,114	3%	8.0×
TJX Companies	TJX	20.1%	$2,318	10.8×	$90,315	7%	14.8×
Total/ Weighted Average		17.9%	$25,661	12.9×	$1,346,308	100%	52.2×

Table AI.4 Valuation of casino and gaming companies, March 2023

Traditional Media							
Company	Ticker Symbol	ROIC	Value Creation ($M)	TEV/ EBITDA	Market Cap. ($M)	Weight	Price/ Book (Current)
Disney	DIS	2.8%	($7,678)	17.0×	$182,918	49%	1.9×
MGM	MGM	0.2%	($2,766)	12.7×	$16,564	4%	3.3×
Caesars	CZR	4.6%	($353)	10.5×	$10,503	3%	2.7×
Las Vegas Sands	LVS	−4.3%	($2,315)	159.8×	$43,907	12%	11.1×
Live Nation	LYV	4.6%	($260)	11.8×	$16,119	4%	NM
Fox	FOX	11.4%	$821	6.6×	$17,551	5%	1.6×
Paramount	PARA	4.3%	($733)	9.7×	$14,657	4%	0.6×
Wynn Resorts, Limited	WYNN	−2.3%	($1,075)	39.4×	$12,722	3%	NM
Boyd Gaming Corporation	BYD	13.1%	$347	7.1×	$6,533	2%	4.2×
Genting Singapore Ltd	GIGNF	4.4%	($303)	13.0×	$10,043	3%	1.6×

(Continued)

(*Continued*)

			Traditional Media				
Company	Ticker Symbol	ROIC	Value Creation ($M)	TEV/ EBITDA	Market Cap. ($M)	Weight	Price/ Book (Current)
Melco Resorts and Entertainment	MLCO	−8.7%	($1,249)	NM	$5,666	2%	NM
Sands China Ltd	SCHYY	−10.9%	($14,016)	NM	$28,224	7%	228.1×
Monarch Casino & Resort Inc.	MCRI	15.7%	$44	8.6×	$1,418	0%	2.8×
Churchill Downs Incorporated	CHDN	7.8%	$44	20.9×	$9,622	3%	15.5×
Total/ Weighted Average		1.5%	($29,492)	31.3×	$376,446	100%	20.1×

APPENDIX II

Top 50 U.S. Hotel GMs and Their Worth (2022)

Table AII.1 Top 50 U.S. Hotel GMs 2022

Rank	General Manager	Worth	Property	Employer Name
1	Pradeep Raman	$472,831	Baccarat Hotel & Residences	SH Hotels & Resorts
2	Mickael Damelincourt	$359,964	Trump International Hotel Washington DC	Trump Hotels
3	Howard Taylor	$217,365	Crowne Plaza Los Angeles	Crescent Hotels & Resorts
4	Sam Basu	$385,046	JW Marriott Orlando Bonnet Creek Resort & Spa	Marriott International
5	Stacy Martin	$328,129	Le Méridien Dallas, The Stoneleigh	HEI Hotels & Resorts
6	Juan Webster	$322,342	Sagamore Pendry Baltimore	Montage Hotels & Resorts
7	Juan Calderon	$328,129	Marriott Dallas Downtown The St. Regis Bal Harbour Resort	Marriott International
8	Winfred van Workum	$472,831	Miami	Marriott International
9	Jorge Tito	$472,831	Yotel New York	Yotel
10	Vivin Kuriakose	$359,964	Marriott Gaithesburg Washingtonian	Marriott International
11	Tamas Vago	$386,733	Hilton Fort Lauderdale Beach Resort	Hilton
12	Vanessa Williams	$399,877	Waldorf Astoria Beverly Hills	Hilton
13	Ernesto Fernandez	$217,365	Andaz Savannah	Hyatt Hotels Corporation
14	Titus Negrescu	$472,831	Gild Hall, a Thompson Hotel	Hyatt Hotels Corporation
15	Marlene Poynder	$472,831	The Carlyle Hotel	Rosewood Hotels & Resorts

(Continued)

(*Continued*)

Rank	General Manager	Worth	Property	Employer Name
16	Kerry Ringham	$336,691	The Westin Houston, Memorial City	Marriott International
17	Michelle Mcclintock	$156,419	Hampton Inn Ann Arbor South	Gulph Creek Hotels
18	Matthew Bailey	$520,000	Montage Kapalua Bay	Montage Hotels & Resorts
19	Nenad Praporski	$327,406	Fairmont Austin	Fairmont Hotels & Resorts
20	Rita Healy	$327,406	Sheraton Austin George-town Hotel	Marriott International
21	Thomas H. Scaramellino	$452,091	Westin Mission Hills Golf Resort & Spa	Marriott International
22	Steven Chou	$336,691	The Post Oak Hotel Uptown Houston	Landry's
23	Fred Sawyers	$385,046	Signia by Hilton Orlando Bonnet Creek and Waldorf Astoria Orlando	Hilton
24	Stefan Gruvberger	$377,690	The LaSalle Chicago	Aimbridge Hospitality
25	Julian Tucker	$399,877	Andaz West Hollywood	Hyatt Hotels Corporation
26	Ramon Ventura-Guzman	$336,691	JW Marriott Houston	Marriott International
27	Danny Williams	$385,046	Trump International Beach Resort	Trump Hotels
28	Jorge Landa	$366,114	InterContinental Houston - Medical Center	Interconti-nental Hotels Group (IHG)
29	Tom M. Segesta	$336,691	Four Seasons Hotel Houston	Four Seasons Hotels & Resorts
30	William Gomes	$228,769	Hilton Garden Inn at Roslyn	Concord Hospitality
31	Perry Ellis H.	$316,554	InterContinental St Paul Riverfront	Interconti-nental Hotels Group (IHG)
32	Mark Irgang	$381,633	Marriott New York JFK Airport	Chartwell Hospitality

Rank	General Manager	Worth	Property	Employer Name
33	Justin Jaramillo	$256,142	Residence Inn Austin North/Parmer Lane, SpringHill Suites Austin North/Parmer Lane	Aimbridge Hospitality
34	Angela Thompson	$334,147	Hotel Vinache	Crescent Hotels & Resorts
35	Brian R. ODay	$322,342	The Hotel Hershey	Hershey Entertainment & Resorts
36	Robert Holmes	$472,831	Iroquois Hotel New York	Triumph Hotels
37	Ronald Lamers	$336,691	St. Regis Houston	Marriott International
38	Charles Shirk	$472,831	Hilton Scranton Conference Center	Welcome Group
39	Paul F. Boudreaux	$327,406	Radisson Hotel Austin	Commonwealth Hotels
40	Jeff Makhlouf	$359,964	The Westin Waltham Boston	Hei Hotels & Resorts
41	Steven M. Wieder	$359,964	Avery Hotel Georgetown	TBC Hotels
42	Scott Selvaggi	$295,451	Sheraton Tampa Brandon	Linchris Hotel Corporation
43	Ian Heffron	$411,212	Hotel 166 - Magnificent Mile Chicago	Fillmore Hospitality
44	Clay R. Andrews	$399,877	The Godfrey Hotel Hollywood	Oxford Capital Group
45	Lee Berthelsen Leon	$472,831	Four Points By Sheraton Manhattan Midtown West	Real Hospitality Group
46	Ian Gee	$369,235	Sheraton Park Hotel at the Anaheim Resort	Aimbridge Hospitality
47	Karan Kakar	$386,733	Cadillac Hotel & Beach Club	Hersha Hospitality Management (HHM)
48	Odyssey Leach	$295,451	Hyatt Place Tampa	Impact Properties

(Continued)

(Continued)

Rank	General Manager	Worth	Property	Employer Name
49	Brenda Kramer	$356,347	Hampton Inn & Suites Portland Pearl District	Raymond Management Company
50	Ann Olsson	$377,690	Driftwood Hospitality Management	Driftwood Hospitality Management

Note: Time period: 2022.

APPENDIX III

Diversity Gap and Target at Regional, GM, and Director Levels

Table AIII.1 Regional operations—diversity opportunity

	Gender		Ethnicity				
	Female	Male	White*	Asian†	Latino/ Hispanic	Black	Other‡
Area Manager	25%	75%	75.40%	6.60%	11.20%	3.90%	2.90%
Regional VP of Food & Beverage	26%	74%	80.90%	1.80%	10.00%	2.70%	4.60%
Regional VP of Hotel Operations	25%	75%	77.60%	9.10%	8.60%	2.10%	2.60%
Regional VP of Sales & Marketing	41%	59%	80.10%	7.20%	8.70%	2.70%	1.30%

*White or Caucasian descent (not Hispanic or Latino).
†Asian includes Native Hawaiian or Pacific Islanders (not Hispanic or Latino).
‡Other includes American Indian, Alaska Native, two or more races, or "I do not wish to provide this information."
Source: Hotel Industry Demographics at Regional Operations Level.
Note: Highlighted cells are the areas with potential for promotion.

We start our analysis of how the gap could be closed at the GM level by assessing assistant GMs, hotel managers who run the rooms side of larger properties, and directors of finance. To begin with, GMs are 80 percent male and 85 percent white with only 6 percent representation among Hispanics and 2.6 percent representation among black people.

The gender gap at the GM level can be reduced to 147 percent by promoting women in assistant GM positions. Likewise, promoting minority talents from assistant GM, hotel manager, and finance director positions will reduce the minority gap to 118 percent at the GM level.

Table AIII.2 GM operations and finance—diversity opportunity

	Gender		Ethnicity				
	Female	Male	White*	Asian†	Latino/ Hispanic	Black	Other‡
Assistant General Manager	31%	69%	83%	4.2%	6.8%	5.0%	1.0%
General Manager	20%	80%	84.9%	4.8%	6.0%	2.6%	1.7%
Hotel Manager	25%	75%	81%	5.6%	8.3%	2.7%	1.4%
Director of Finance	29%	71%	75.4%	9.6%	9.5%	3.1%	2.4%

*White or Caucasian descent (not Hispanic or Latino).
†Asian includes Native Hawaiian or Pacific Islanders (not Hispanic or Latino).
‡Other includes American Indian, Alaska Native, two or more races, or "I do not wish to provide this information."
Source: Hotel Industry Demographics at Regional Operations Level.
Note: Highlighted cells are the areas with potential for promotion.

Next, we analyzed the primary director roles reporting to the GM which could offer significant opportunities to improve diversity in the near future. Directors of sales and spa have remarkable gender diversity while rooms and revenue management are far below the target.

Promoting female talents from sales and spa director positions could reduce the gender gap at the GM level to 96 percent. Promoting minority talents from revenue management, rooms director, and spa director positions would reduce the minority gap at the GM level to 106 percent.

Table AIII.3 Property-level directors reporting to the GM

	Gender		Ethnicity				
	Female	Male	White*	Asian†	Latino/ Hispanic	Black	Other‡
Director of Revenue Management	36%	64%	75.3%	10.3%	9.5%	2.9%	2%
Director of Room	35%	65%	69.8%	10.8%	12.1%	4.4%	2.9%

	Gender		Ethnicity				
	Female	Male	White*	Asian[†]	Latino/ Hispanic	Black	Other[‡]
Director of Sales & Marketing	68%	32%	76.8%	7.4%	10.8%	3.8%	1.2%
Director of SPA	74%	26%	78.6%	6%	12.5%	2.1%	0.8%

*White or Caucasian descent (not Hispanic or Latino).
[†]Asian includes Native Hawaiian or Pacific Islanders (not Hispanic or Latino).
[‡]Other includes American Indian, Alaska Native, two or more races, or "I do not wish to provide this information."
Source: Hotel Industry Demographics at Regional Operations Level.
Note: Highlighted cells are the areas with potential for promotion.

We then proceeded to analyze the secondary director roles reporting to the GM, typically in full-service properties, which could offer significant opportunities to improve diversity in the near future. While directors of catering and human resources have considerable gender diversity, housekeeping and food and beverage director roles have considerably less.

Promoting female talents from catering and HR director positions to GM positions can reduce the gender gap to 125 percent. Promoting Latino/Hispanic talents from F&B, housekeeping, and HR director positions and black talents from housekeeping director positions could reduce the diversity gap to 109 percent.

Table AIII.4 Property-level directors reporting to the GM

	Gender		Ethnicity				
	Female	Male	White*	Asian[†]	Latino/ Hispanic	Black	Other[‡]
Director of Food & Beverage	20%	80%	72.9%	6.5%	12.1%	4.4%	4.1%
Director of Catering & Conference Services	71%	29%	80.4%	5.4%	10.8%	2.2%	1.2%

(Continued)

(*Continued*)

	Gender		Ethnicity				
	Female	Male	White*	Asian†	Latino/ Hispanic	Black	Other‡
Director of House- keeping	40%	60%	56.3%	9.9%	21.7%	9.3%	2.8%
Director of Human Resources	74%	26%	67.4%	10.1%	14.4%	6.3%	1.8%

*White or Caucasian descent (not Hispanic or Latino).
†Asian includes Native Hawaiian or Pacific Islanders (not Hispanic or Latino).
‡Other includes American Indian, Alaska Native, two or more races, or "I do not wish to provide this information."
Source: Hotel Industry Demographics at Regional Operations Level.
Note: Highlighted cells are the areas with potential for promotion.

In order to promote these employees from within and build for the future, the industry must backfill and retain or build upon the diverse talent pool that already exists in the heart of the operation. This includes supervisor roles where talents manage teams, such as front-office supervisors and restaurant managers that have relatively high representation of women and black people, more in line with their respective frontline representation. Additionally, there are some areas of improvement potential such as restaurant management, which is otherwise a remarkably diverse department. Restaurant management lags in terms of Latino/Hispanic representation and there are few women in culinary management roles in U.S. hotels (see Table 3.5).

Promoting qualified women from front office, guest relations/experience supervisor, and restaurant management positions to director roles would backfill women in director roles by only 20 percent overall. Similarly, promoting Latino/Hispanic talents from front office, guest relation, and executive chef positions as well as black talents from front office and restaurant management positions would backfill with minorities in director roles by 32 percent. This implies that one of the biggest hurdles for the industry to achieve its diversity targets internally is to do three times as well in training, developing, and retaining the remarkably diverse front line, whose turnover averages between 75 and 115 percent depending on the type of hotel and market. If this is not achieved, then the hotel industry must recruit a very large pool of diverse talents at the supervisor level from other industries and internationally.

Table AIII.5 Property-level supervisor positions

	Gender		Ethnicity				
	Female	Male	White*	Asian[†]	Latino/Hispanic	Black	Other[‡]
Front Office Supervisor	42%	58%	62.7%	12.9%	11.4%	10.2%	2.8%
Guest Relations/ Experience Supervisor	42%	58%	62.6%	13.9%	13%	4.4%	6.1%
Executive Chef	9%	91%	68.6%	8.6%	11.7%	5.7%	5.4%
Restaurant Manager	40%	60%	66.1%	10%	6%	14.1%	3.8%

*White or Caucasian descent (not Hispanic or Latino).

[†]Asian includes Native Hawaiian or Pacific Islanders (not Hispanic or Latino).

[‡]Other includes American Indian, Alaska Native, two or more races, or "I do not wish to provide this information."

Source: Hotel Industry Demographics at Regional Operations Level.

Note: Highlighted cells are the areas with potential for promotion.

APPENDIX IV

Table IV.1 Typology of displaced people

Type of Movement	Description	Cases
Substate	Attempt by group(s) within an existing state to establish autonomy, in the form of either more autonomy or a new state; based on historical, ethnic, or other factors	Serbs, Croatia, Muslims in former Yugoslavia; Albanians in Kosovo; Somali clans; Khmer Rouge in Cambodia; Shia in Iraq; Tamils in Sri Lanka
Trans-state	Independence movements involving a concentrated grouping of a people situated across international boundaries	Kurds in Iraq, Iran, and Syria; Armenians in Nagorno-Karabakh
Dispersed peoples	Ethnically or culturally, or distinct peoples, intermixed through the same territory	Tatarstan and Volga Regions in Russia; Bosnia-Hercegovina
Representative	A population seeks to transform its form of governance, usually toward a more democratic one	South Africa; Cambodia; Haiti; Angola; Nigeria

Note: Self-determination movements often fall into more than one of the categories outlined above.

Source: Morton Halperin, David Scheffer, and Partricia L. Small, eds., *Self-Determination in the New World Order* (Washington: Carnegie Endowment, 1992).

Notes

Chapter 1

1. Hamel (1994).
2. Ortiz (2023).

Chapter 2

1. Bartlett and Ghoshal (1989).
2. Effler (2022).
3. Bhojwani (2023).
4. Fuller, Raman, Sage-Gavin, and Hines (2021).
5. Fortune (2022).

Chapter 4

1. Lewis (2004).
2. Data Source: www.spotrac.com

Chapter 5

1. *Building the Assets of Low and Moderate Income Workers and Their Families* (2019).
2. Gelsi (2023).
3. Dudley and Rouen (2021).
4. Sutherland (2022).
5. Morgan (2022).
6. Coburn and Liberson (2023).

Chapter 6

1. Bhattacharjee and Ferdous (2018).
2. Sapong (2012).

3. Starr (2016).
4. Baskas (2023).

Chapter 7

1. O'Neill (2022).
2. Hamel and Prahalad (1985).
3. Freedom House (2023).
4. Khanna (2018).
5. ZAWYA (2019).
6. Economist (2003), pp. 56–57.

Chapter 9

1. OECD (2019).

Chapter 10

1. World Economic Forum (2024).
2. Center for MIT Entrepreneurship (2018).
3. Restaurant Business (2023).
4. Heinrich Böll Foundation (2020).
5. The White House (2023)
6. University World News (2023)
7. World Economic Forum (2023)
8. Sheehan, M (2023)

References

Bartlett, C.A. and S. Ghoshal. 1989. *Managing Across Borders: The Transnational Solution*. Boston, MA: Harvard Business School Press.

Baskas, H. March 8, 2023. "That 'Bed Tax' on Your Hotel Bill Isn't Going Anywhere, but the Things It Funds Are Changing." *NBC News*. www.nbcnews.com/business/travel/hotel-bed-tax-biden-junk-fees-rcna70405 (accessed June 2023).

Bhattacharjee, Y. and I. Ferdous. September 4, 2018. "How Indian Americans Came to Run Half of All U.S. Motels." *National Geographic*. www.nationalgeographic.com/culture/article/south-asia-america-motels-immigration (accessed June 2023).

Bhojwani, R. January 15, 2023. "Narrowing of Bid-Ask Spread to Result in Record Hotel Sales, Plus Six Other Predictions for 2023." *CoStar*. www.costar.com/article/1504568489/narrowing-of-bid-ask-spread-to-result-in-record-hotel-sales-plus-six-other-predictions-for-2023 (accessed June 2023).

Building the Assets of Low and Moderate Income Workers and Their Families. 2019. Rutgers.

Center for MIT Entrepreneurship. 2018. *Spyce, MIT-Born Robotic Kitchen Startup, Launches Restaurant*.

Coburn, B. and D. Liberson. June 7, 2023. "The Untapped Opportunity of Broad-Based Ownership." *Harvard Advanced Leadership Initiative*. www.sir.advancedleadership.harvard.edu/articles/the-untapped-opportunity-of-broad-based-ownership (accessed June 2023).

Dudley, T. and E. Rouen. May 13, 2021. "The Big Benefits of Employee Ownership." *Harvard Business Review*. https://hbr.org/2021/05/the-big-benefits-of-employee-ownership (accessed June 2023).

Heinrich Böll Foundation. 2020. *Multilateralism 2.0 In Search of New Partnerships for the German and European Foreign Policy*.

The Economist. June 8, 2023. "Why Sequoia Capital is sawing off its Chinese branch." *The Economist*. https://economist.com/business/2023/06/08/why-sequoia-capital-is-sawing-off-its-chinese-branch (accessed June 2023)

The White House. 2023. *Executive Order on the Safe, Secure, and Trustworthy Development and Use of Artificial Intelligence*.

Effler, G. September 15, 2022. *Third-Party Hotel Management Companies Facing Higher Guest Expectations as Room Rates Increase, J.D. Power Finds*. J.D. Power. www.jdpower.com/business/press-releases/2022-north-america-third-party-hotel-management-guest-satisfaction (accessed June 2023).

Fortune. 2022. "100 Best Companies to Work For." *Fortune.* https://fortune
.com/ranking/best-companies/ (accessed June 2023).

Freedom House. 2023. "New Report: Global Freedom Declines for
17th Consecutive Year, but May Be Approaching a Turning Point." *Freedom
House.* https://freedomhouse.org/article/new-report-global-freedom-
declines-17th-consecutive-year-may-be-approaching-turning-point (accessed
June 2023).

Fuller, J., M. Raman, E. Sage-Gavin, and K. Hines. 2021. *Hidden Workers:
Untapped Talent.* Harvard Business School. www.hbs.edu/managing-the-
future-of-work/Documents/research/hiddenworkers09032021.pdf (accessed
June 2023).

Gelsi, S. February 6, 2023. "KKR Brings Employee Ownership to Latest
Mega Buyout." *Private Equity News.* www.penews.com/articles/kkr-brings-
employee-ownership-to-latest-mega-buyout-20230206 (accessed June 2023).

Hamel, G. 1994. *Competing for the Future.* Harvard Business School Press.
https://hbr.org/1994/07/competing-for-the-future (accessed June 2023).

Hamel, G. and C. Prahalad. July 1985. "Do You Really Have a Global Strategy?"
Harvard Business Review. https://hbr.org/1985/07/do-you-really-have-a-
global-strategy (accessed June 2023).

Khanna, T. 2018. *Billions of Entrepreneurs: How China and India Are Reshaping
Their Futures and Yours.* Boston, MA: Harvard Business School Press.

Lewis, M. 2004. *Moneyball.* WW Norton.

Morgan, A. March 3, 2022. "The Venetian Resort Hotel Casino to Launch
'Equity-Like' Sharing Scheme." *World Casino News.* https://news
.worldcasinodirectory.com/the-venetian-resort-hotel-casino-to-launch-
equity-like-sharing-scheme-100087 (accessed June 2023).

OECD. 2019. *ARTIFICIAL INTELLIGENCE & RESPONSIBLE BUSINESS
CONDUCT.* OECD.https://mneguidelines.oecd.org/RBC-and-artificial-
intelligence.pdf (accessed October 2023)

O'Neill, S. November 8, 2022. *Global Hotel Sector Is Turning a New Corner:
New JLL Report.* Skift. https://skift.com/blog/global-hotel-sector-has-turned-
a-corner-says-new-jll-report/ (accessed June 2023).

Ortiz, R. March 28, 2023. "Rising Labor Costs: Drivers Include Inflation,
High Minimum Wage, and More Hours Worked." *Lodging.* https://
lodgingmagazine.com/rising-labor-costs-drivers-include-inflation-high-
minimum-wage-and-more-hours-worked/ (accessed June 2023).

Restaurant Business. 2023. *Sweetgreen's robotic Infinite Kitchen is Finally Open.*

Sapong, E. May 13, 2012. "The 'Patel-Motel' Phenomenon; Immigrant
Entrepreneurs From India, Many With the Same Last Name, Now Dominate
the Hospitality Industry Here and Around the Nation." *The Buffalo News.*

https://buffalonews.com/news/the-patel-motel-phenomenon-immigrant-entrepreneurs-from-india-many-with-the-same-last-name-now/article_ b5404a8b-1e03-5632-9dbb-e197d9ee3254.html (accessed June 2023).

Sheehan, M. 2023. *China's AI Regulations and How They Get Made.*

Starr, A. March 5, 2016. "Here to Stay: How Indian-Born Innkeepers Revolutionized America's Motels." *npr.* www.npr.org/2016/03/05/46918 0918/here-to-stay-how-indian-born-innkeepers-revolutionized-americas-motels (accessed June 2023).

Sutherland, B. May 31, 2022. "KKR Wins by Treating Workers More Like Owners." *The Washington Post.* www.washingtonpost.com/business/kkr-wins-by-treating-workers-more-like-owners/2022/05/31/04e9c9bc-e0da-11ec-ae64-6b23e5155b62_story.html (accessed June 2023).

University World News. 2023. *Education and research minister unveils AI Action Plan.*

World Economic Forum. 2023. *The AI Governance Summit: Key sessions, talking points and how to livestream the event.*

World Economic Forum. 2024. *Emerging tech, like AI, is poised to make healthcare more accurate, accessible and sustainable.*

Zawya. July 26, 2019. *Labor Ministry: 100% Saudization of 20 Hospitality Jobs as of Next Year.* Zawya. www.zawya.com/en/economy/labor-ministry-100-saudization-of-20-hospitality-jobs-as-of-next-year-l33hrx5v (accessed June 2023).

Sources

Employee Ownership

Ferguson, D., F. Berger, and P. Francese. 1987. "Intrapreneuring in Hospitality Organizations." *International Journal of Hospitality Management* 6, no. 1, pp. 23–31.

Godoy, K. March 21, 2018. "In With the New: Intrapreneurship and Innovation in Hospitality." *Cornell SC Johnson College of Business.* https://business.cornell .edu/hub/2018/03/21/intrapreneurship-innovation/ (accessed June 2023).

Mogelonsky, L. March 30, 2016. "Intrapreneurs Are the Lifeblood of a Hotel." *HospitalityNet.* www.hospitalitynet.org/opinion/4075102.html (accessed June 2023).

Molla, R. November 1, 2021. "Service Workers Are Getting Paid More Than Ever: It's Not Enough." *Vox Magazine.* www.vox.com/recode/22748448/ service-food-hotel-workers-pay-raise-resignation-jobs-wages-benefits (accessed June 2023).

Diversity, Equity, and Inclusion

Geller, J. 2011. *Global Business Driven HR Transformation: The Journey Continues.* Deloitte. www2.deloitte.com/content/dam/Deloitte/de/Documents/human-capital/global-business-driven-hr-transformation.pdf (accessed June 2023).

Friedersdorf, C. January 18, 2023. "The Paradox of Diversity Trainings." *The Atlantic.* www.theatlantic.com/newsletters/archive/2023/01/diversity-training-paradox-intolerance/672756/ (accessed June 2023).

Frost, S. and D. Kalman. 2016. *Inclusive Talent Management: How Business Can Thrive in an Age of Diversity.* Kogan Page.

Mirza, A. August 11, 2022. "The End of Labor as We Know It: Implications for Hotel CEOs." *Hospitalitynet.* www.hospitalitynet.org/external/4111946.html (accessed June 2023).

Nieves, J. and A. Quintana. 2018. "Human Resource Practices and Innovation in the Hotel Industry: The Mediating Role of Human Capital." *Tourism and Hospitality Research* 18, no. 1, pp. 72–83.

Franchise Business Models and Business Strategy

Berger, R. April 21, 2023. "Private Equity Makes Inroads Into the Hospital Sector." *Globest.com.* www.globest.com/2023/04/21/%E2%80%8Bprivate-equity-makes-inroads-into-the-hospital-sector/#:~:text=PESP%20found%20that%20at%20least,all%20proprietary%20for%2Dprofit%20hospitals (accessed June 2023).

Fleron, A. and S. Singhal. September 16, 2022. *The Gathering Storm: The Uncertain Future of US Healthcare.* McKinsey & Company. www.mckinsey.com/industries/healthcare/our-insights/the-gathering-storm-the-uncertain-future-of-us-healthcare (accessed June 2023).

Kreimer, S. December 14, 2021. *Health Systems Reap Big Rewards by Acquiring Practices, but Physicians Aren't Sharing in Those Benefits, Study Finds.* Fierce Healthcare. www.fiercehealthcare.com/practices/health-systems-reap-big-rewards-by-acquiring-practices-but-physicians-aren-t-sharing (accessed June 2023).

Lagasse, J. March 10, 2023. "Hospitals' Labor Costs Increased 258% Over the Last Three Years." *HIMSS.* www.healthcarefinancenews.com/news/hospitals-labor-costs-increased-258-over-last-three-years (accessed June 2023).

Lodging Staff. August 2, 2021. "2021 Guide to Franchising." *Lodging Magazine.* https://lodgingmagazine.com/2021-guide-to-franchising/ (accessed June 2023).

Pace, G., N. Janiga, and D. Lo. October 16, 2020. *The Value of Branding in Healthcare.* Healthcare Appraisers. https://healthcareappraisers.com/the-value-of-branding-in-healthcare/ (accessed June 2023).

Russell, K. and B. Kim. January 12, 2021. *HVS U.S. Hotel Franchise Fee Guide 2020.* HVS. www.hvs.com/article/8966-HVS-US-Hotel-Franchise-Fee-Guide-2020 (accessed June 2023).

Employer Ranking

Arpita. October 31, 2021. *Infosys Reskilling Employees on War-Scale via Talent Marketplace; 34% Hiring via Reskilling.* Trak.in. https://trak.in/tags/business/2021/10/31/infosys-reskilling-employees-on-war-scale-via-talent-marketplace-34-hiring-via-reskilling/ (accessed June 2023).

Service Profit Chain

Walters, R. 2018. *Reevaluating the Service Profit Chain Model: With Special Consideration to the HRT Segment.* California State Polytechnic University.

Hotel Valuation/Economic Trend

CBRE. March 7, 2023. *U.S. Cap Rate Survey H2 2022.* CBRE. www.cbre.com/insights/reports/us-cap-rate-survey-h2-2022 (accessed June 2023).

Deloitte. 2021. *The Future of Hospitality: Uncovering Opportunities to Recover and Thrive in the New Normal.* Deloitte. www2.deloitte.com/content/dam/Deloitte/ca/Documents/consumer-industrial-products/ca-future-of-hospitality-pov-aoda-en.pdf (accessed June 2023).

Deloitte. 2021. *The Future of HR in the Face of COVID-19.* Deloitte. www2.deloitte.com/lu/en/pages/human-capital/articles/accelerating-digital-HR-during-and-post-covid-19.html (accessed June 2023).

Galun, J. April 2, 2019. *How Can Hospitality Join the Agile Movement?* The Hospitality Technology. https://hospitalitytech.com/how-can-hospitality-join-agile-movement (accessed June 2023).

Lawler, E. and J. Boudreau. 2015. *Global Trends in Human Resource Management: A Twenty-Year Analysis.* Stanford Business Books.

Pine, B. and J. Gilmore. 1999. *The Experience Economy: Work Is Theater and Every Business Is a Stage.* Harvard Business School Press.

PwC. 2023. *RevPAR to Finish 2022 at Record Highs, but Economic Headwinds Strengthen for 2023.* PwC. www.pwc.com/us/en/industries/consumer-markets/hospitality-leisure/us-hospitality-directions.html (accessed June 2023).

Simons, R. 2011. *Human Resource Management: Issues, Challenges, and Opportunities*. Apple Academic Press.

Sperance, C. 2020. *Accor Just Restructured the Company in the Middle of a Pandemic: Why Now?* Skift. https://skift.com/2020/09/11/accor-just-restructured-the-company-in-the-middle-of-a-pandemic-why-now/ (accessed June 2023).

STR. February 8, 2023. *U.S. Hotel Revenues, Profits and Labor Costs Reached Record-Highs in 2022*. STR. https://str.com/press-release/us-hotel-revenues-profits-and-labor-costs-reached-record-highs-2022 (accessed June 2023).

Globalization

Burke, R., M. Koyuncu, W. Jing, and L. Fiksenbaum. 2009. "Work Engagement Among Hotel Managers in Beijing, China: Potential Antecedents and Consequences." *Tourism Review* 64, no. 3, pp. 4–18.

Garcia-Herrero, A. 2022. "Slowbalisation in the Context of US-China Decoupling." *Intereconomics* 57, no. 6, pp. 352–358.

Gates, S. 1994. *The Changing Global Role of the Human Resource Function*. Conference Board Inc.

Ghoshal, S. 1987. "Global Strategy: An Organizing Framework." *Strategic Management Journal* 8, no. 2, p. 425.

Kar, A. and I. Mahapatra. 2018. "HR Practices and Trends: Understanding Global HR Practices." *International Journal of Multidisciplinary Education and Research* 3, no. 4, pp. 15–21.

Kramer, R. J. 1996. *Organizing for Global Competitiveness: A Research Summary*. Conference Board.

Prahalad, C.K. and K. Lieberthal. 2003. "The End of Corporate Imperialism." *Harvard Business Review* 81, no. 8, pp. 109–117.

Robinson, J. 2001. *Jack Welch on Leadership: Executive Lessons From the Master*. Prima Lifestyles.

Roudometof, V. 2016. *Glocalization: A Critical Introduction*. Routledge.

Roudometof, V. 2016. "Theorizing Glocalization: Three Interpretations." *European Journal of Social Theory* 19, no. 3, pp. 391–408.

Ruzagiriza, A.U. 2017. "Does Cross-Culture Human Resource Management Affect Performance of International Organizations? Evidence From Rwanda." *International Journal of Innovation and Economics Development* 2, no. 6, pp. 14–28.

Yin, X., Y. Yang, H. Kim, and Y. Zhang. 2022. "Examining the Job Burnout of Chinese Hospitality Management Students in Internships via the Transactional Model." *Frontiers of Psychology* 13.

Disruptive Innovation

Christensen, C. 2011. *The Innovator's Dilemma: The Revolutionary Book That Will Change the Way You Do Business*. HarperBusiness.

Craig, W. October 23, 2018. "The Nature of Leadership in a Flat Organization." *Forbes*. www.forbes.com/sites/williamcraig/2018/10/23/the-nature-of-leadership-in-a-flat-organization/?sh=b8bae615fe19 (accessed June 2023).

EHL Faculty. "Business Model Innovation: An Exciting Sector?" *EHL Hospitality Insights*. https://hospitalityinsights.ehl.edu/hospitality-business-model-innovation-competitive-advantage (accessed June 2023).

Heskett, J. L., W.E. Sasser, and L.A. Schlesinger. 2015. *What Great Service Leaders Know and Do: Creating Breakthroughs in Service Firms*. Berrett-Koehler.

Johansen, B. 2017. *The New Leadership Literacies: Thriving in a Future of Extreme Disruption and Distributed Everything*. Berrett-Koehler Publishers.

Jooss, S., R. Burbach, and H. Ruel. 2021. *Talent Management Innovations in the International Hospitality Industry*. Emerald Publishing.

Laloux, F. and N. Parker. 2016. *Reinventing Organizations: An Illustrated Invitation to Join the Conversation on Next-Stage Organizations*. Nelson Parker.

Raj, W. 2021. *Running the Agile and Lean Hotel*. Hotel Intel.co. https://hotelintel.co/running-an-agile-and-lean-hotel/ (accessed June 2023).

Ridderstróale, J. and K. Nordström. 2005. *Karaoke Capitalism: Daring to be Different in a Copycat World*. Praeger Publishers.

Stadler, C., J. Hautz, K. Matzler, and S. von den Eichen. 2021. *Open Strategy: Mastering Disruption From Outside the C-Suite*. The MIT Press.

Wickhamn, W. 2019. "Innovation, Sustainable HRM and Customer Satisfaction." *International Journal of Hospitality Management* 76, pp. 102–110.

HR Tech, AI, and Machine Learning

Batra, N., D. Betts, and S. Davis. April 30, 2019. *Forces of Change*. Deloitte. www2.deloitte.com/us/en/insights/industry/health-care/forces-of-change-health-care.html (accessed June 2023).

Bissola, R. 2019. *HRM 4.0 for Human-Centered Organizations*. Emerald Publishing

Eddy, N. February 7, 2023. "The Future of HR Tech: How AI Is Transforming Human Resources." *InformationWeek*. www.informationweek.com/big-data/the-future-of-hr-tech-how-ai-is-transforming-human-resources (accessed June 2023).

Eubanks, B. 2018. *Artificial Intelligence for HR: Use AI to Support and Develop a Successful Workforce*. Kogan Page.

Frankiewicz, D. and T. Chamorro-Premuzic. May 6, 2020. "Digital Transformation Is About Talent, Not Technology." *Harvard Business*

Review. https://hbr.org/2020/05/digital-transformation-is-about-talent-not-technology (accessed June 2023).

Guldenberg, S., E. Ernst, and K. North. 2021. *Managing Work in the Digital Economy: Challenges, Strategies, and Practices for the Next Decade.* Springer.

Kover, A. March 10, 2020. *A New Perspective on Hospitality: How Hilton Uses VR to Teach Empathy.* Meta. https://tech.facebook.com/reality-labs/2020/3/a-new-perspective-on-hospitality-how-hilton-uses-vr-to-teach-empathy/ (accessed June 2023).

May, J. 2017. *Rewriting the Rules for the Digital Age.* Deloitte University Press. www2.deloitte.com/content/dam/Deloitte/global/Documents/Human Capital/hc-2017-global-human-capital-trends-gx.pdf (accessed June 2023).

Meister, J. May 21, 2012. "The Future of Work: How to Use Gamification for Talent Management." *Forbes.* www.forbes.com/sites/jeannemeister/2012/05/21/the-future-of-work-how-to-use-gamification-for-talent-management/?sh=7142c45a98d3 (accessed June 2023).

Newman, D. August 20, 2018. "2018 Digital Transformation Trends: Where Are We Now?" *Forbes.* www.forbes.com/sites/danielnewman/2018/08/20/2018-digital-transformation-trends-where-are-we-now/?sh=4d4fb41bc647 (accessed June 2023).

Sen, S. 2020. *Digital HR Strategy: Achieving Sustainable Transformation in the Digital Age.* Kogan Page.

Shivakumar, K. and S. Sethii. 2019. *Building Digital Experience Platforms.* Springer

Zielinski, D. January 10, 2023. *2023 HR Technology Trends: Talent Marketplaces, Expanding AI and Optimizing Existing Systems.* SHRM. www.shrm.org/resourcesandtools/hr-topics/technology/pages/2023-hr-technology-trends.aspx (accessed June 2023).

Talent Marketplaces

Basch, S. January 12, 2022. "INTOO's Career Mobility Capabilities Included in Deloitte's Internal Mobility and Talent Marketplace Solutions Report." *Cision.* www.prweb.com/releases/intoos_career_mobility_capabilities_included_in_deloittes_internal_mobility_and_talent_marketplace_solutions_report/prweb18425306.htm (accessed June 2023).

Bersin, J. July 3, 2020. *Talent Marketplace Platforms Explode Into View.* Josh Bersin. https://joshbersin.com/2020/07/talent-marketplace-platforms-explode-into-view/ (accessed June 2023).

Carnetec Brasil. March 25, 2021. *Is Your Hotel Ready to Hire Post-Pandemic?* Carnetec Brasil. www.carnetec.com.br/Industry/TechnicalArticles/Details/98046 (accessed June 2023).

EY. 2020. *Will HR Transformation Be the Thread That Ties Value to Experiences?* Ernst & Young. www.ey.com/en_ua/workforce/future-hr (accessed June 2023).

Field, E., B. Hancock, and B. Schaningr. April 26, 2022. *Stave Off Attrition With an Internal Talent Marketplace.* McKinsey&Company. www.mckinsey.com/capabilities/people-and-organizational-performance/our-insights/stave-off-attrition-with-an-internal-talent-marketplace (accessed June 2023).

Fulton, A. December 15, 2021. "Learning New Set of Skills Through a Talent Marketplace Can Revitalize Employees." *HR.com.* www.hr.com/en/magazines/all_articles/learning-new-set-of-skills-through-a-talent-market_kx7evbjl.html (accessed June 2023).

Gantcheva, I., R. Jones, and D. Manolatos. 2019. *Activating the Internal Talent Marketplace.* Deloitte. www2.deloitte.com/content/dam/Deloitte/at/Documents/human-capital/at-internal-talent-markets.pdf (accessed June 2023).

Gantcheva, I., R. Jones, and D. Kearns-Manolatos. 2020. *Activating the Internal Talent Marketplace: Accelerate Workforce Resilience, Agility and Capability, and Impact the Future of Work.* Deloitte. www2.deloitte.com/us/en/insights/focus/technology-and-the-future-of-work/internal-talent-marketplace.html (accessed June 2023).

Hameed, I., Z. Riaz, G. Arain, and O. Farooq. 2016. "How Does Internal and External CSR Affect Employees' Organizational Identification? A Perspective From the Group Engagement Model." *Frontiers of Psychology* 7, no. 788.

Marinakou, E. and C. Giousmpasoglou. 2019. "Talent Management and Retention Strategies in Luxury Hotels: Evidence From Four Countries." *International Journal of Contemporary Hospitality Management* 31, no. 10, pp. 3855–3878.

Maurer, R. April 16, 2021. *Internal Marketplaces Are the Future of Talent Management.* SHRM. www.shrm.org/resourcesandtools/hr-topics/talent-acquisition/pages/internal-marketplaces-future-of-talent-management.aspx (accessed June 2023).

Schwartz, J. October 11, 2021. *Talent Marketplaces and the Challenges of 2022: Time for Real Innovation in Workforce Strategies.* Alm Benefits Pro. www.benefitspro.com/2021/10/11/talent-marketplaces-and-the-challenges-of-2022-why-the-2020s-require-real-innovation-in-workforce-strategies/?slreturn=20230222152246 (accessed June 2023).

Smith, L., J. Kohan, and I. Pilewska. May 10, 2022. "What Stops Employees From Applying for Internal Roles." *Harvard Business Review.* https://hbr.org/2022/05/what-stops-employees-from-applying-for-internal-roles (accessed June 2023).

Stroh, L.K. and P.M. Caligiuri. 1998. "Increasing Global Competitiveness Through Effective People Management." *Journal of World Business* 33, no. 1, pp. 1–16.

Suhag, N. 2017. "The Impact of Training on Team Effectiveness in the Hotel Industry." *SSRN Electronic Journal*. https://papers.ssrn.com/sol3/papers .cfm?abstract_id=3065770 (accessed June 2023).

TNN. October 29, 2021. "Infy Starts Internal Talent Marketplace to Meet Demand." *The Times of India*. https://timesofindia.indiatimes.com/city/ bengaluru/infy-starts-internal-talent-marketplace-to-meet-demand/ articleshow/87348954.cms (accessed June 2023).

Ulrich, D. 1998. "A New Mandate for Human Resources." *Harvard Business Review* 76, no. 1, pp. 124–134.

Vaduganathan, N., C. McDonald, A. Bailey, and R. Laverdiere. June 8, 2022. *Tapping Into Fluid Talent*. BCG. www.bcg.com/publications/2022/tapping- into-fluid-talent (accessed June 2023).

Vaduganathan, N., C. McDonald, and G. Novacek. July 15, 2022. *Internal Talent Mobility Programs Can Advance Gender Equity. Do Yours?* BCG. www .bcg.com/publications/2022/how-companies-can-improve-gender-equity (accessed June 2023).

Vaduganathan, N., B. Zweig, C. McDonald, and L. Simon. October 17, 2022. "What Outperformers Do Differently to Tap Internal Talent." *MIT Sloan Management Review*. https://sloanreview.mit.edu/article/what-outperformers- do-differently-to-tap-internal-talent/ (accessed June 2023).

Wilson, M., M. Shannon, and D. Moulton. 2020. *Internal Mobility and Talent Marketplace Solutions: Market Primer*. Deloitte. www2.deloitte.com/content/ dam/Deloitte/us/Documents/human-capital/us-internal-mobility-and- talent-marketplace-solutions-market-primer.pdf (accessed June 2023).

Government Policies and Organized Labor

Hamilton, H. September 20, 2022. "Once Upon a Time, 'Waitress' Was a Union Job. Could History Repeat Itself?" *Slate*. https://slate.com/news-and- politics/2022/09/history-of-hospitality-unions-united-states.html (accessed June 2023).

Martin, H. August 25, 2022. "Chateau Marmont Agrees to Let Workers Unionize, Cancels Plans for Members-Only Hotel." *Los Angeles Times*. www .latimes.com/business/story/2022-08-25/chateau-marmont-agrees-to-let- workers-unionize (accessed June 2023).

McNicholas, C., H. Shierholz, and M. Poydock. January 22, 2021. *Union Workers Had More Job Security During the Pandemic, but Unionization Remains Historically Low*. Economic Policy Institute. www.epi.org/publication/union-workers-had-more-job-security-during-the-pandemic-but-unionization-remains-historically-low-data-on-union-representation-in-2020-reinforce-the-need-for-dismantling-barriers-to-union-organizing/ (accessed June 2023).

Workplace Conditions and Safety

Dowell, E. October 14, 2020. *Census Bureau's 2018 County Business Patterns Provides Data on Over 1,200 Industries.* United States Census Bureau. www.census.gov/library/stories/2020/10/health-care-still-largest-united-states-employer.html (accessed June 2023).

Dresser, L., A. Bernhardt, and E. Parker. June 2000. *The Restructuring of Hotel Jobs and the Role of Institutions.* Russell Sage Foundation. www.russellsage.org/awarded-project/restructuring-hotel-jobs-and-role-institutions (accessed June 2023).

Lee, P. and N. Krause. 2002. "The Impact of a Worker Health Study on Working Conditions." *Journal of Public Health Policy* 23, no. 2, pp. 268–285.

Neber, J. March 2, 2023. *City's Health Care Labor Moment Comes at an Inconvenient Time for Strained Hospitals.* Crain's New York Business. www.crainsnewyork.com/health-care/new-yorks-health-care-labor-push-comes-inconvenient-time-strained-hospitals (accessed June 2023).

Streit, D. February 23, 2023. *Bronx Frontline Doctors Overwhelmingly Vote to Re-Establish Union.* The Committee of Interns and Residents. www.cirseiu.org/bronx-frontline-doctors-overwhelmingly-vote-to-re-establish-union/#:~:text=Bronx%2C%20New%20York%20City%2C%20NY,Residents%20(CIR%2FSEIU) (accessed June 2023).

About the Author

Alexander Mirza is Founder and CEO of Mogul Hotels, a technology and branding company based in Los Angeles. He has over 25 years' experience, starting at Deloitte Consulting and Accenture where he was a Partner. As a management consultant, Alex advised CEOs, government leaders, and international organizations. He subsequently led corporate strategy at Starwood Hotels and held senior management roles overseeing corporate development and business units at Hilton, Ticketmaster, and Caesars. He is one of the few entrepreneurs to build a hotel company in China, cofounding Cachet Hotels, which scaled across Asia. Mirza was awarded the Sasakawa Peace Fellowship for doctoral studies in international economics at York University, holds an MBA from Harvard Business School where he received the McArthur Fellowship for Canadians, and has Master's and Bachelor's degrees from Queen's University at Kingston, where he was an Aga Khan Foundation Scholar. He has authored books and articles featured in the Library of Canada, *Harvard Real Estate Review, Entrepreneur Magazine*, Phocuswright, and the World Economic Forum. www.alexandermirza.com

Index

OTHER TITLES IN THE TOURISM AND HOSPITALITY MANAGEMENT COLLECTION

Betsy Bender Stringam, New Mexico State University, Editor

- *Talent Disruption* by Alexander Mirza
- *How a Global Pandemic Changed the Way We Travel* by Jacqueline Jeynes
- *Hotel Revenue Management* by Dave Roberts
- *Astrotourism* by Michael Marlin
- *Enhancing Joy in Travel* by Virginia Murphy-Berman
- *Healthy Vines, Pure Wines* by Pamela Lanier and Jessica Nicole Hughes
- *Overtourism* by Helene von Magius Mogelhoj
- *Food and Beverage Management in the Luxury Hotel Industry* by Sylvain Boussard
- *Targeting the Mature Traveler* by Jacqueline Jeynes
- *Hospitality* by Chris Sheppardson
- *A Time of Change in Hospitality Leadership* by Chris Sheppardson
- *Food and Architecture* by Subhadip Majumder and Sounak Majumder
- *Improving Convention Center Management Using Business Analytics and Key Performance Indicators* by Myles T. McGrane
- *Improving Convention Center Management Using Business Analytics and Key Performance Indicators* by Myles T. McGrane
- *A Profile of the Hospitality Industry, Second Edition* by Betsy Bender Stringam

Concise and Applied Business Books

The Collection listed above is one of 30 business subject collections that Business Expert Press has grown to make BEP a premiere publisher of print and digital books. Our concise and applied books are for...

- Professionals and Practitioners
- Faculty who adopt our books for courses
- Librarians who know that BEP's Digital Libraries are a unique way to offer students ebooks to download, not restricted with any digital rights management
- Executive Training Course Leaders
- Business Seminar Organizers

Business Expert Press books are for anyone who needs to dig deeper on business ideas, goals, and solutions to everyday problems. Whether one print book, one ebook, or buying a digital library of 110 ebooks, we remain the affordable and smart way to be business smart. For more information, please visit www.businessexpertpress.com, or contact sales@businessexpertpress.com.

www.ingramcontent.com/pod-product-compliance
Lightning Source LLC
Chambersburg PA
CBHW061145220326
41599CB00025B/4358